LEAD GUITAR WORKSHOP

Lead Guitar: Level 2

Library of Congress Control Number:

Any references to historical events, real people, or real places are used fictitiously. Names, characters, and places are products of the author's imagination.

Front cover image by Suke Cerulo
Book design by Suke Cerulo
Front Cover Photo by Jessica Maceli
About Author Photo by Paul Citone
Back cover/Inside cover Photo by Paul Citone
Student Reviewer: Linda Ameroso

Printed by Lead Guitar Workshop, Inc., in the United States of America.

First edition 2021

SCAN FOR MORE

for all backing tracks and videos

www.LeadGuitarWorkshop.com

PREFACE

I always enjoyed music as a kid but my immediate family was not musical. There wasn't a lot of music playing in the house and we were never the type of family to sing. But my Grandfather George Lane was a Big Band musician and bandleader in the 1950's in Boston and New York. I don't have any memories of him playing music but he would have hilarious stories "from the road" traveling with the band. Later in life I really learned to appreciate them as I toured extensively.

It was 1984 and I heard Van Halen for the first time. I knew right then and there that I wanted to play music. I got my first guitar for Christmas in that year and quickly took lessons because I had no idea what to do. At the time I was really into playing football and I was good at it. I realized I was never going to be in the NFL or make a career out of it. But I did realize there was no NFL of music, anybody could play! That was so exciting. I knew I was going to play music for my whole life. I just had to figure out how to make it a career.

I had weekly guitar lessons from the time I was twelve until I graduated High School. For most of this time my teacher was Sandy Prager. He played "third stream jazz" on a nylon string guitar. This was as far away from Van Halen as possible without being a classical guitarist. But I learned so much about music, how to think about it and improvise. He constantly had me creating. Once I finished High School I went to **Berklee College of Music**. It was the only school I wanted to go to. After four years I got my Bachelors Degree in Professional Music.

My one goal upon graduating was to join a band. Fortunately for me I met my future bandmates of 30 plus years. We formed the band **"Schleigho"** in 1993 and toured full time within a year or so. We toured 200 plus dates a year for almost five years straight and still play to this day. We recorded and released 5 albums. We signed a label with the **Allman Brothers Band**, toured with **Derek Trucks**, and played with so very many people all over the country. This was my "real world" music education.

But even though I had lessons in High School and a great experience at Berklee I still felt like I was slow learning and still really didn't get the true nature of music and guitar. I struggled to connect the musical dots.

I had to build confidence to make my own conclusions about music. I heard so many different ideas, terms, explanations and they were confusing. I was perplexed that music had been around for hundreds of years and there was still so much indecision about ideas and terminology.

I had to separate music from the instrument. This was one of my biggest realizations. It came into fruition when I started playing flute. I realized the music was its own language independent of the instrument that plays it. When I started really practicing flute my guitar playing got better! I was stunned, but I realized my musicianship was better and it was now translating to guitar.

Once my band started touring I had guitar players (and flute players) asking me for lessons. I think I gave my first lesson in 1995. It was very casual and it was new to me but I was just trying to help people out. I realized I had a good way of explaining things and I was able to connect with people. Over the years I kept teaching. It was rewarding and I was learning a lot by having to explain music to people in many different ways.

About six months after I moved to NYC in 2003 I got my first real teaching job at a guitar school in NYC. I was touring and teaching full time. I was engulfed in playing and teaching music and it was wonderful. As touring slowed down the teaching picked up. I was teaching ten classes and about thirty private students. Close to eighty folks a week were coming to see me to learn about guitar and music. After years of teaching groups and private students I was able to refine my approach to teaching and to understanding music and how it relates to the guitar. Years ago I estimated that I hit my 10,000 hours as a guitar player. Now I was hitting my 10,000 hours as a teacher.

In 2003 I wrote my first book "Lead Guitar Basics" for me to use at the guitar school. Over the years this grew into five complete books and a number of rewrites. I also became the Director of the Lead Guitar Department. I train other teachers to teach my material and musically evaluate all incoming teachers to the school.

I was amassing an unprecedented amount of teaching experience and gaining access to hundreds, if not thousands, of guitar players struggling in the same way I had. Over years of refinement I was able to develop this entire pedagogy for learning lead guitar.

These books have three decades of experience behind them and seventeen years of in-classroom development. I believe in these books, and I think they will help you immensely as you become a better guitarist and musician. These are all the things I wish I had when I was starting my journey.

HOW TO USE BOOK

Each book is written as ten lessons continually building on each other. The books all work together and are meant to extend and expand your knowledge as you work and grow with them. Go through them in order and go back later to revisit topics.

These books were initially created as 10 week courses, one chapter per week. You can use it in the same way. Each Chapter is about an hour long. There are enough warm-ups, exercises, new skills and practice to last you for a week. There is overlap and repetition in the books to really help reinforce the core ideas.

Every lesson is structured the same way. It is meant to optimize your learning, efficiency, and time. The repetition creates good habits.

Tune in: First you have to get in the right head space. You must remind yourself that you are a musician and a guitar player. That music is Melody, Harmony, and Rhythm; and that rhythm is the number one factor to sounding good. It's like a mantra.

Warm-up: These are exercises to get your musical blood flowing and synchronize your internal clock. There are usually up to three warm-ups; *Muted String Ladders, Shells*, and *Changing Gears*. They are all music based and are like push-ups and jumping jacks to athletes.

Exercises: These are straight up music exercises like scales, arpeggios and more.

Review: This is part of the learning circle. You must review everything you learn. Eventually that will become part of your everyday language.

New Topic: Learn something new. It can be big or small, but it should expand your knowledge, even if it's learning something new about something you already know.

Practice: Play! Get better by playing music. Use your new idea/technique, concept in real time in the music you are playing, even if it is a one chord jam by yourself. Self Generating music and backing tracks are a focal point.

Summary: A reminder of what has been learned so far. Summaries compound with each chapter.

Going through each word and each note as written in these books is only part of the bigger picture. You have to imagine how music is working and how it relates to your instrument. You have to have a desire to grow and a never ending curiosity about music. If you keep questioning music you will find more answers and go deeper and deeper. You have to "drive" music, start a song yourself, jam on it and make it music all by yourself. When you're playing by yourself and someone walks in they should ask you "What song are you playing?" not "What are you practicing?" Learning music and playing is not about checking off a list of requirements. It's about sounding like a musician playing good music, and not someone noodling at the guitar store.

At a certain point in your musical life, you will learn all the information about music that you will ever use. Then your growth is about becoming closer to that information and growing deeper with it every time you revisit it. There isn't a learning path in music, it's a learning circle. An ever expanding circle is like rings in a tree. It's the growth in the rings, in the trunk of the tree that allows those branches to grow and extend.

Music is just a language and a guitar is just an instrument. Both are silent without you, you are music!

As guitarists Pat Martino and Mike Stern both told me, and I will tell you, "Just keep playing." Enjoy!

Suke Cerulo

Table of Contents

Lead Guitar-Level 2

This book is for those who have completed Level One and are familiar with playing a Major or minor pentatonic scale in any key. This book is for those who are comfortable with the basic guitar techniques of hammer-ons, pull-offs, slides and bends and want to improve overall as a guitar player and a musician. It is also for those who want to learn the five patterns that cover the entire fretboard, and learn the neck so they can use the whole instrument in a more musical way.

CHAPTER 1

TUNE IN

Whenever you grab your guitar and start to play, two separate worlds are active. One is the instrument you are playing, wood and wire plucked at specific times and making sounds. Then there are the notes, the actual tones being created and combined in the air molecules. This is a language of 12 notes that every instrument is built to play. This is a language older than any instrument that currently plays it except the voice.

You are growing as a musician and a guitar player. As a musician you are learning about notes and scales and how they relate to chords and especially their Relatives. As a guitar player you are a craftsperson learning scale patterns and how to navigate them on the fretboard according to what musical scale you need. As guitar players we learn hammer-ons, pull-offs, bends, slides and so many different ways to make our notes sound cool, lyrical.

Music has three elements: MELODY, HARMONY, and RHYTHM.

"I am a musician and a guitar player. Music is my language and my guitar is my voice. Music is Melody, Harmony and Rhythm. I develop my language skills and my instrument skills. They are two separate worlds working together to complete the circle of music."

Rhythm is the number one factor to sounding great as a musician.

MUTED STRING LADDERS (MSL)

Muted String Ladders are a fantastic warm up that exercise the picking hand and your rhythmic abilities. Mute the strings with your fretboard hand.

- Choose how many strings (1-6) and mute strings with fretboard hand.
- Start with quarter-notes, then change gears (eighth-notes, triplets, sixteenth-notes).
- Start with ALL DOWN picks.
- Change to ALL UP picks.
- Change to ALTERNATE picking. *(You can just do alternate picking if time is limited.)*
- Change to NEXT GEAR.

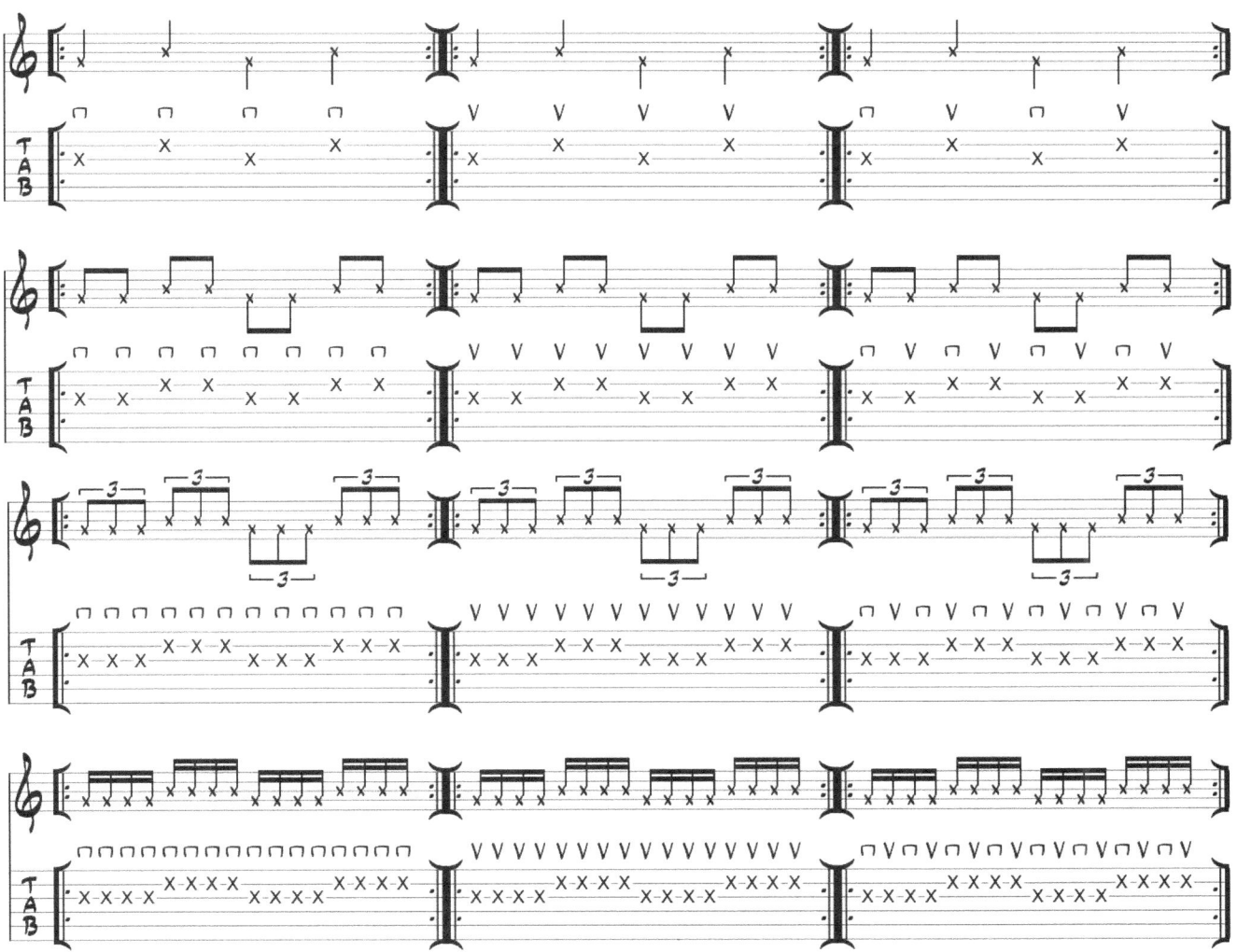

SHELLS

Shells are like "wax on, wax off." They are actions that practice real world moves. They are scale segments. These exercises help you in real musical situations and help overcome guitar hindrances. These are *not* scale exercises *but* **dexterity exercises**. Any time you are having a fingering issue you can make a shell out of it to help you.

Your musicianship should not be dictated by your finger habits.

- Choose any combination of fingers (for example 1 3).
- Pick a RHYTHM and a starting fret (8th notes and 5th fret).
- You will use that fingering (1 3) to ascend and (1 3) to descend.
- Then REVERSE the fingering (3 1) and ascend and descend with (3 1).

SHELL 1 3 Eighth-notes

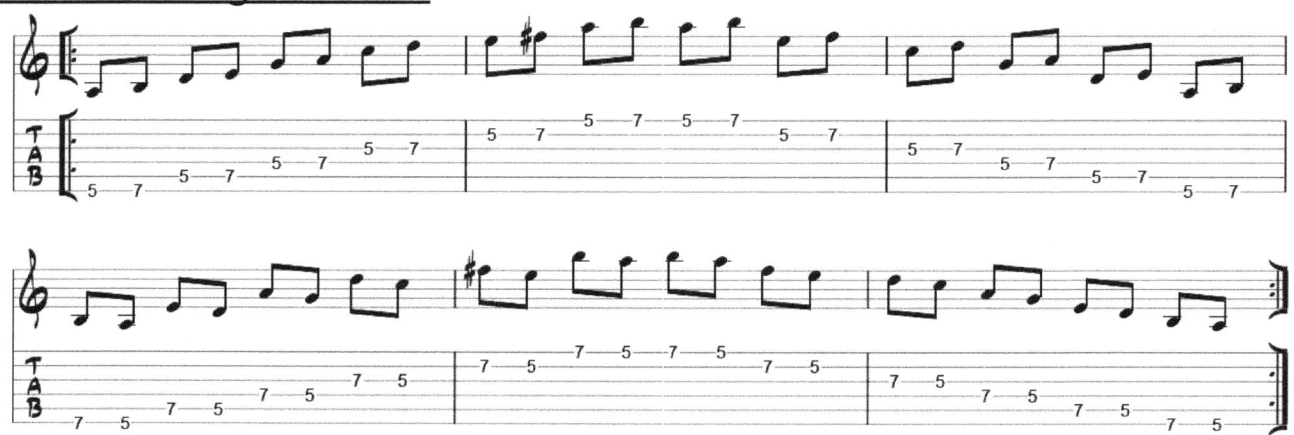

SHELL 1 4 Eighth-notes

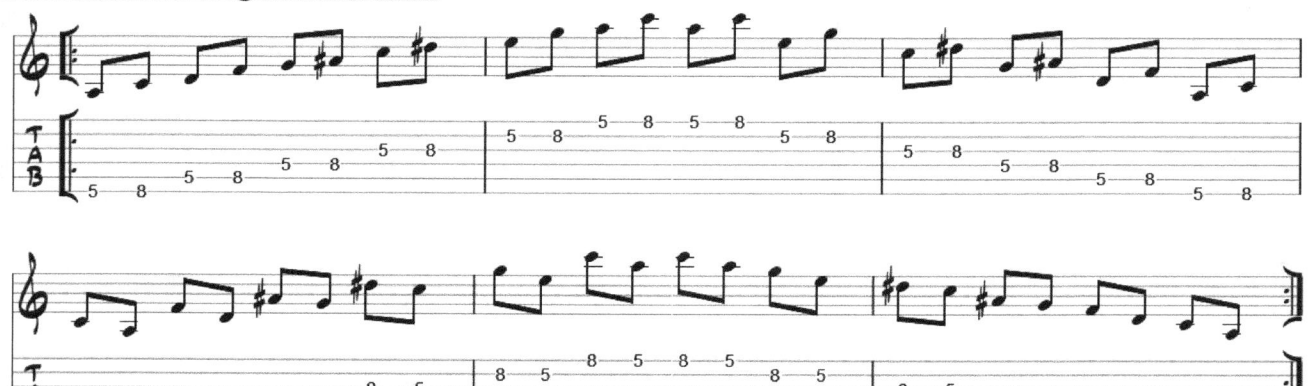

PENTATONICS

Pentatonic scales are five note scales that have been part of human culture for hundreds of years, much older than the guitar itself. There are two fundamental types/sounds of pentatonic scales. One is **Major** and one is **minor**.

The Major pentatonic scale is a very happy and upbeat sounding scale. It is 5 notes of our traditional seven note scale. It utilizes the 1 2 3 5 6 notes of a scale. If you ever learned Do Re Me Fa So La Ti Do, then it would be Do, Re, Me So, and La.

G Major pentatonic scale would be **G A B D E.**

As a guitar player our instrument has notes moving on and X and Y axis. This causes a lot of redundant notes all over the fretboard. It can be hard to see and very visually disorienting. The guitar is not intuitive to look at.

You can see below how the G Major pentatonic scale on the G string can be played in position and in _multiple_ other places _(two shown here for example)._

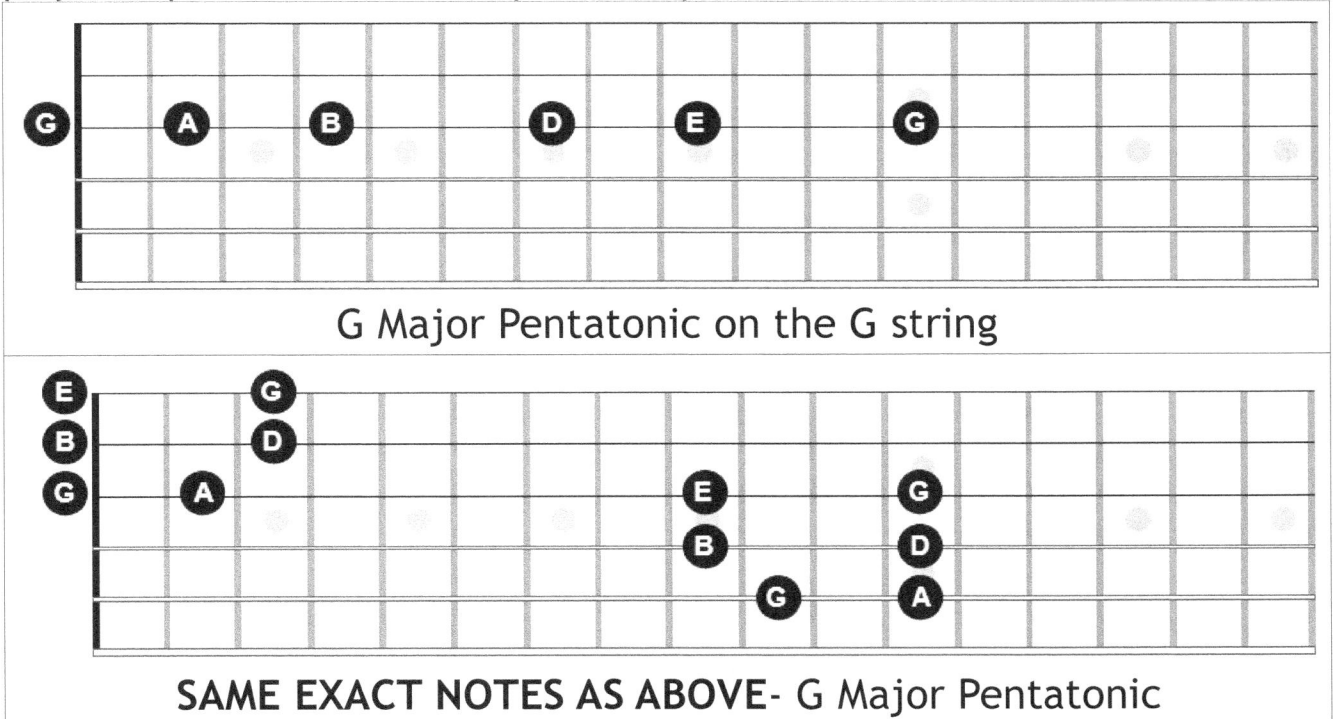

G Major Pentatonic on the G string

SAME EXACT NOTES AS ABOVE- G Major Pentatonic

RELATIVE MAJOR AND RELATIVE MINOR

As a musician we need to understand that for every Major Key there is a relative minor key. They have the same notes and the same chords, but they start and resolve to a different note. I like to think of this as a house. It has a front door and a back door. Each door looks and feels different but they are both entries into the same house with the same family inside.

The two scales we have looked at, G Major and E minor pentatonic, are relatives. They share the same notes and come from the same key in which they share the chords.

The **G Major pentatonic scale** is: **G A B D E**
The **E minor pentatonic scale** is: **E G A B D**

They are the same notes and they contain the notes of both chords.

G Major chord: G B D
E minor chord: E G B

The relationship of relative Major and relative minor is one of the most fundamental and beneficial things to know in music, it doubles your knowledge. *This relationship happens 12 times in music, one for each note.*

The 12 **Keys** have relatives. (Key of G Major *IS* the key of E minor.)
The 12 **chords** have relatives. (G and Em chords)
the 12 **scales** have relatives. (G and E minor pentatonic)

Relative chords are often swapped out for one another in songs. They also create sections of the song. For example the verse of the song could be in E minor and the chorus in G Major (Relative Major). Neil Young does this in "Rockin' in the Free World."

Relative Major and relative minor is what I call a "**Musical Truth,**" or one of the many common things in the musical language that all musicians know despite what instrument they play.

PATTERN #1

MUSICIAN	GUITAR PLAYER
There are **12 notes** in all of music (7 natural notes and 5 accidental notes). Each one of them is key/chord/scale. There are 12 Major pentatonic scales (one for each note) and 12 minor pentatonic scales (one for each note). As a musician, you know that it's a two-for-one deal. Every Major has a relative minor and vice-versa. There are **12 Relative Major-minor relationships** in all of music. **TRIANGLE=*minor* ROOT** **SQUARE=*Major* ROOT**	*Rock and Roll Rule* 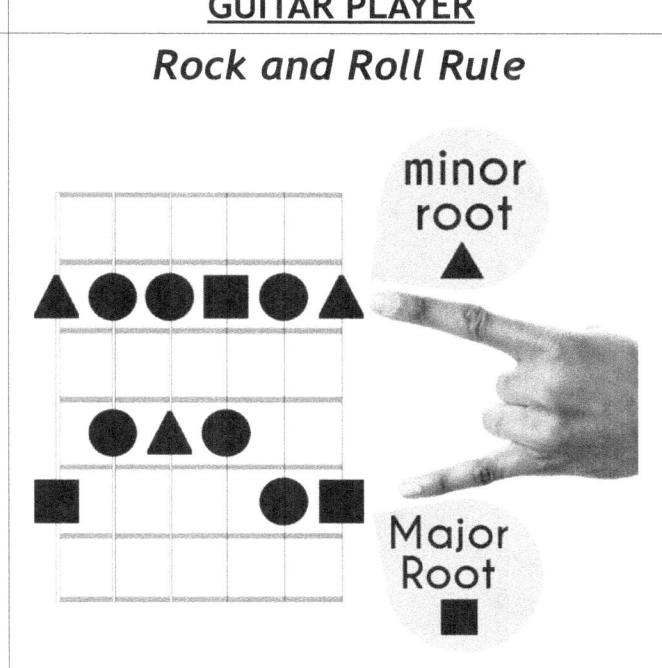
Once you know the chord progression you are going to solo over, you must decide on the **"MAIN" CHORD**, or the chord the others revolve around and want to resolve to. Then you **match the scale** to the chord, Major=Major and minor=minor. Find the ROOT of the chord (6th string). Decide on **INDEX for minor** or **PINKY for Major**. Match the finger to the fret and lay down pattern #1.	**Pattern #1 MOVEABLE** 

EXERCISE

Exercising scales and licks are an effective bridge between physical warm-ups and musical duties. It's really helpful to Self-Generate (SELF-GEN) the chord and then the scale/lick. It's great for your ear, your rhythm, your feel, and overall ability to carry a tune.

G Major

E minor

HOW TO NAVIGATE SCALE

1. Pick chord. (for example A Major)

2. Find the ROOT note on the E string. (A=5th fret)

3. Decide if scale is Major or minor (depending on chord). Place either the FIRST finger (for minor) or the PINKY (for Major). (pinky for A Major)

4. Lay down PATTERN #1. (2nd fret to 5th fret for A Major) (BONUS: A Major is also F# minor pentatonic)

Key of C Major/A minor

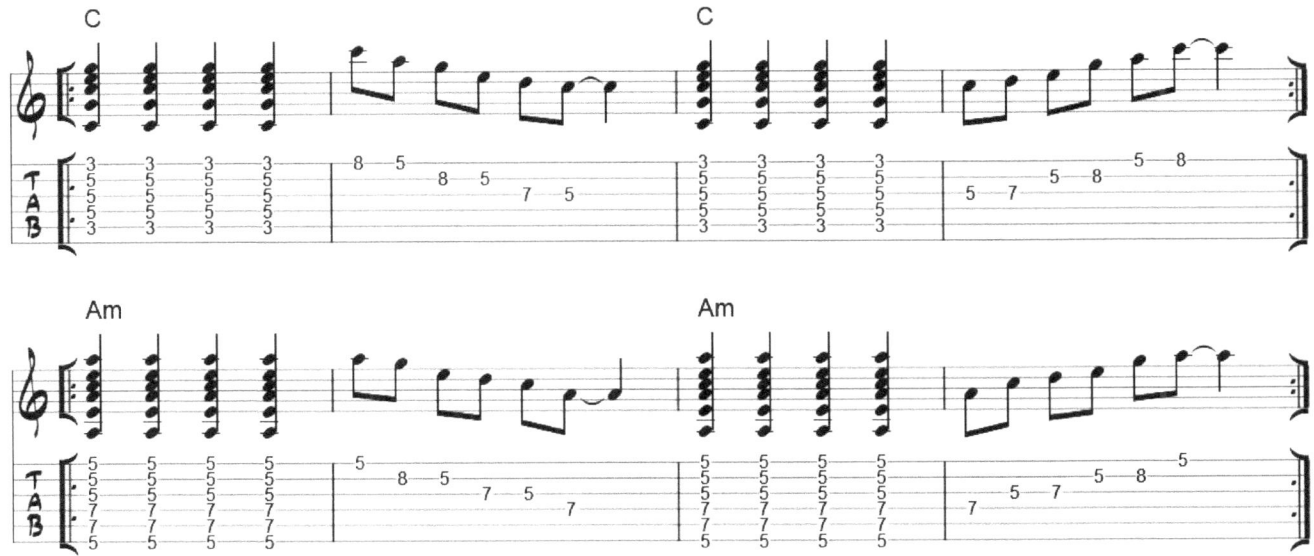

PRACTICE

Pattern #1 Major and minor LICK #1 Key G/Em

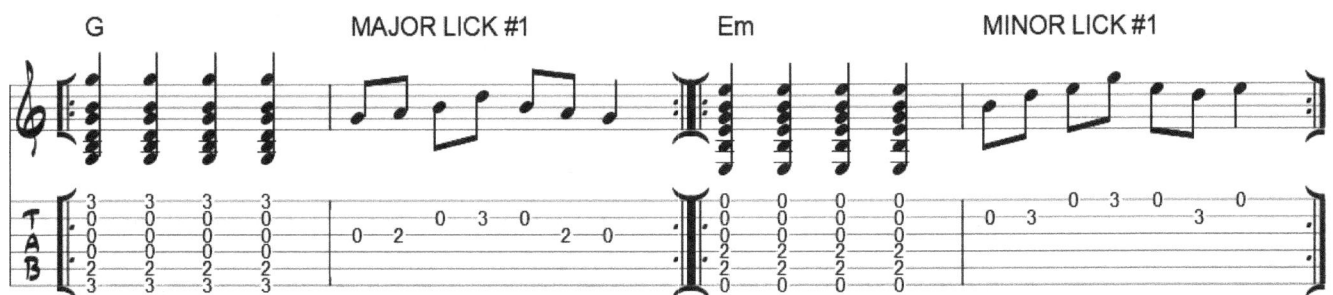

Pattern #1 Major and minor LICK #1 Key G/Em with Hammer-ons and Pull-offs

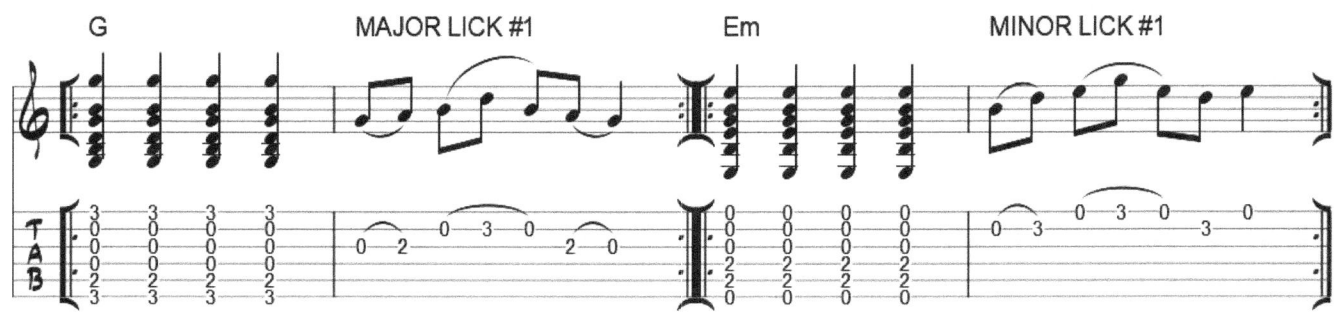

Pattern #1 Major and minor LICK #1 Key A/F#m

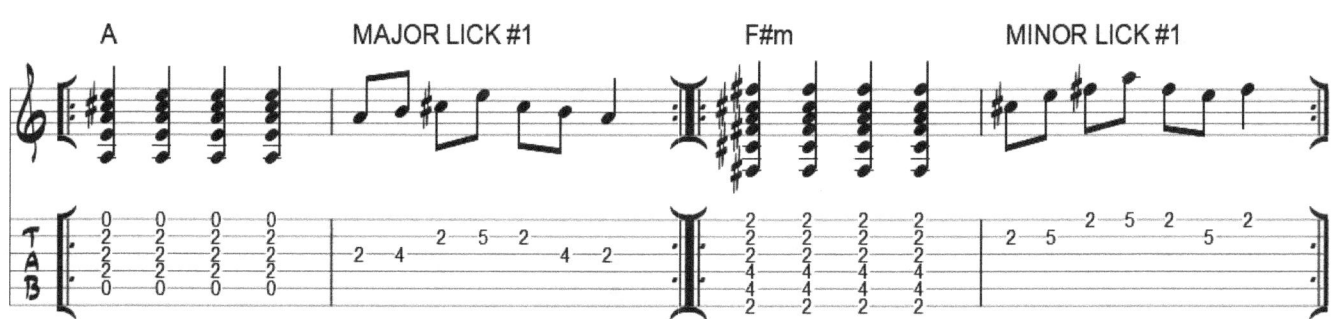

Pattern #1 Major and minor LICK #1 Key C/Am

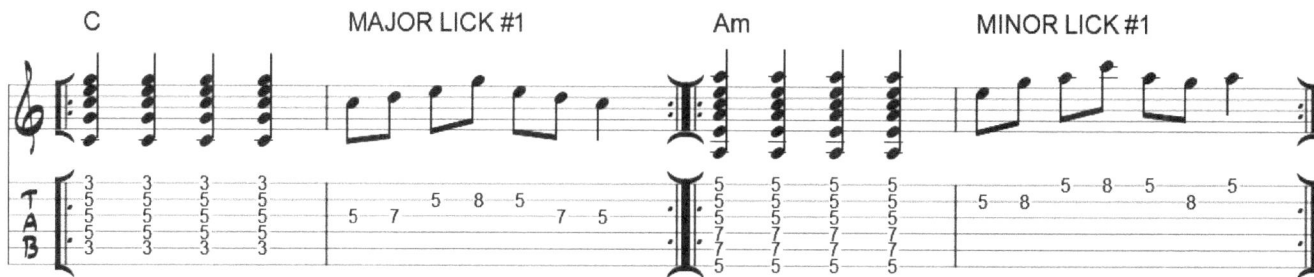

Pattern #1 Major and minor LICK #1 Key D/Bm

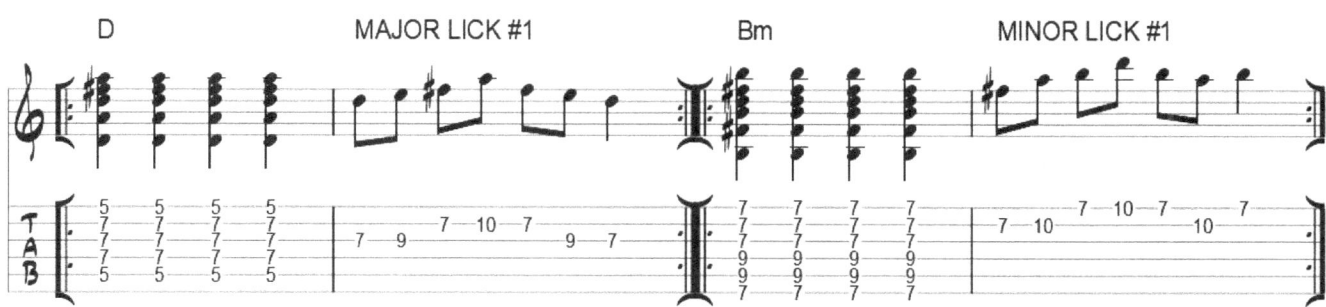

ROOT LOCATIONS in PATTERN #1

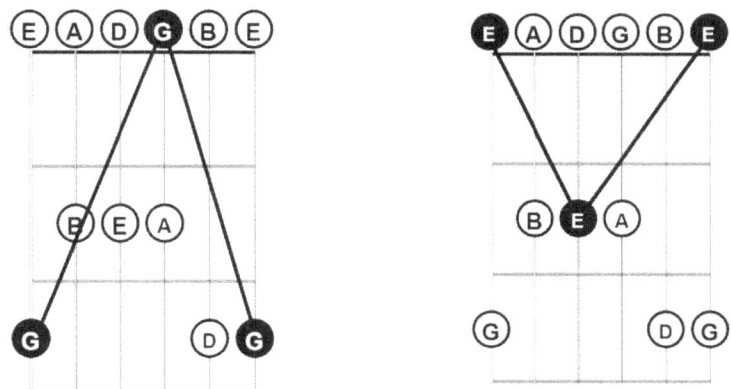

It's really important to remember the locations of the ROOTS of the RELATIVE MAJOR and RELATIVE MINOR in Pattern #1. They are ALWAYS in the same locations. The above example is G Major and E minor.

They make V shapes in the opposite direction. This relationship is really important as it stays true for ALL notes on any fret on the fretboard.

BACKING TRACKS

Another extremely enjoyable way to play is to jam along with backing tracks. I call backing tracks HARMONIC METRONOMES. They not only keep a beat but they offer a harmonic backdrop (chords in the background) to give perspective to your melody notes.

The backing tracks at Lead Guitar Workshop are specifically created to learn with and enjoy. The tracks are mostly performed live so they don't have a "cut and paste" sound to them. Tracks feel like a real band. They also highlight the chords as they go for more advanced practice such as playing the changes or using arpeggios.

Backing Track- G Major G Major pentatonic scale G Major licks	RELATIVES G Major/E minor Pattern #1 OPEN
Backing Track- E Minor E minor pentatonic scale E minor licks	
Backing Track- C Major C Major pentatonic C Major licks	RELATIVES C Major/A minor Pattern #1 (5th-8th fret)
Backing Track- A minor A minor pentatonic scale A minor licks	

FOR ALL BACKING TRACKS

www.LeadGuitarWorkshop.com

SUMMARY

We are musicians. We are guitar players.
We learn the language of music. Melody, Harmony, and Rhythm
We learn the craft of playing the guitar as an instrument.

We warm up with Muted String Ladders (MSL) and SHELLS.

RHYTHM is most important.

We Exercise our scales and licks.

We learn musical ideas (LICKS) to start to build "musical conversation."

We learn about relative Major and relative minor, as a two-for-one in music. One scale is two. We use the ROCK AND ROLL RULE for pattern #1 to help us guitarists see this musical relationship.

We learned what LEGATO is as a MUSICIAN and how to use it as a GUITAR PLAYER with HAMMER-ONS, PULL-OFFS, SLIDES, and BENDS.

We use BACKING TRACKS and SELF GENERATE to give a real time context to our playing.

We use PATTERN #1 ROCK AND ROLL RULE to navigate our scales and to easily see the relationship between the relative Major and relative minor.

You will use Pattern #1 to navigate ALL 12 Major pentatonic scales and ALL 12 minor pentatonic scales (one for each fret).

Don't forget that at the 12th fret the guitar (an music world) starts over again an octave higher. That means for the Keys of Em/G (12th-15th fret) up to Bm/D (19th-22nd fret) you get Pattern #1 an octave higher.

CHAPTER 2

TUNE IN

"I am a musician and a guitar player. Music is my language and my guitar is my voice. Music is Melody, Harmony and Rhythm. I develop my language skills and my instrument skills. They are two separate worlds working together to complete the circle of music."

Rhythm is the number one factor to sounding great as a musician.

WARM UP

Muted String Ladder: Top 2 strings 4 rhythms (gears)

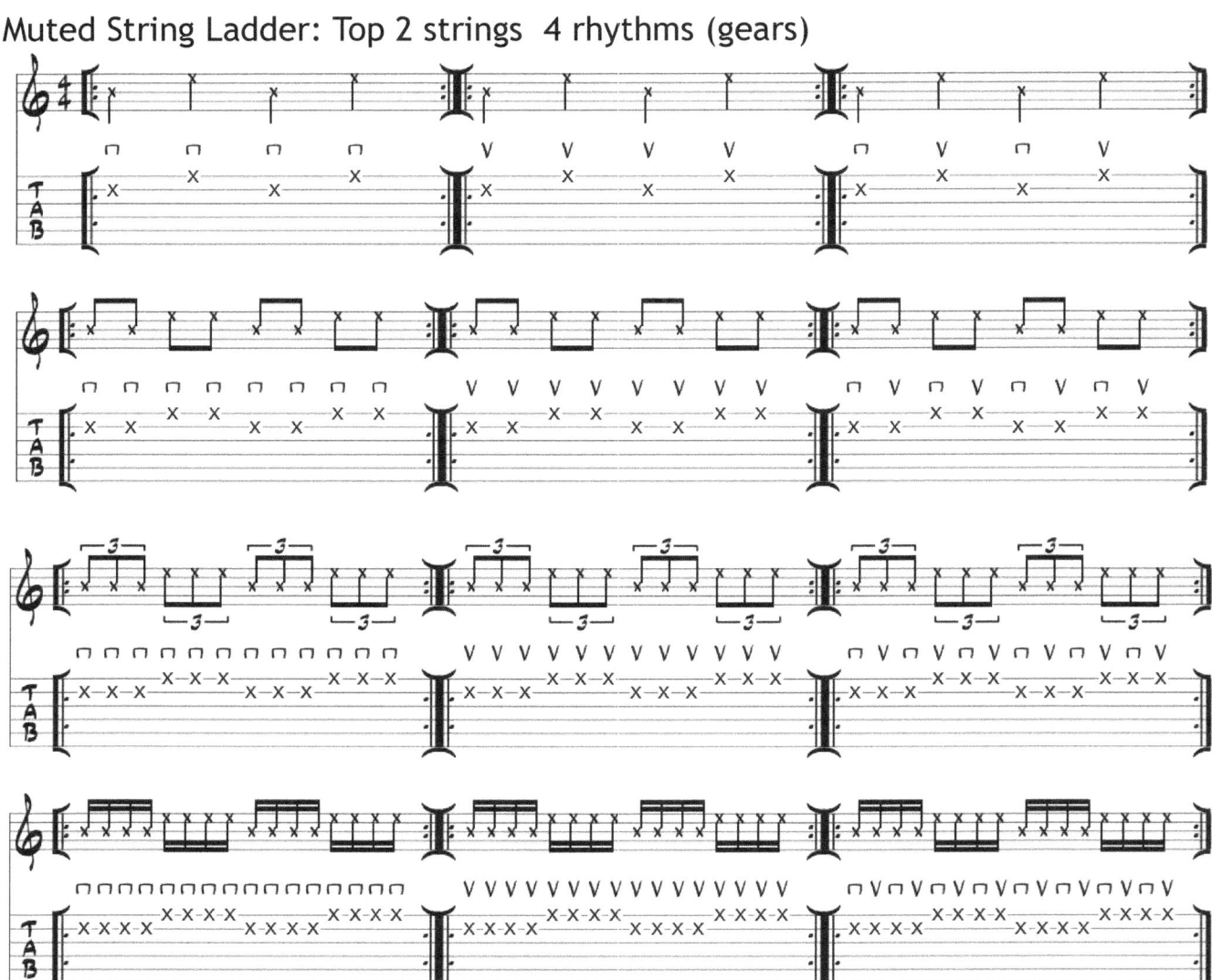

SHELLS

Shells are actions that practice real world moves. They are scale segments. These exercises help you in real musical situations to overcome guitar hindrances. These are *not* scale exercises *but* **dexterity exercises**. Any time you are having a fingering issue you can make a shell out of it to help you.

Your musicianship should not be dictated by your finger habits.

- Choose any combination of fingers. (for example 1 3)
- Pick a RHYTHM and a starting fret (8th notes and 5th fret)
- Use that fingering (1 3) to ascend and (1 3) to descend
- Then REVERSE the fingering (3 1) and ascend and descend with (3 1).

SHELL 1 3 Eighth-notes

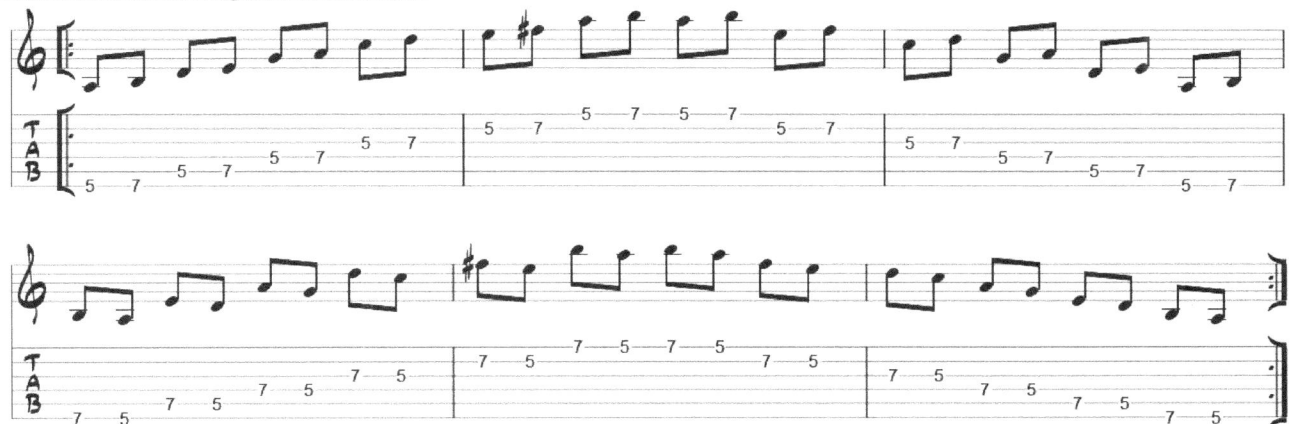

SHELL 1 4 Eighth-notes

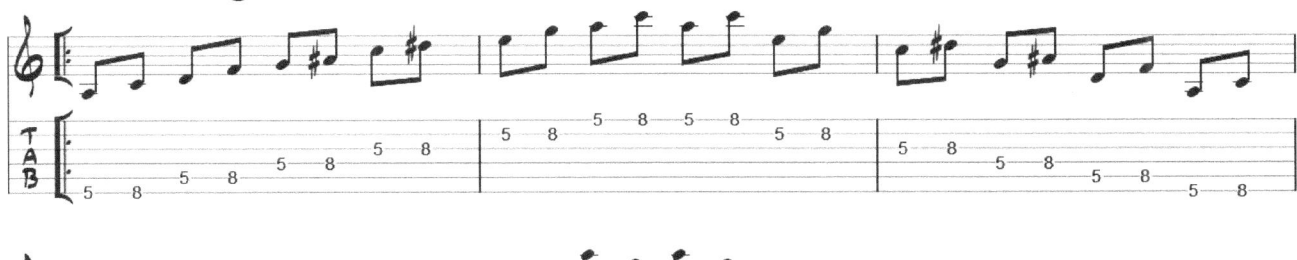

REVIEW

MUSICIAN	GUITAR PLAYER
There are **12 notes** in all of music (7 natural notes and 5 accidental notes). Each one of them is a key/chord/scale. There are 12 Major pentatonic scales (one for each note) and 12 minor pentatonic scales (one for each note). As a musician, you know that it's a two-for-one deal. Every Major has a relative minor and vice-versa. There are **12 Relative Major-minor relationships** in all of music. **TRIANGLE=*minor* ROOT** **SQUARE=*Major* ROOT**	*Rock and Roll Rule* 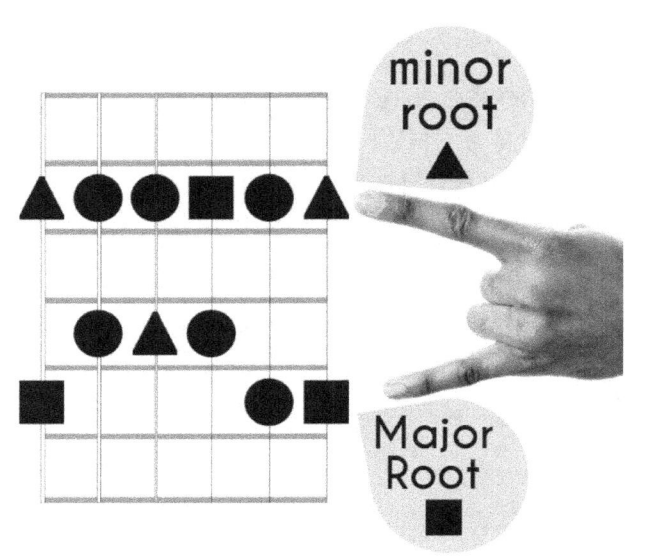
Once you know the chord progression you are going to solo over, you must decide on the **"MAIN" CHORD,** or the chord the others revolve around and want to resolve to. Then you **match the scale** to the chord, Major=Major and minor=minor. Find the ROOT of the chord (6th string). Decide on **INDEX for minor** or **PINKY for Major.** Match the finger to the fret and lay down pattern #1.	**Pattern #1 MOVEABLE** 

EXERCISE

Pattern #1 Two Octaves   Keys: C/Am, G/Em, D/Bm, A/F#m
Pick Relative Major or minor, pick a tempo (60 bpm) and pick a rhythm (8ths).
Play them ascending and descending for one or two octaves in each pattern.

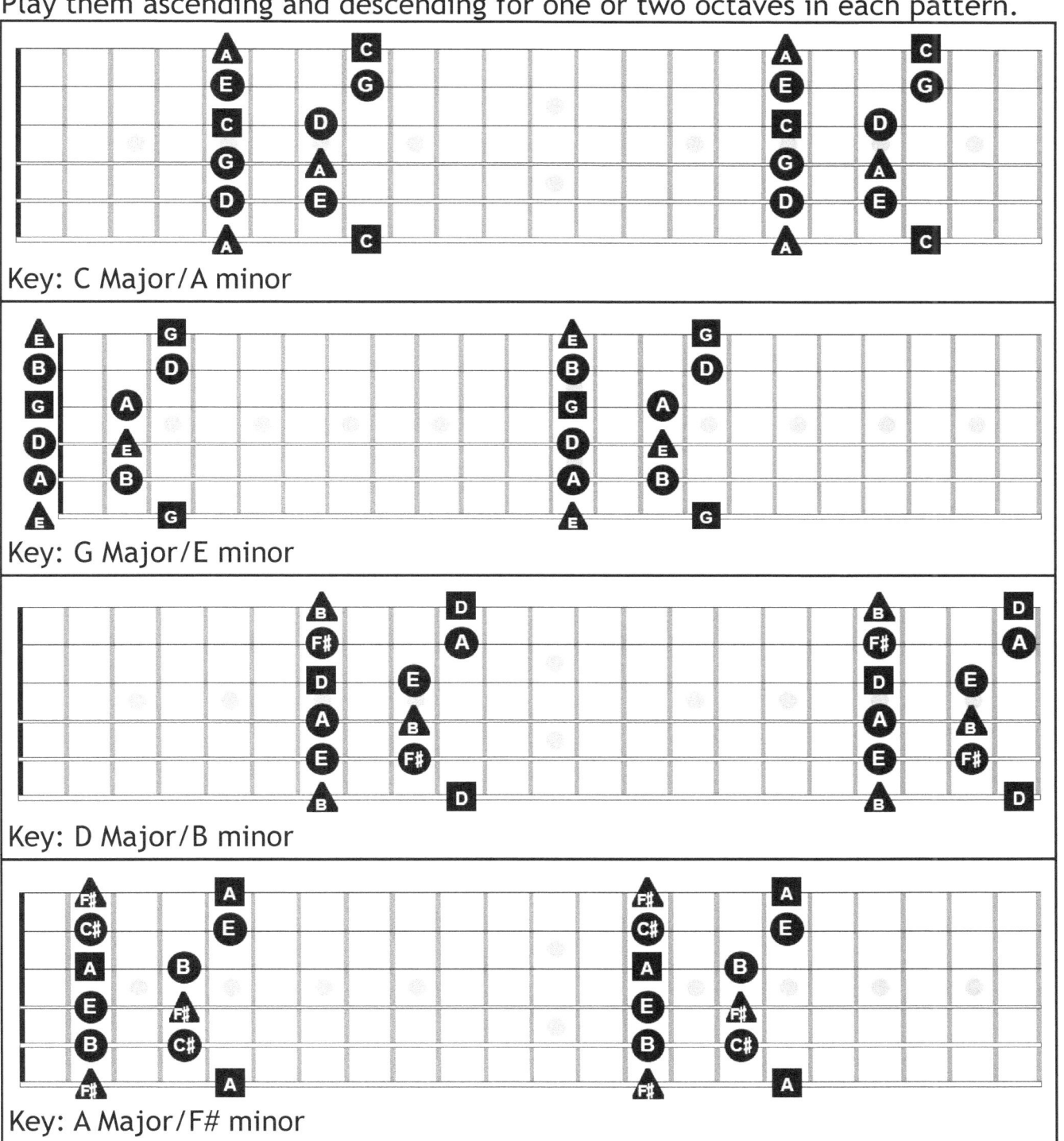

Key: C Major/A minor

Key: G Major/E minor

Key: D Major/B minor

Key: A Major/F# minor

Pattern #1 Major and minor LICK #1 C/ Am

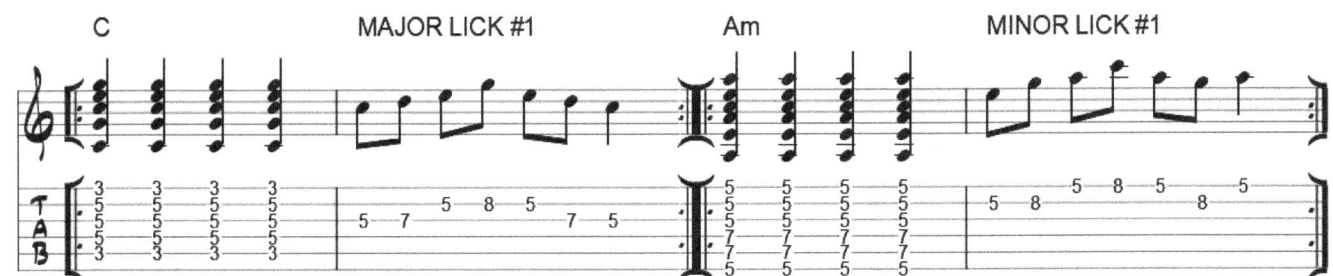

Pattern #1 Major and minor LICK #1 Key G/Em

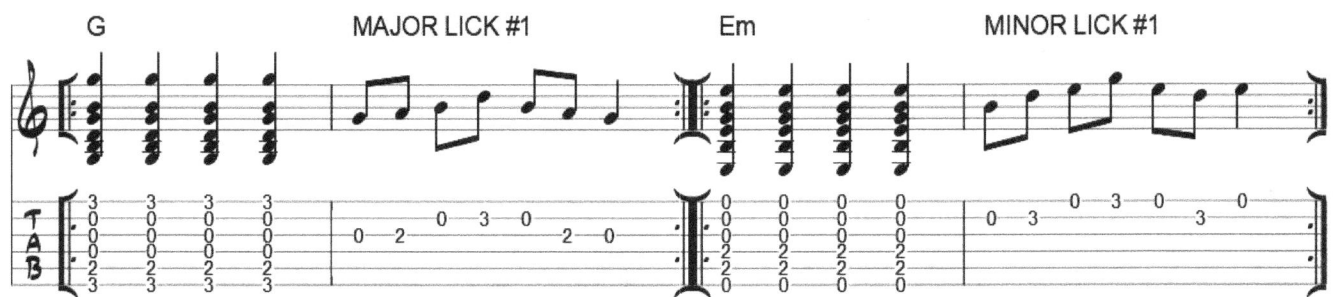

Pattern #1 Major and minor LICK #1 Key-D/Bm

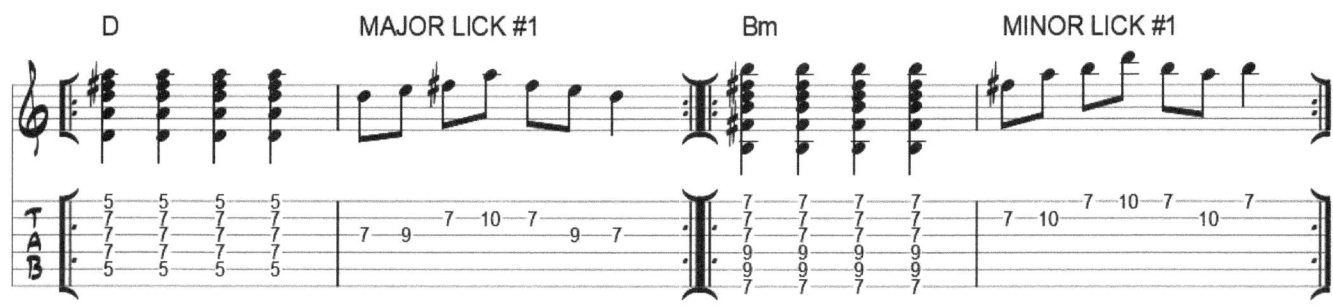

Pattern #1 Major and minor LICK #1 Key-A/F#m

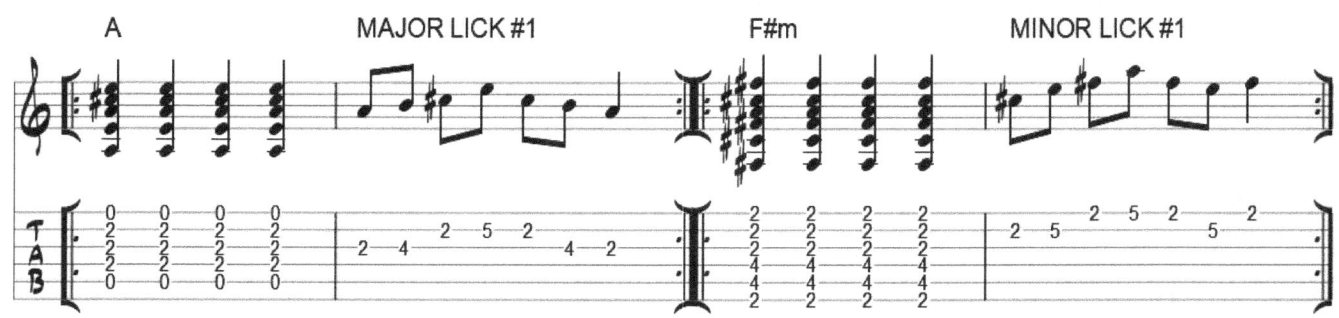

PATTERN #2

Once we make our musical decisions and properly navigate Pattern #1 on the fretboard we use the other patterns to extend the range of the scale and use the entire fretboard. Every pattern has the same 5 notes. Here is Pattern #2.

Major=Square   minor=Triangle

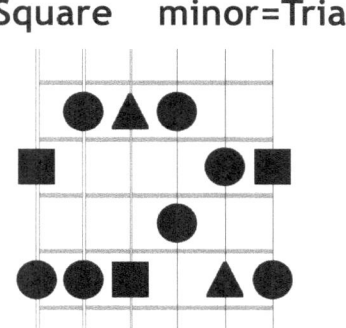

Pattern #2 is ALWAYS connected to and right above Pattern #1.

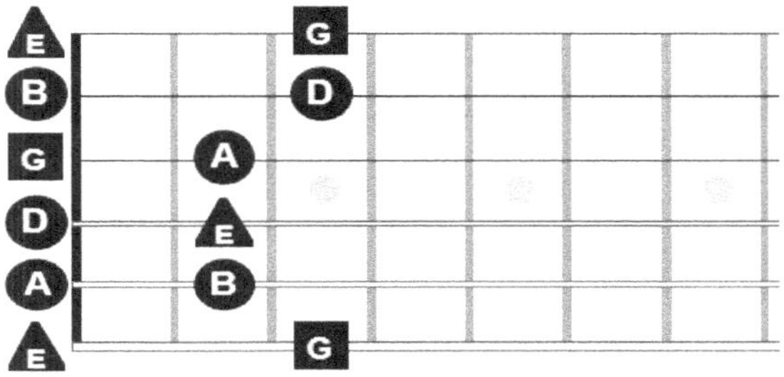

Pattern #1 G/Em

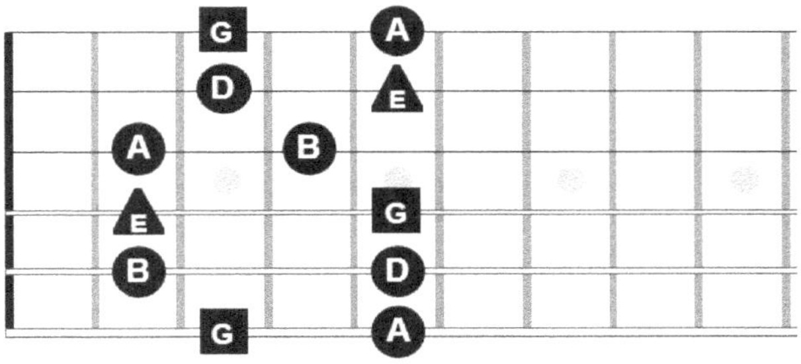

Pattern #2 G/Em

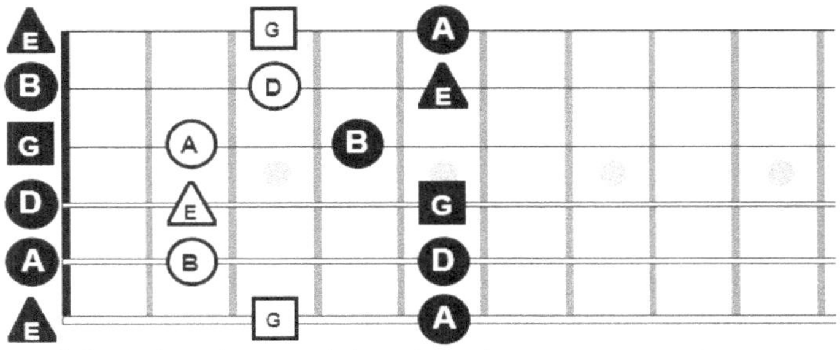

Pattern #1 + #2 G/Em *(white is shared by both patterns)*

Here are the first four keys with patterns #1 + #2. As you can see pattern #2 is ALWAYS available to you above pattern #1. It is an extension of the scale that you choose for pattern #1. They are the same notes.

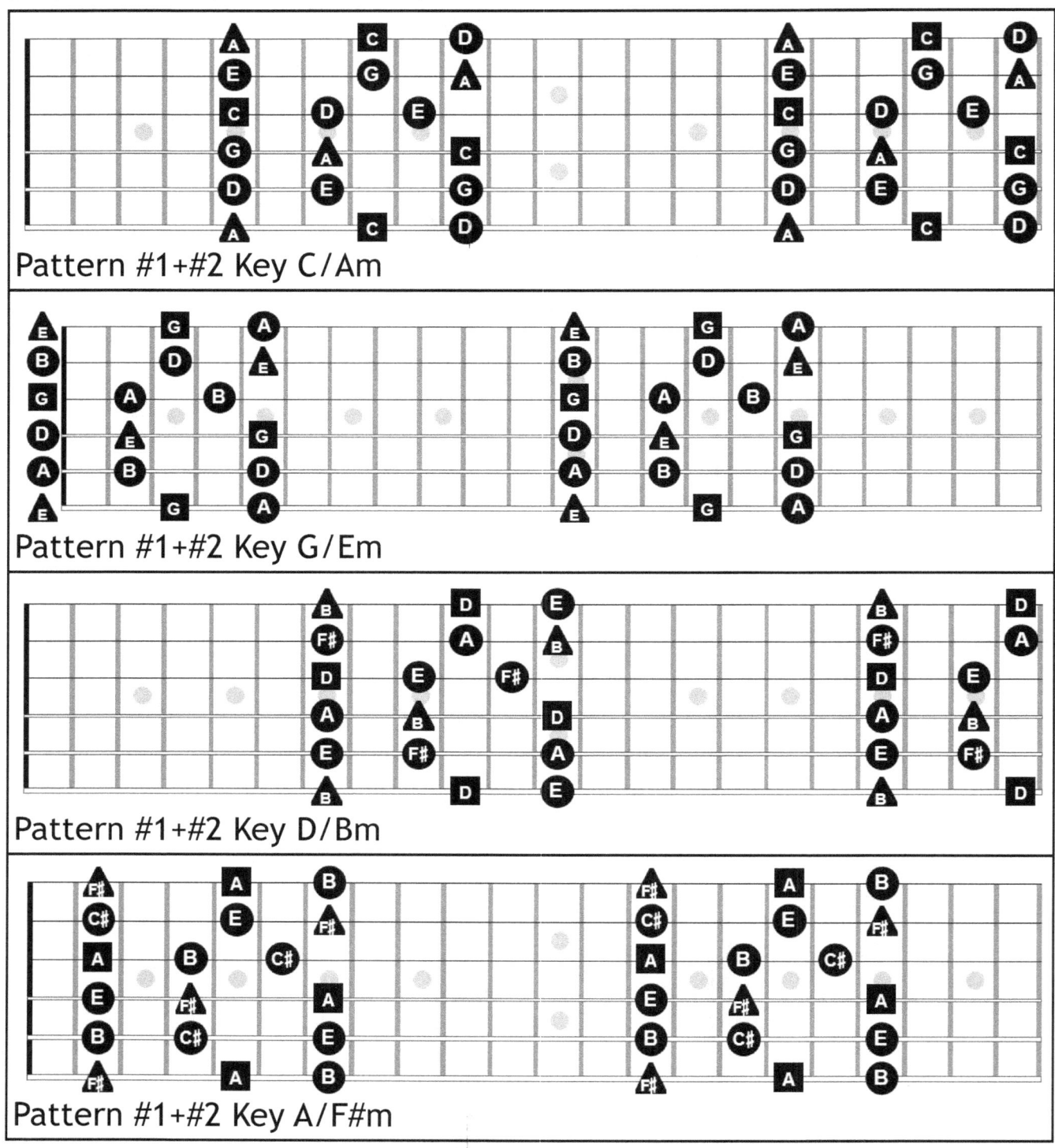

Pattern #1+#2 Key C/Am

Pattern #1+#2 Key G/Em

Pattern #1+#2 Key D/Bm

Pattern #1+#2 Key A/F#m

BLUES SCALE VS. THE BLUE NOTE

There is so much confusion surrounding the idea of a "Blues scale" and the "Blue Note." They both add an obviously bluesy sound but in different ways. A lot of people equate the two but to me they are very different ideas.

THE BLUES SCALE

The Blues scale is a slang term and people define it and use it in different ways. Some people think the blues scale happens once you add a blue note. Some add more than a blue note and some even play the scale different with different notes depending on what octave they are in.

To me, the Blues Scale is simply a matter of context.

Play a minor pentatonic over a Major chord.

It is an optional scale sound when you play in Major. The mismatch between the notes in a minor scale and its Major chord cause a really recognizable sound that we love. It's really important to understand that it is ABOUT CONTEXT and NOT NEW NOTES.

As a musician we ask ourselves what is the "main" chord and what is the scale for that chord. If a chord is minor we match it with a minor pentatonic. The same is true if it is a Major chord. If it is a Major chord we match it with a Major pentatonic.

Now, if the chord is Major we can ALSO use a BLUESY scale sound along with that HAPPY chord sound. That gives us two options for Major chords. Minor chords just get minor pentatonics.

I think of minor pentatonic as a SAD sound and a Major pentatonic HAPPY. I think of the Blues scale as simply BLUESY.

CHORD	SCALE
Em	E minor pentatonic-SAD
G	G Major pentatonic-HAPPY G minor pentatonic-BLUESY
E	E Major pentatonic-HAPPY E minor pentatonic-BLUESY
Am	A minor pentatonic-SAD

BLUES SCALE CONTINUED

If we compare the the notes we can see what is happening. If you have a G Major chord the notes of the chord are

G B D

The notes of the G Major pentatonic scale are

G A B D E

All of the notes in the chord (GBD) are in the scale. The Major pentatonic has the three notes of the chord and two more color tones.

The notes of a G minor pentatonic (G Blues Scale) are

G B*b* C D F

You can see that the B note became a B*b*. That is a minor third in the scale clashing with the Major third of the chord. This is what causes the the "Bluesy" sound. The F note creates a *b*7 interval which really helps it work with Dominant 7th chords (G7).

- The Blues scale doesn't always work. Sometimes it reveals its "wrongness." You just have to try it.
- You can mix Major (HAPPY) and minor(BLUESY) over a major chord. You can start in one and switch to the other, or craftily blend the two.
- The "Blues scale" sounds bluesy, whether you want it to or not. As soon as you play a minor pentatonic over a major chord it happens.
- Minor just gets minor. If you play a Major pentatonic over a minor chord it sounds awful. Try it.

THE BLUE NOTE

Contrary to the Blues Scale, the Blue Note is an additional note that is added to a pentatonic scale and can be added at any point that the sound would work. The Blue note is not part of the scale of even the key but it works wonderfully (most of the time). I like to think of the Blue Note like hot sauce. I love hot sauce on most things, but sometimes it just doesn't work, like on pancakes. Also, too much hot sauce with ruin its effect. Both are true with the Blue Note. The Blue Note is in ALL styles of music, not just blues. From Classical to metal to punk, pop, bluegrass, don't let the word blue fool you.

As a guitar player it is easy to remember the Blue Note as it lives in the same physical place in the pentatonics regardless of what key you are in. There is only one Blue Note in a scale and it lives in multiple places (octaves).

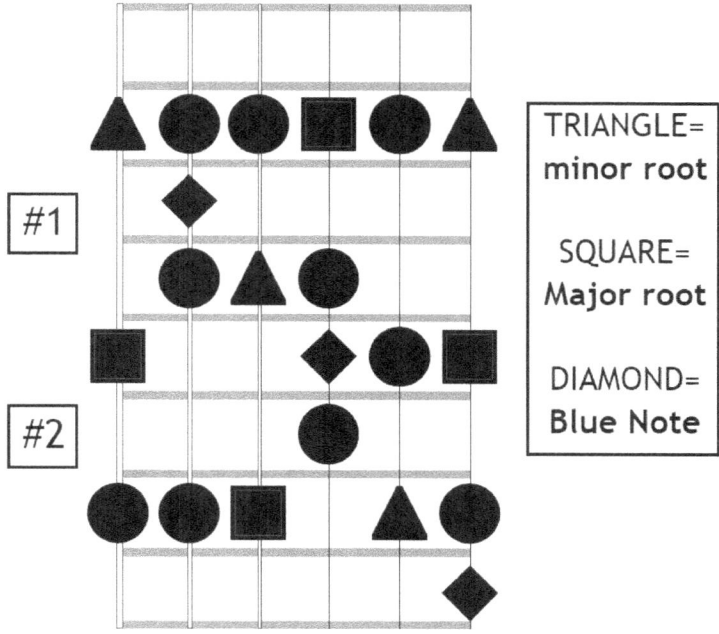

TRIANGLE=
minor root

SQUARE=
Major root

DIAMOND=
Blue Note

- The Blue Note is an artificial additive, season to taste.
- The Blue Note works in Major, minor and Blues but sounds different in each. It can be sassy and swanky to dirty and evil.
- ALL styles of music use the Blue note not just Blues.

WATCH video about Blues Scale vs the Blue Note
www.LeadGuitarWorkshop.com

PRACTICE

Round the Block

A great way to practice the patterns is what I call "Round the Block." Simply ascend pattern #1, shift up, and descend pattern #2. You can also reverse that. Descend pattern #1, shift up and ascend pattern #2.

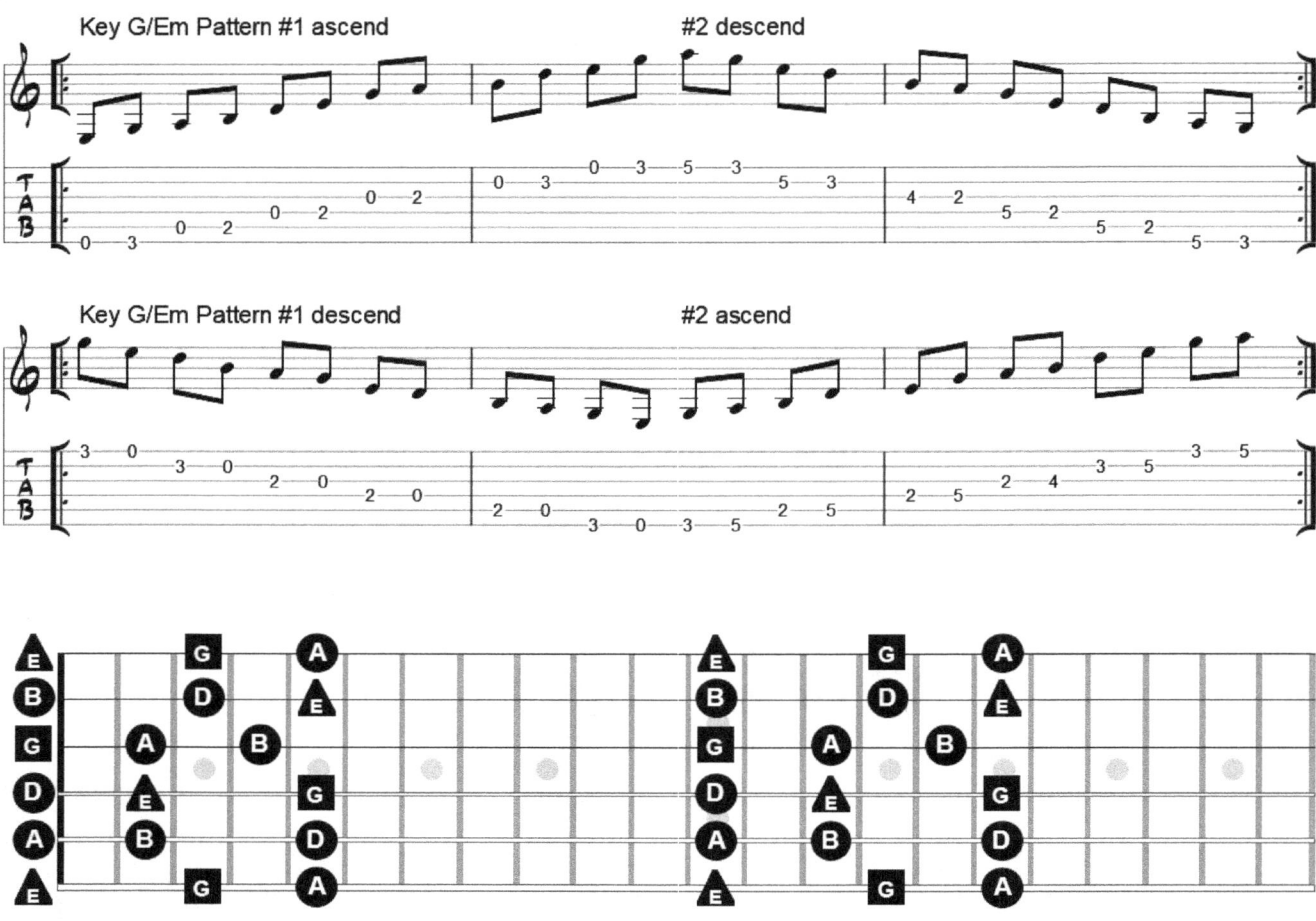

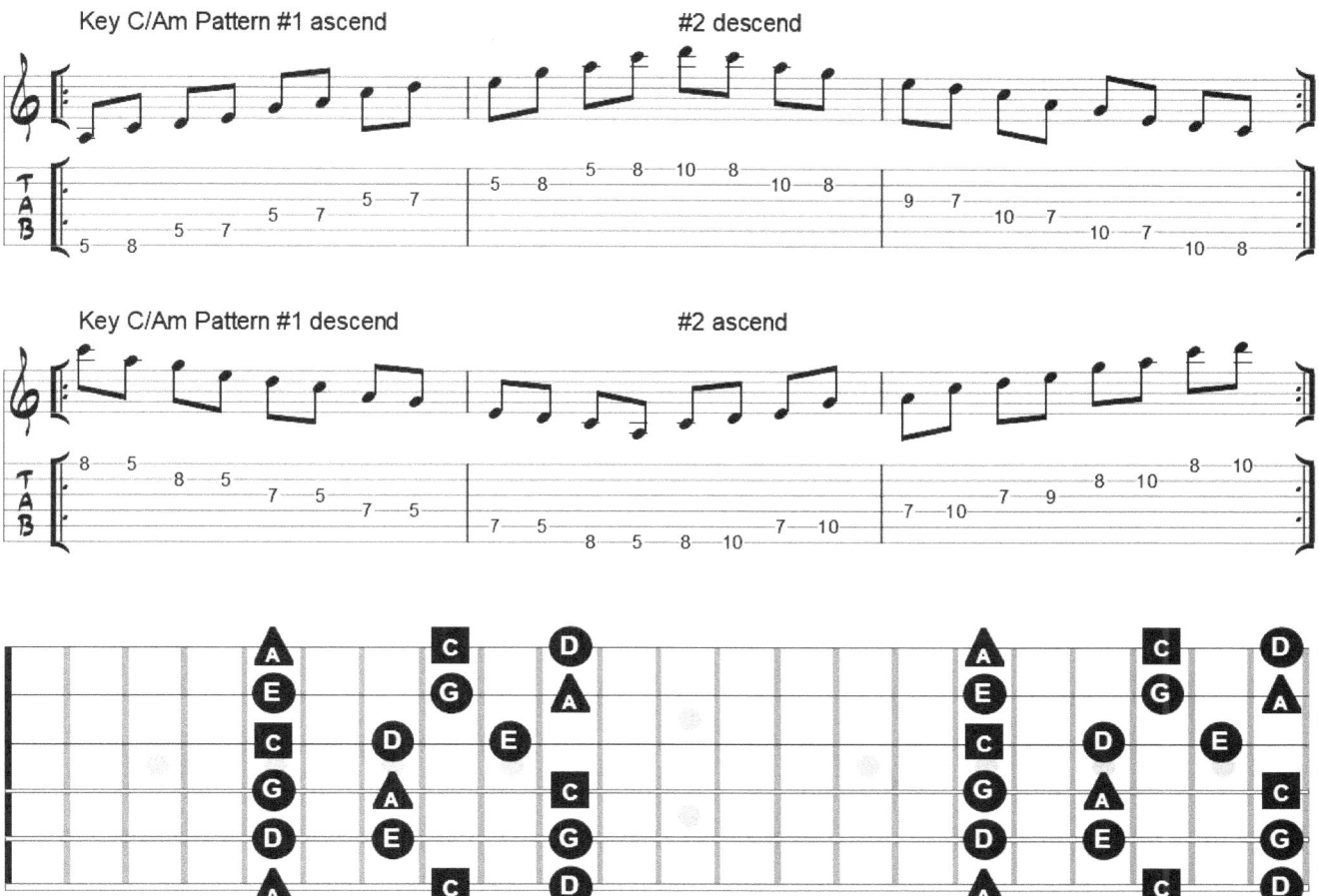

- There are 12 notes in any pentatonic pattern (two notes per string for six strings).

- Round the Block goes up one pattern, shifts and goes down the next. You can eventually zig-zag through all five patterns.

- You can start on any pattern and ascend or descend first.

- Always do everything in time (with a rhythm).

LICKS

KEY OF G MAJOR - E MINOR

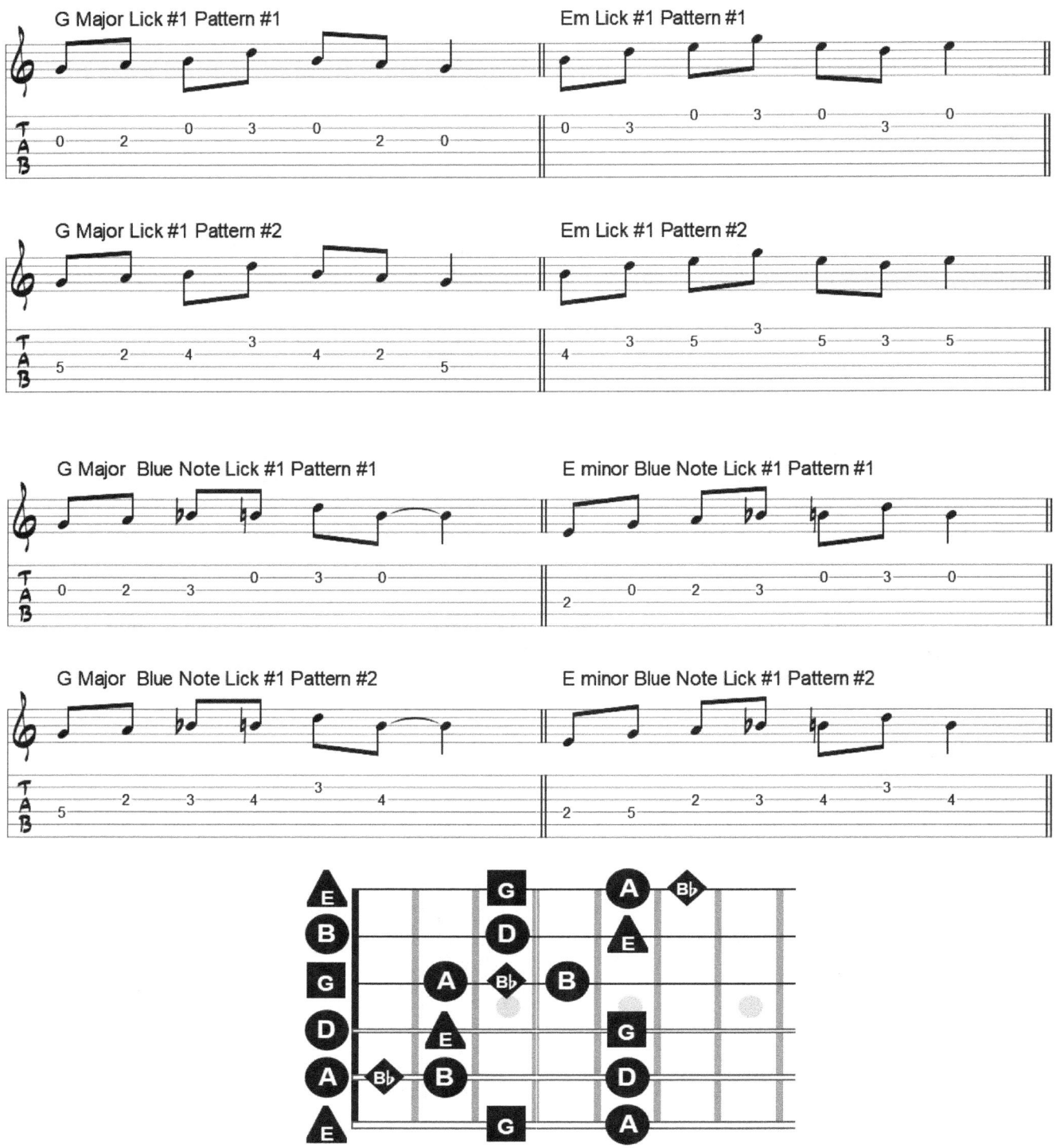

KEY OF C MAJOR - A MINOR

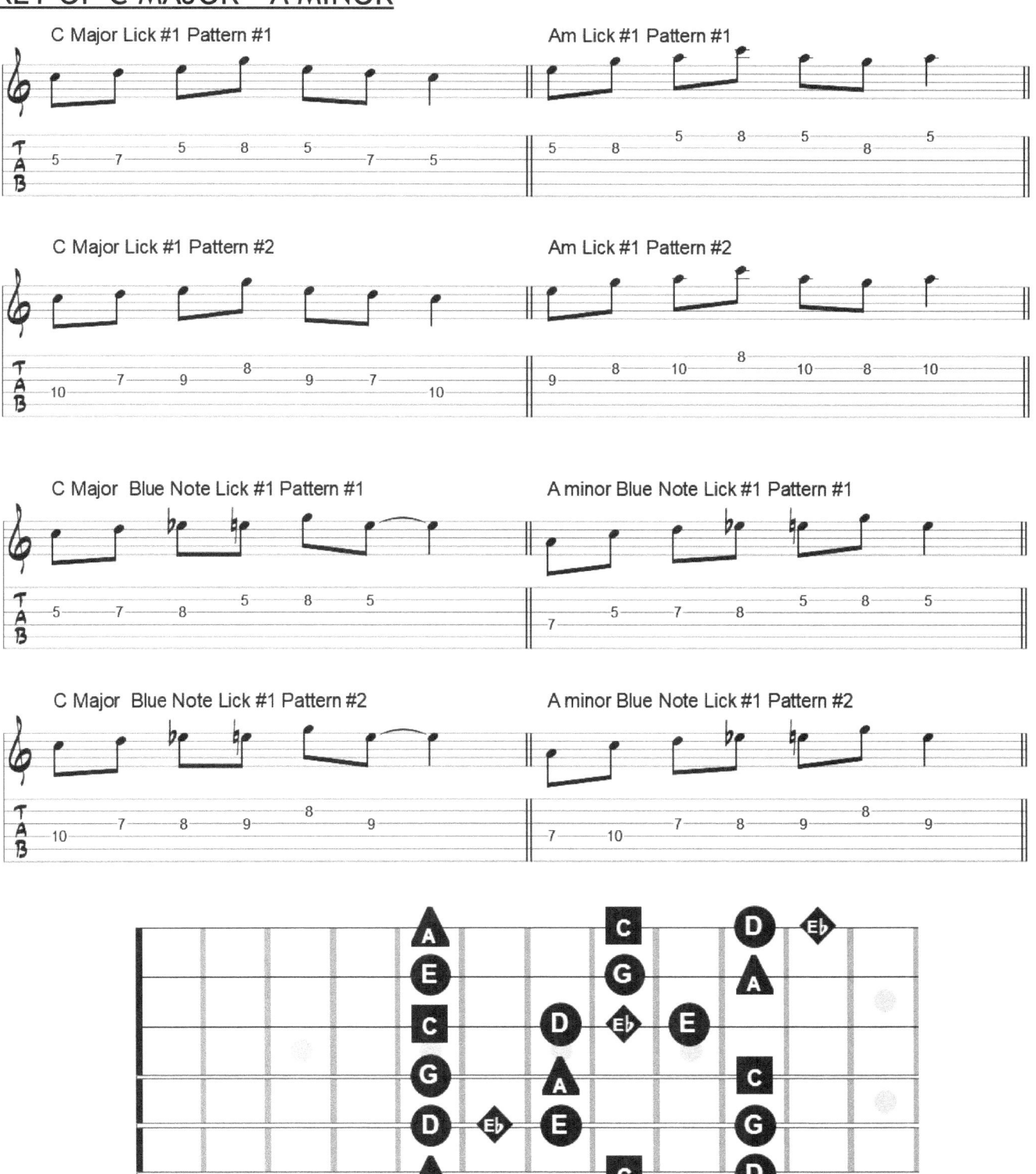

C Major Lick #1 Pattern #1

Am Lick #1 Pattern #1

C Major Lick #1 Pattern #2

Am Lick #1 Pattern #2

C Major Blue Note Lick #1 Pattern #1

A minor Blue Note Lick #1 Pattern #1

C Major Blue Note Lick #1 Pattern #2

A minor Blue Note Lick #1 Pattern #2

BACKING TRACKS

Knowing a 12 bar blues is an essential skill for any musician. And for guitar players the key of E and key of A are the two most prominent. I assume this is because of the benefit of the open strings.

In an E blues the main chord is an E7 chord (which is major). The best scale for all three chords (especially when all three are 7th chords) is the minor pentatonic of the main chord. This would be an E minor pentatonic and it would act like an E Blues scale.

SOLO IDEAS:
- E minor pentatonic and improvise
- Pattern #1 in the open position and Pattern #2 on the 3rd fret
- Use E minor Licks
- Add the Blue Note
- Play one bar, rest one bar
- Repeat ideas
- Use same patterns #1 and #2 at 12th fret (and 15th)

12 BAR BLUES IN E

E^7	E^7	E^7	E^7	
A^7	A^7	E^7	E^7	
B^7	A^7	E^7	B^7	‖

BACKING TRACK: 12 BAR BLUES IN E
www.LeadGuitarWorkshop.com

12 BAR BLUES IN A

SOLO IDEAS:
- A minor pentatonic and improvise
- Pattern #1 on the 5th fret and Pattern #2 on the 8th fret
- Use A minor Licks
- Add the Blue Note
- Play one bar, rest one bar
- Repeat ideas
- Use same patterns #1 and #2 at 17th fret (and 20th)

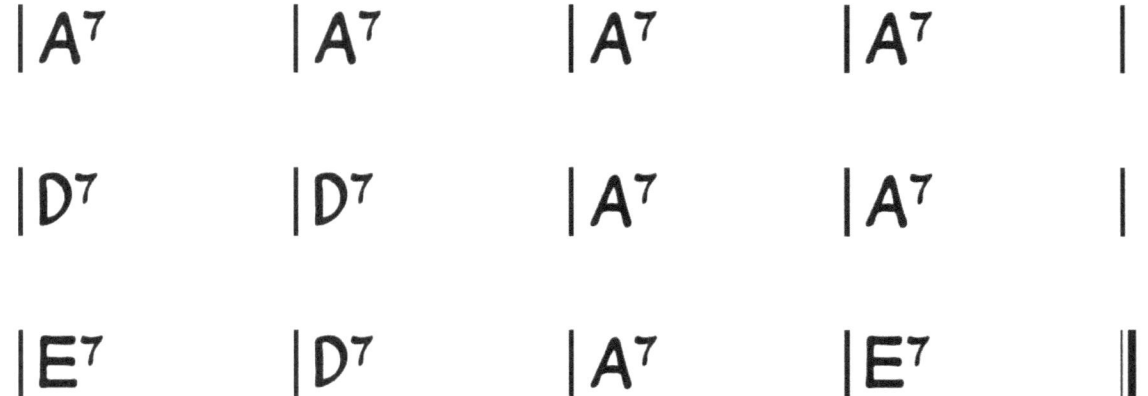

BACKING TRACK: 12 BAR BLUES IN A
www.LeadGuitarWorkshop.com

SUMMARY

We are musicians. We are guitar players.
We learn the language of music. Melody, Harmony, and Rhythm
We learn the craft of playing the guitar as an instrument.

We warm up with Muted String Ladders (MSL) and SHELLS.

RHYTHM is most important.

We Exercise our scales and licks.

We learn musical ideas (LICKS) to start to build "musical conversation" to learn to improvise.

AS A MUSICIAN:

- We decide on the "main" chord and base the scale upon that chord.
- MINOR chord gets a MINOR scale.
- MAJOR chord can get either the MAJOR pentatonic and/or the BLUES pentatonic.

AS A GUITAR PLAYER:

- Once we know the music scale we need to find the ROOT note on the low E string.
- Then we decide on the the FIRST FINGER for MINOR or BLUES or we use the PINKY for MAJOR.
- Once Pattern #1 is on the fretboard everything is relative to it.
- Add Pattern #2, always connected to pattern #1, to extend the range of the scale further up the fretboard. (more octaves of the same notes)
- Add the Blue Note for extra color.

CHAPTER 3

TUNE IN

"I am a musician and a guitar player. Music is my language and my guitar is my voice. Music is Melody, Harmony and Rhythm. I develop my language skills and my instrument skills. They are two separate worlds working together to complete the circle of music."

Rhythm is the number one factor to sounding great as a musician.

WARM UP

Muted String Ladder (MSL) top 3 strings all gears

First ALL DOWN picked
Second ALL UP picked
Third ALTERNATE pick.
If limited by TIME (In the day, or fast tempo) then ALTERNATE pick ALL.

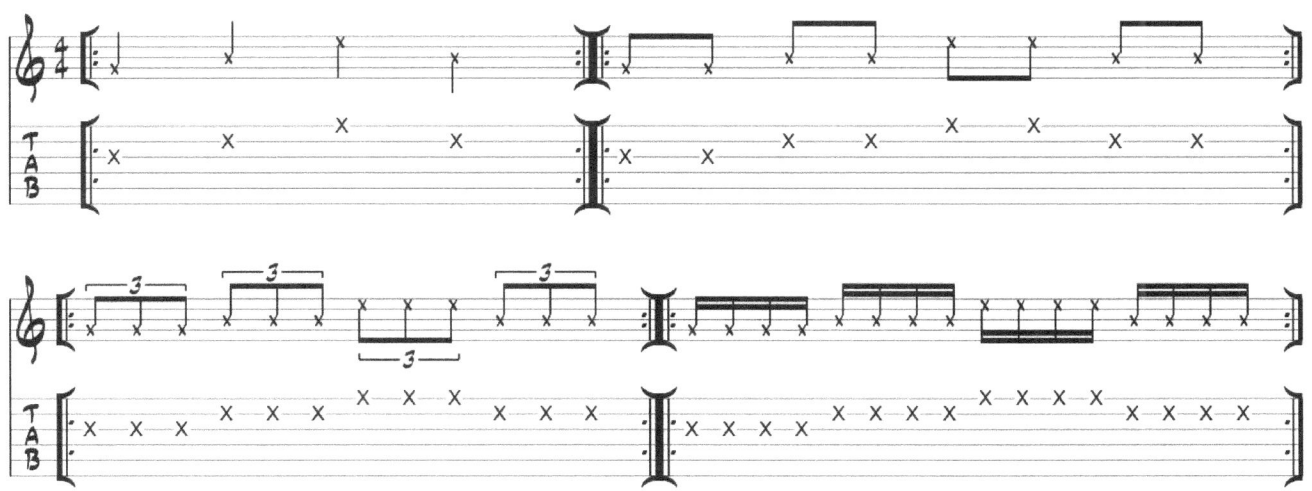

SHELL 2 4

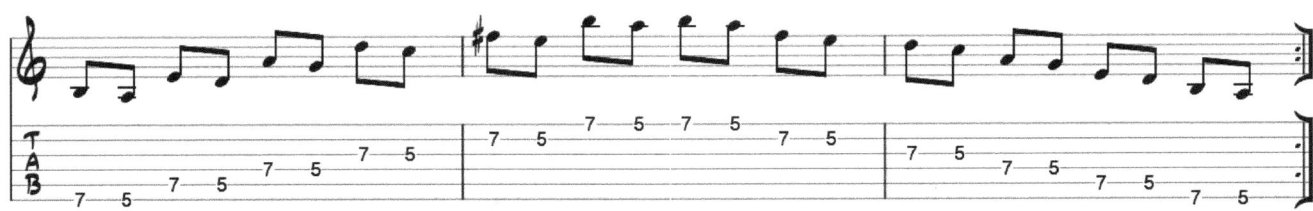

SHELL 1 3 Triplets

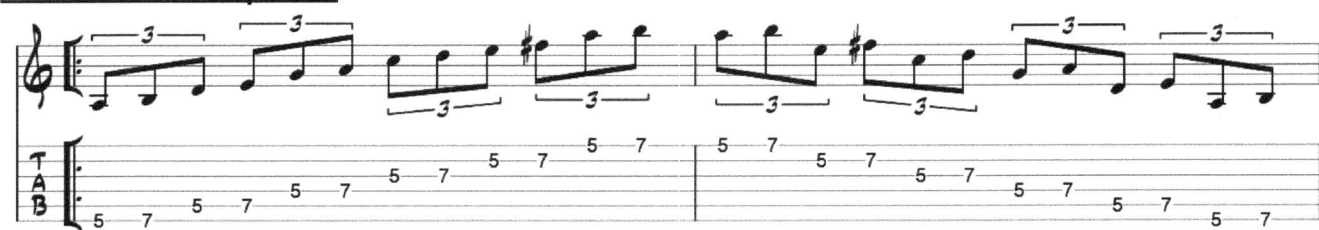

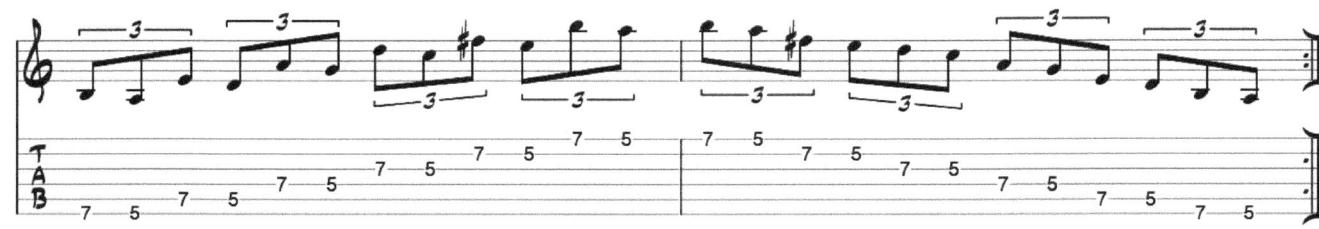

SHELL 1 3 STRETCH (for pentatonic scales high on the neck)

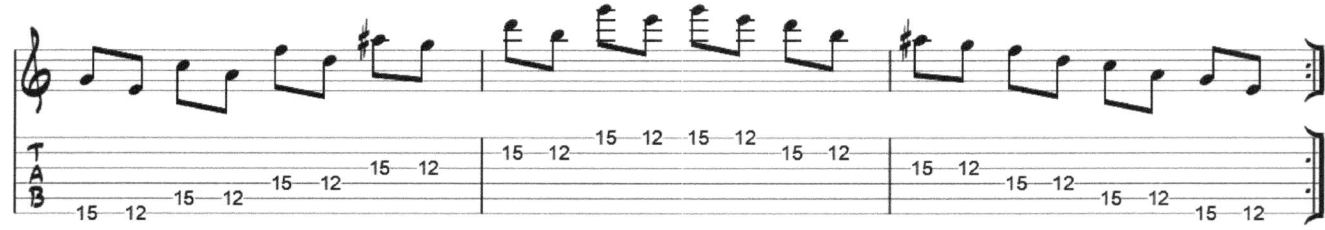

EXERCISE

ROUND THE BLOCK   Patterns #1 and #2   ascend #1 and descend #2 (**=shift)

KEY: G Major/E minor

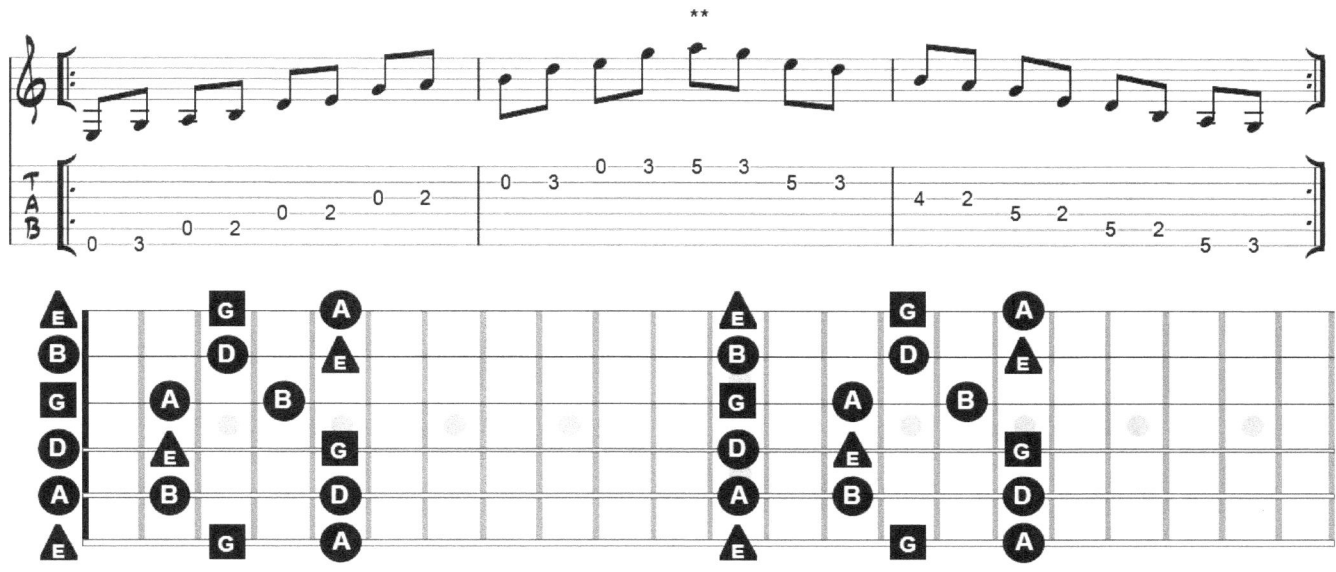

KEY: D Major/B minor

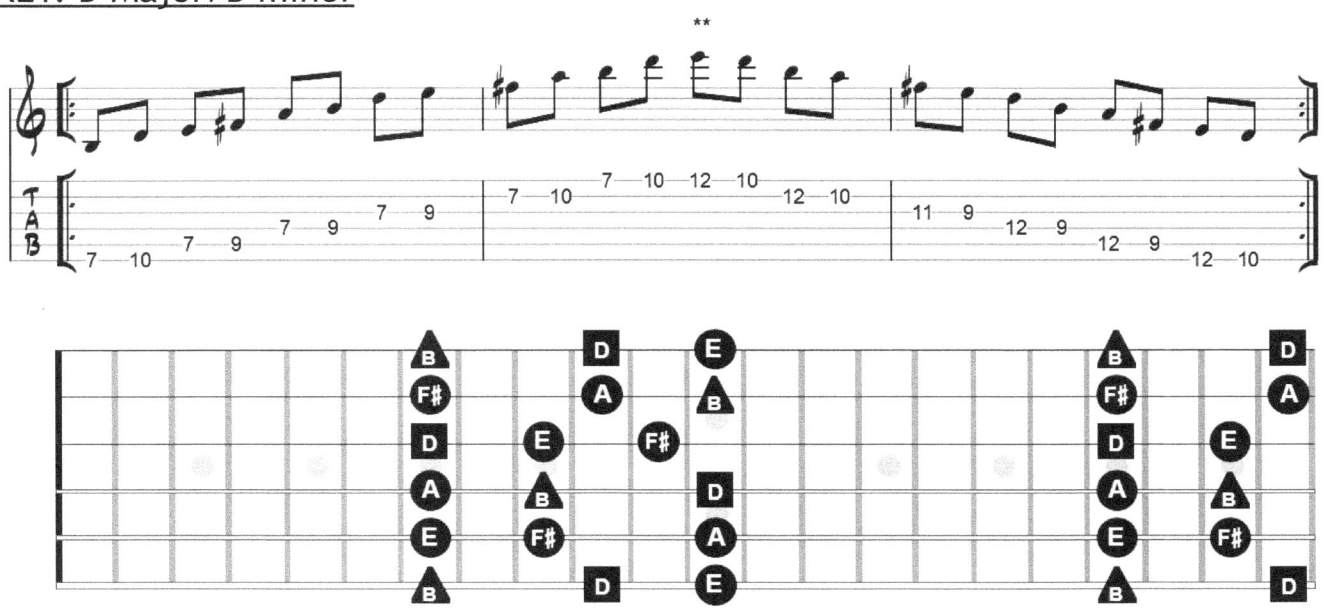

KEY: G Major/E minor   add Blue Note

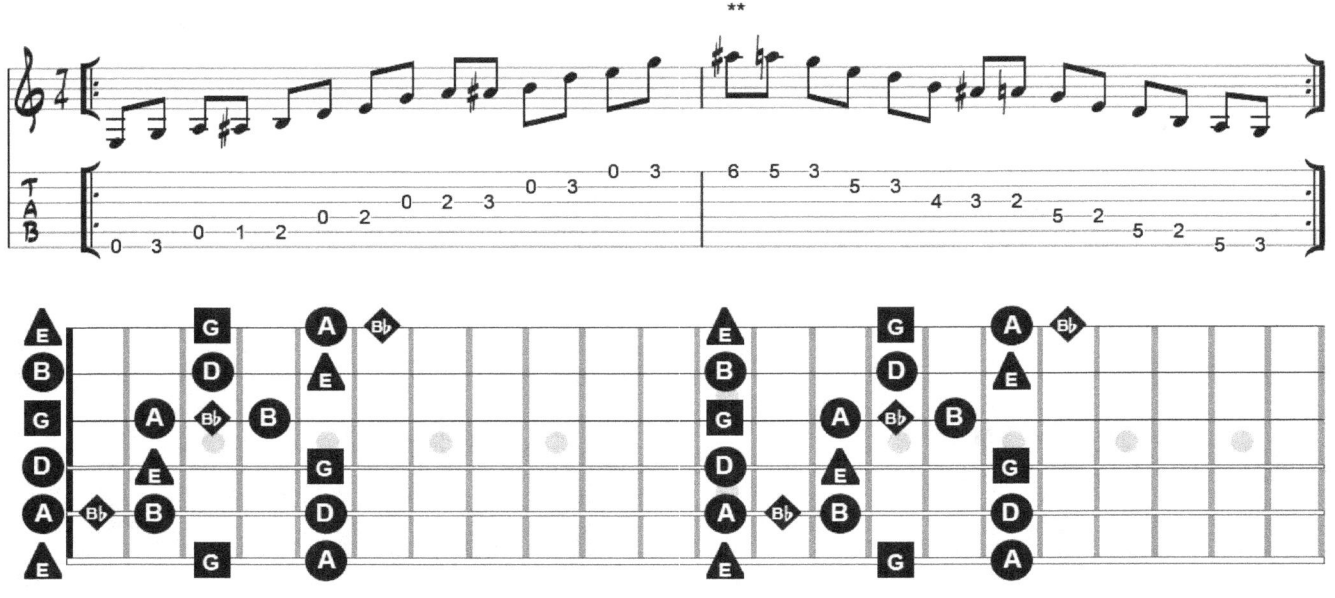

KEY: D Major/B minor   add Blue Note

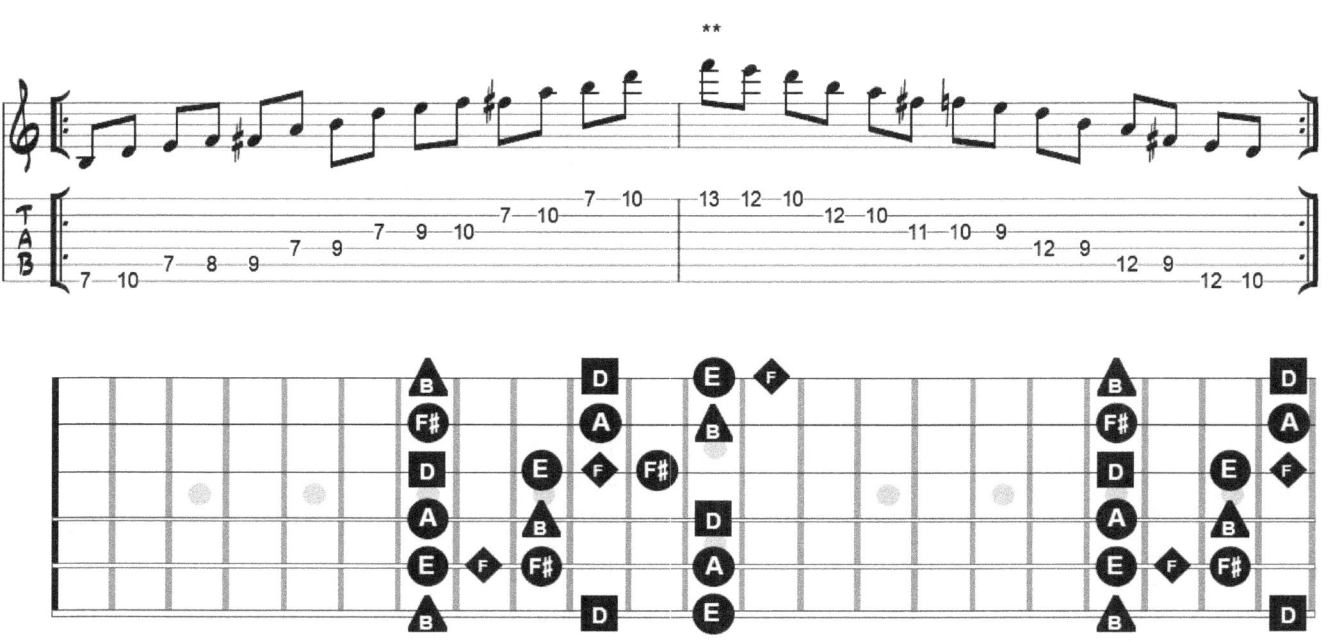

REVIEW

As a musician, we know there are only 12 notes. There are only 12 keys, 12 Major chords, 12 minor chords, 12 Major pentatonic scales, and 12 minor pentatonic scales. We also know about Relative Major and minor relationships. For every Major there is a relative minor. This is true as a chord, a pentatonic scale, Major and minor scales (7 note scale Ionian/Aeolian).

C/Am	G/Em	D/Bm	A/F#m	E/C#m	B/G#m
F#/E*b*	D*b*/B*b*m	A*b*/Fm	E*b*/Cm	B*b*/Gm	F/Dm

Every chord has a pentatonic that matches it. G Major chord get a G Major pentatonic. C# minor chord gets a C# minor pentatonic.

Every chord progression has a "main" chord. It is the one chord the others revolve around. It is the chord you want to end on. That main chord is often the key but not always. The main chord might be the one you see the most often or it might be the first chord. The only way to really know is to listen and see what chord the song wants to stop on, as if you were onstage performing it.

We match a pentatonic scale to the main chord of the chord progression. I call this playing "globally." We are using one pentatonic scale for all of the chords in the progression. This almost always works.

Minor chords always get a minor pentatonic. A Major chord can get either. If you play a Major pentatonic scale over a Major chord (G Major pentatonic scale over a G Major chord) then you get a very upbeat, happy, nice sound. But, if you played a G minor scale over the G Major chord, it would be the BLUES SCALE. The Blues scale is the minor pentatonic scale over the Major chord (of the same Root).

The Blues Scale is an extremely common sound and works well in so many places. It works great over the "main" chord in a progression. It's not supposed to work, but it usually does. You will know pretty quickly if it doesn't because it just sounds wrong.

Compare the songs "Can't You See" By Marshall Tucker and "Sympathy for the Devil" by the Rolling Stones. They both have the same progression V IV I V. The Major flute melody greatly contrasts Keith Richards Blues scale solo.

In contrast to the contextual nature of the BLUES SCALE, we also looked at the BLUE NOTE. It is an "artificial additive" that we can add to our pentatonic at any time to add cool color. It works wonderfully in ALL THREE ways we use a pentatonic scale; as a MAJOR scale, a MINOR scale and a BLUES scale.

As Guitar players we have focused on how to properly navigate pattern #1 on the fretboard once we have made our musical decision about what scale to play. We learned that Pattern #1 is special because it happens to contain the Relative Major and relative minor note on the same string (E string). Once pattern #1 is correctly placed everything else fits relative to that.

We must know the 12 notes on the low (and high) E string to navigate our pattern #1. We remember that EF and BC have no space (or fret) between them.

First finger for the minor root, and pinky for the Major root, that's the "ROCK AND ROLL RULE" for Pattern #1. This rule reminds us where the ROOTS are for the RELATIVE MAJOR and RELATIVE MINOR.

Once pattern #1 is on the fretboard, then Pattern #2 is ALWAYS connected to pattern #1 higher up on the fretboard. All five patterns are relative to each other. We will see how #5 is ALWAYS *behind* pattern #1. Patterns #5 and #2 "bookend" pattern #1.

The SHELLS can helps us practice the most common fingerings. For pentatonic scales there only two intervals (distance between notes); a WHOLE STEP and WHOLE+HALF STEP. On guitar this translates to a distance of either 2 or 3 frets. Our fretboard hand will play these in one of four ways. For the WHOLE STEP you will use either 1 3 or 2 4 fingers. (Some even use 1 2 for the whole step.) For the WHOLE+HALF STEP you will use either 1 4 or 1 3 stretch. The SHELLS help us exercise all the potential permutations of these fingerings.

The Blue Note is available in 3 octaves in patterns #1 and #2. It is the same note, just occurring in different octaves. It is always in the same physical place in the scale patterns no matter the key. It is in the same place regardless of whether we are thinking Major, minor, or Blues.

HAMMER-ONS, PULL-OFFS, SLIDES

Legato is a term in the music world for making a smooth consistent sound between all of your notes. There should be an even volume with no silence between notes and that will soften the attack of the notes and even them out into one stream of sound. Different instruments deal with this differently. On the guitar we have four techniques to achieve this; Hammer-ons, Pull-offs, Slides, and Bends. We will explore bending more deeply in a future chapter.

It is extremely important to maintain the rhythm of the original phrase when you enhance it with legato techniques.

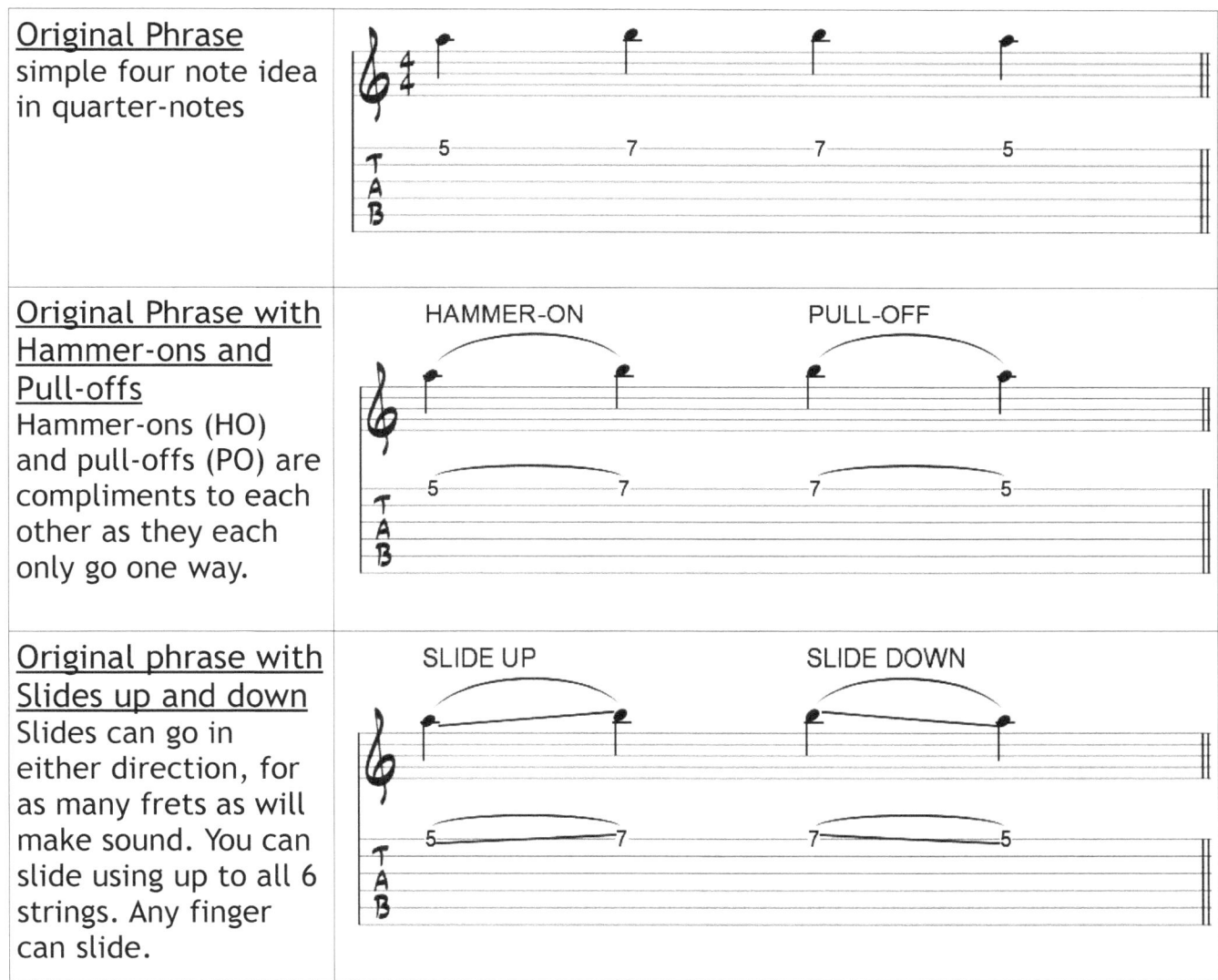

Original Phrase simple four note idea in quarter-notes	
Original Phrase with Hammer-ons and Pull-offs Hammer-ons (HO) and pull-offs (PO) are compliments to each other as they each only go one way.	
Original phrase with Slides up and down Slides can go in either direction, for as many frets as will make sound. You can slide using up to all 6 strings. Any finger can slide.	

PATTERN #5

In the same way that pattern #2 is always above pattern #1, Pattern #5 is
ALWAYS *behind* pattern #1. It is still the same five notes as patterns #1 and #2.
It just helps us move our scale sound further around the fretboard.

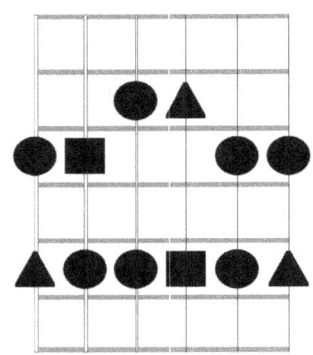

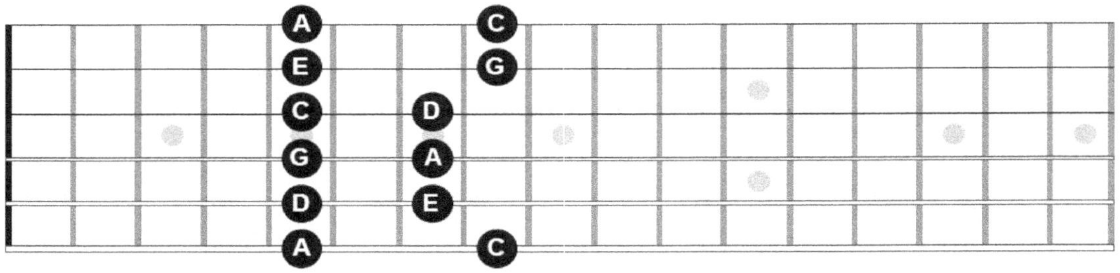

Pattern #1 C Major / A minor

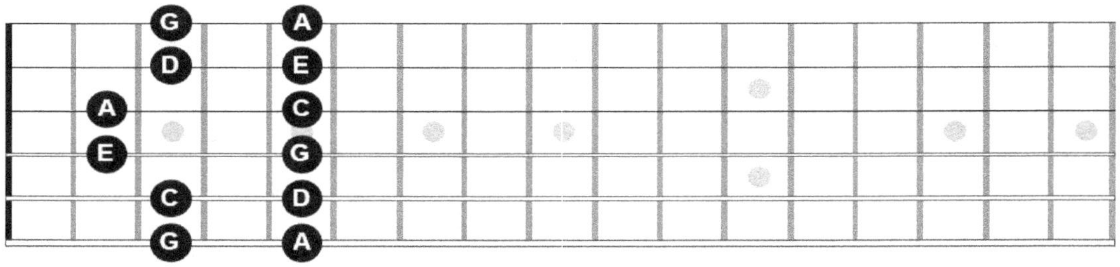

Pattern #5 C Major / A minor

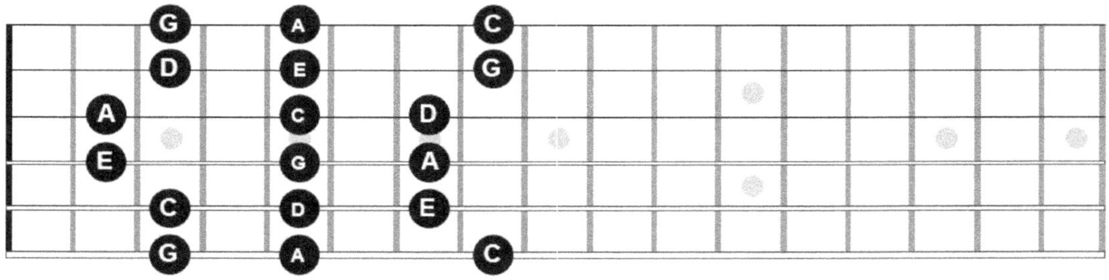

Pattern #5 + #1 C Major / A minor

PRACTICE

ROUND THE BLOCK   Key C Major A minor   ascend #1 descend #5

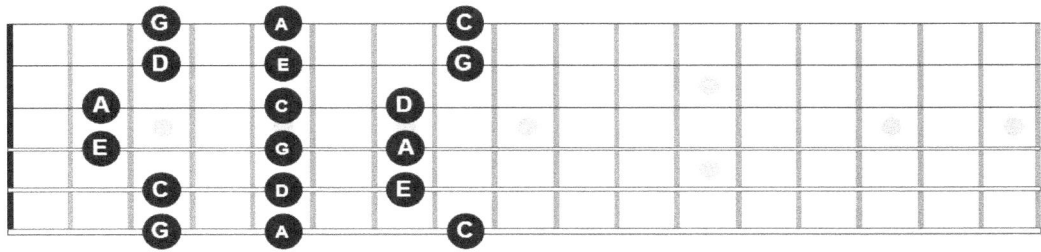

Pattern #1 C Major A minor   Pattern #5 C Major A minor

SELF GEN   C Major Chord (can use Am too)   HO PO SLIDE

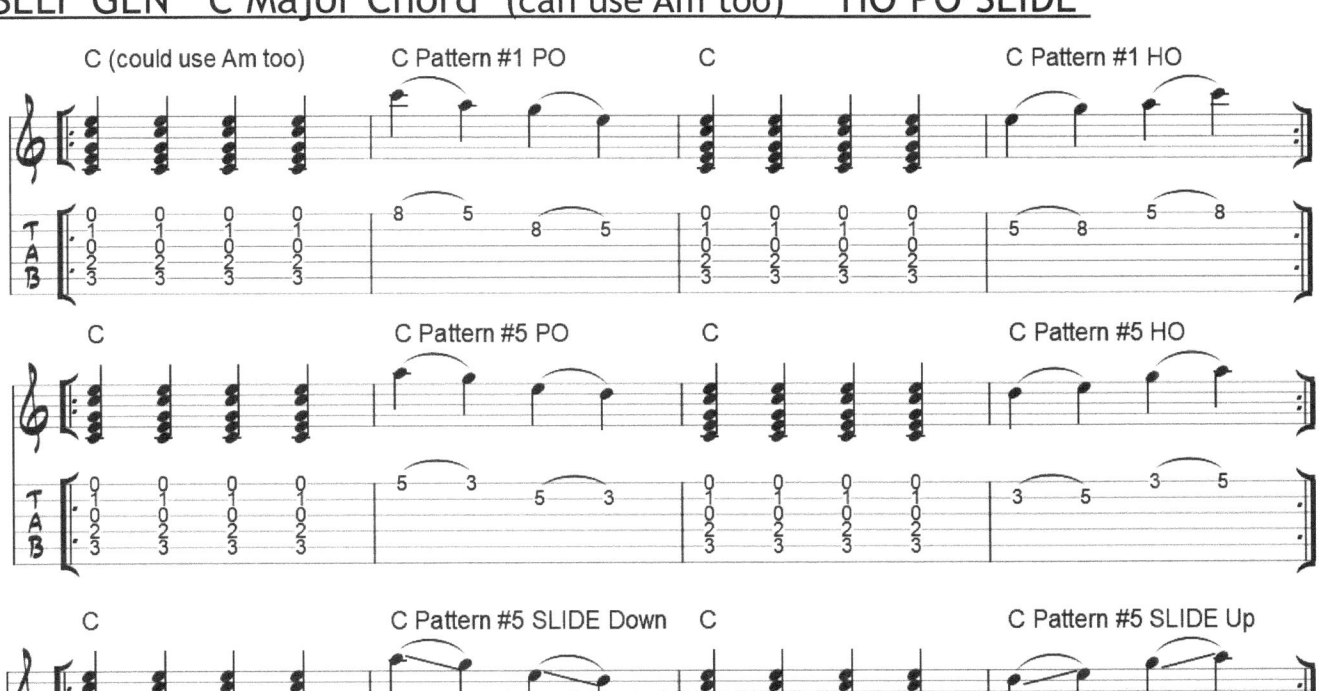

C (could use Am too)   C Pattern #1 PO   C   C Pattern #1 HO

C   C Pattern #5 PO   C   C Pattern #5 HO

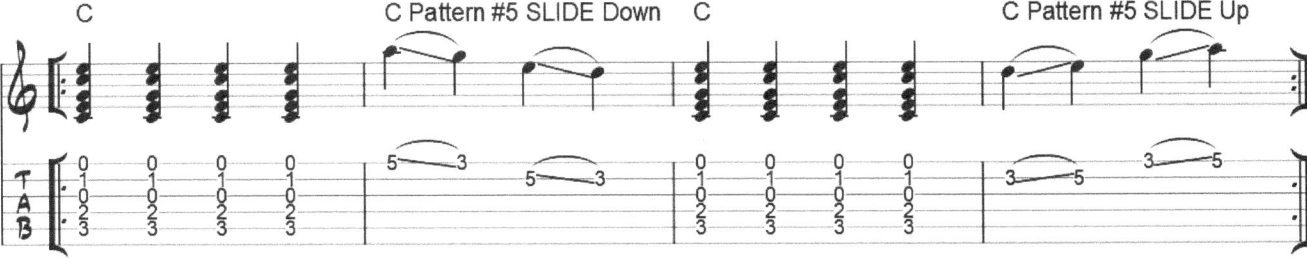

C   C Pattern #5 SLIDE Down   C   C Pattern #5 SLIDE Up

ROUND THE BLOCK

<u>KEY G Major E minor   Higher octave   ascend #1 descend #5</u>

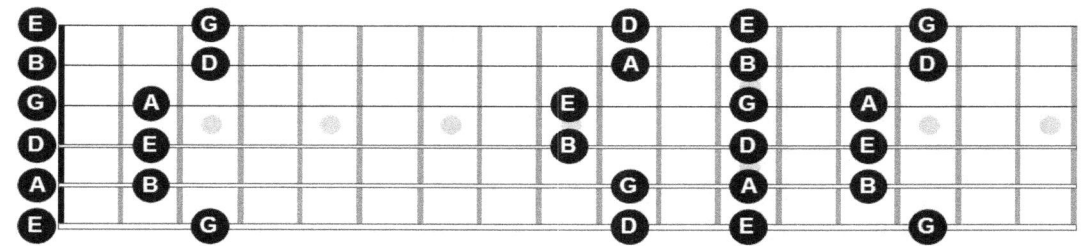

Pattern #1 G Major E minor   Pattern #5 G Major E minor

<u>SELF GEN E minor Chord</u> (Can use G Major too)   HO PO SLIDE

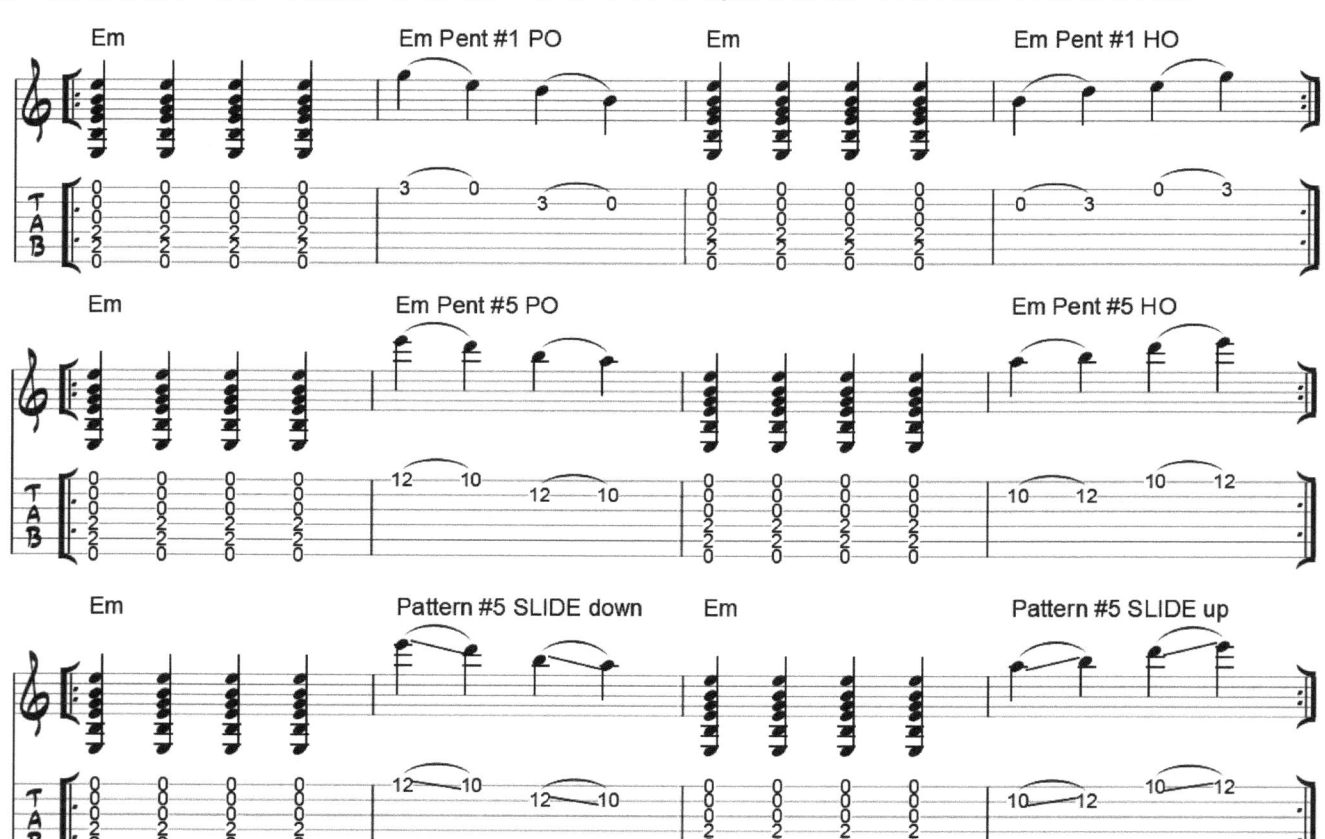

ROUND THE BLOCK
KEY D Major B minor   ascend #1 descend #5

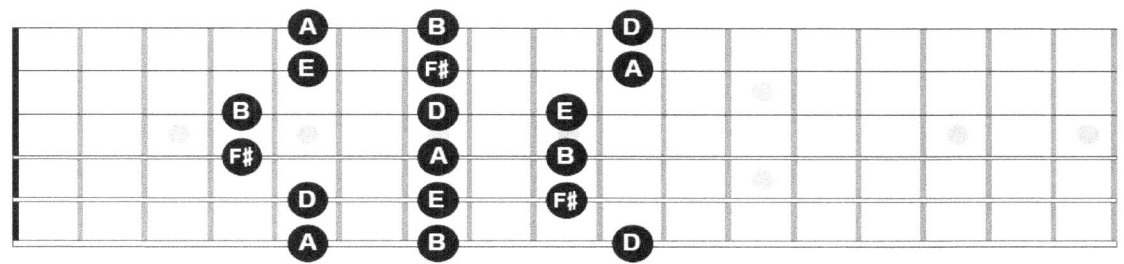

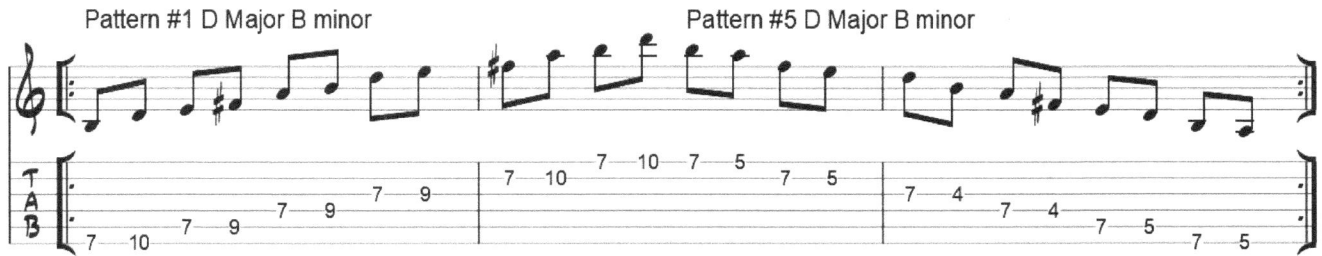

Pattern #1 D Major B minor   Pattern #5 D Major B minor

SELF GEN   D Major Chord (Can use Bm too) HO PO SLIDE

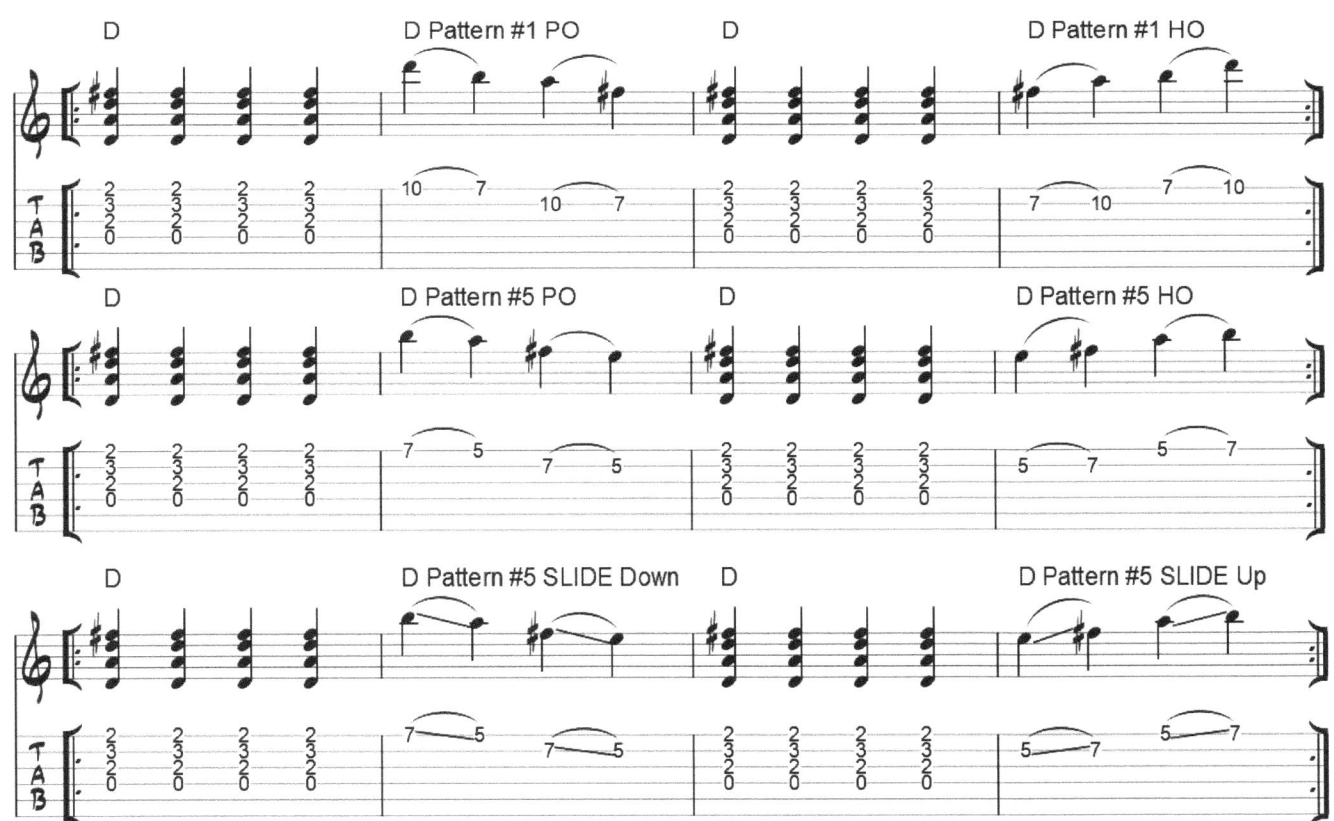

LICKS

Licks by the NOTES:

Find them in any octave and move them in any direction the notes will allow. Change the rhythm and phrasing. They are all within the span of an octave. The first lick is one of the most classic sounds on guitar. It usually happens between patterns #1 and #2 on the G string. You can play this in many ways. It's a great musical idea.

The slide is particular to this lick. *(S)=slide*

You can freely add HO, PO, and SLIDES between any notes that are on the same string.

C MAJOR	_A MINOR_
CD*(S)*EG (the 1-2 Slide)	ACD*(S)*EG (the 1-2 Slide)
CDEG	EGA
CAC	AGA
GACDC	ACDE
CGAC	EGCA
CDEC	CAGA
CDEGE	EGACA
GADC	CAE

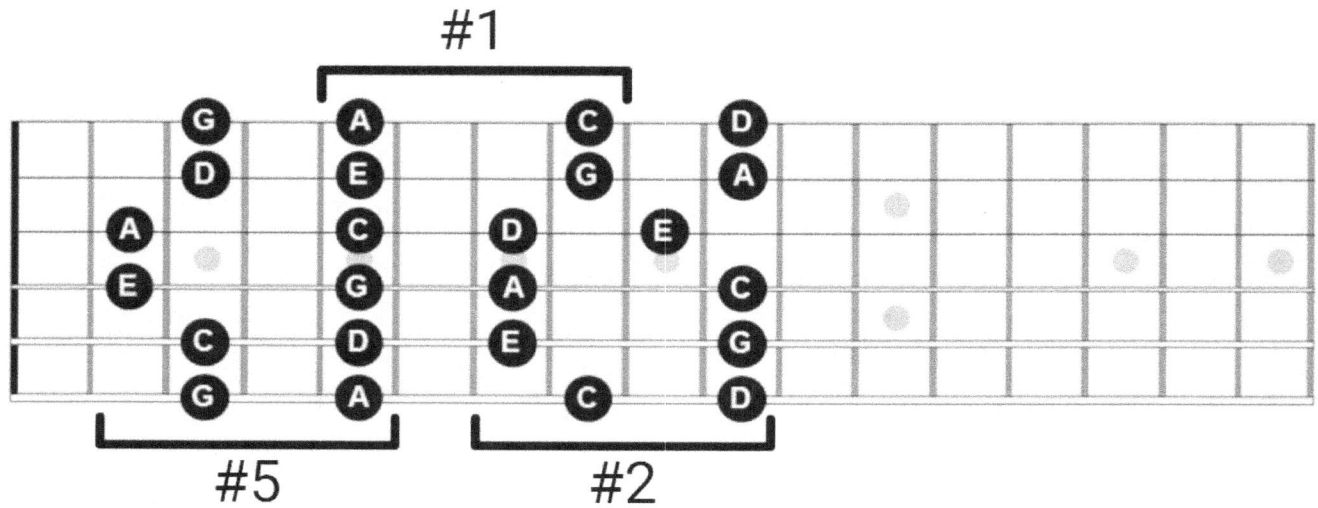

SUMMARY

We are musicians. We are guitar players.
We learn the language of music. Melody, Harmony, and Rhythm
We learn the craft of playing the guitar as an instrument.

We warm up with Muted String Ladders (MSL) and SHELLS.

RHYTHM is most important.

We Exercise our scales and licks. Round the Block is an easy and effective way to memorize and run the patterns.

We learn musical ideas (LICKS) to start to build "musical conversation" to learn to improvise.

AS A MUSICIAN:

- We decide on the "main" chord and base the scale upon that chord.
- MINOR chord gets a MINOR scale.
- MAJOR chord can get either the MAJOR pentatonic and/or the BLUES pentatonic.
- Add the Blue Note for extra color.

AS A GUITAR PLAYER:

- Once we know the music scale we need to find the ROOT note on the low E string.
- Then we decide on the the FIRST FINGER for MINOR or BLUES or we use the PINKY for MAJOR.
- Once Pattern #1 is on the fretboard everything is relative to it.
- Add Pattern #2 and #5, always connected on either side of pattern #1 to extend the range of the scale further up and down the fretboard.

CHAPTER 4

TUNE IN

"I am a musician and a guitar player. Music is my language and my guitar is my voice. Music is Melody, Harmony and Rhythm. I develop my language skills and my instrument skills. They are two separate worlds working together to complete the circle of music."

Rhythm is the number one factor to sounding great as a musician.

WARM UP

MSL 3 Strings DGB   all gears

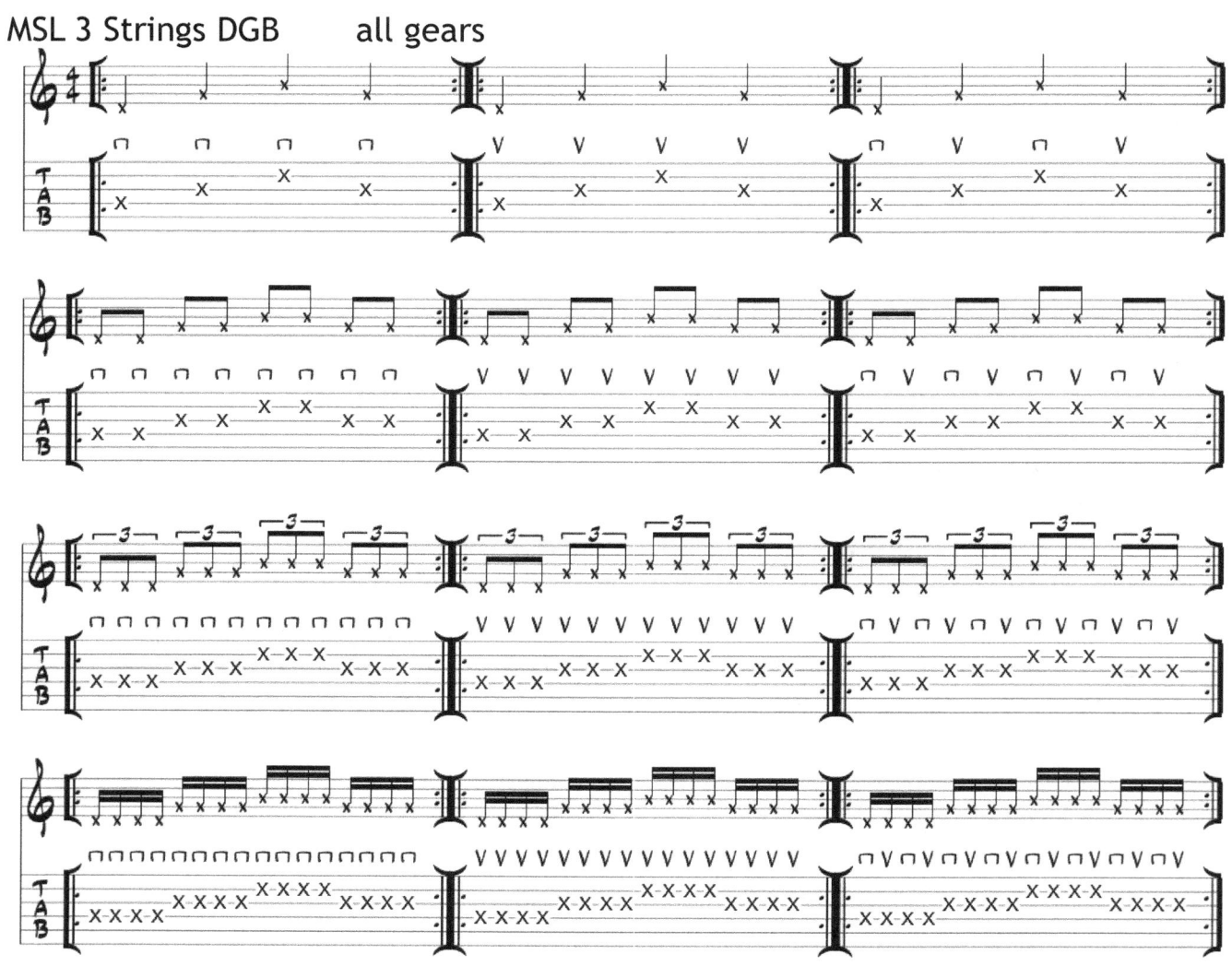

SHELL 1 3 Hammer-ons and Pull-offs (HO PO)

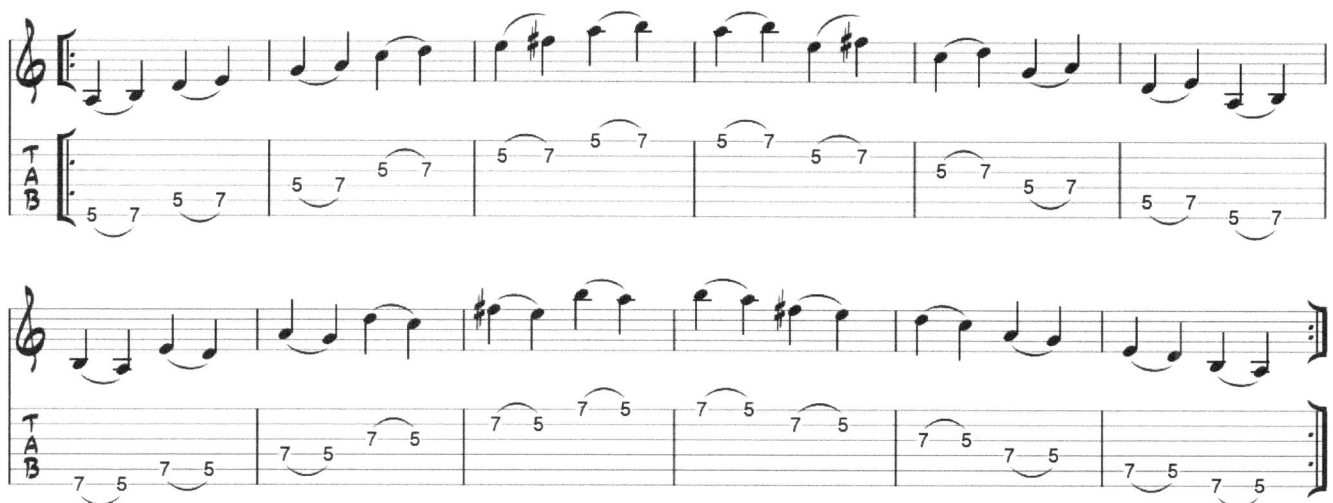

SHELL 1 3 SLIDES

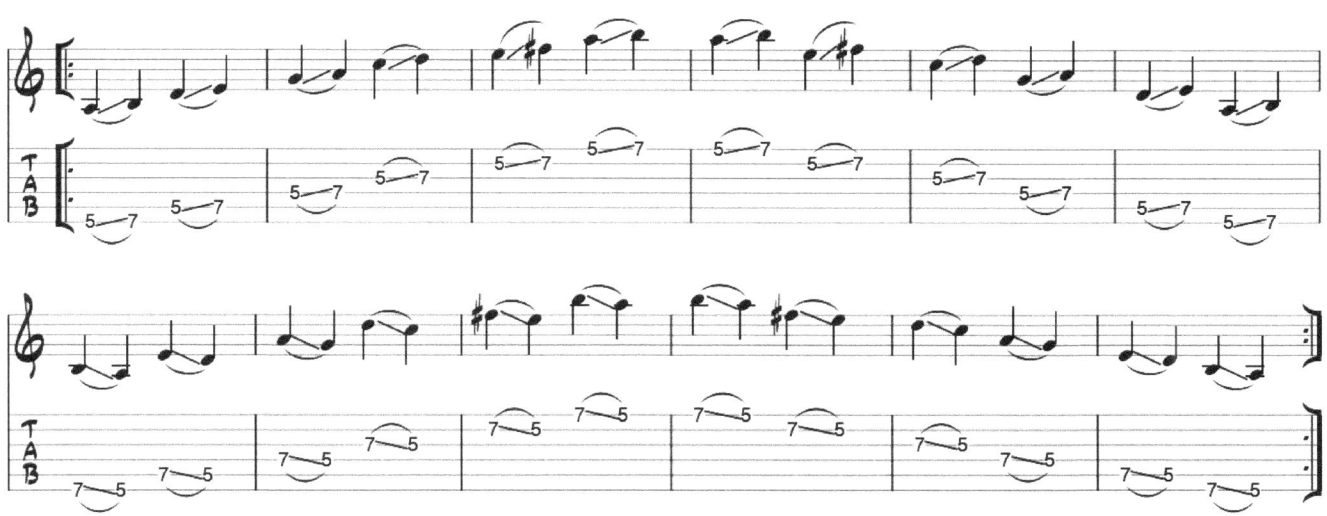

EXERCISE

Patterns #5, #1, #2   up and down and Round the Block

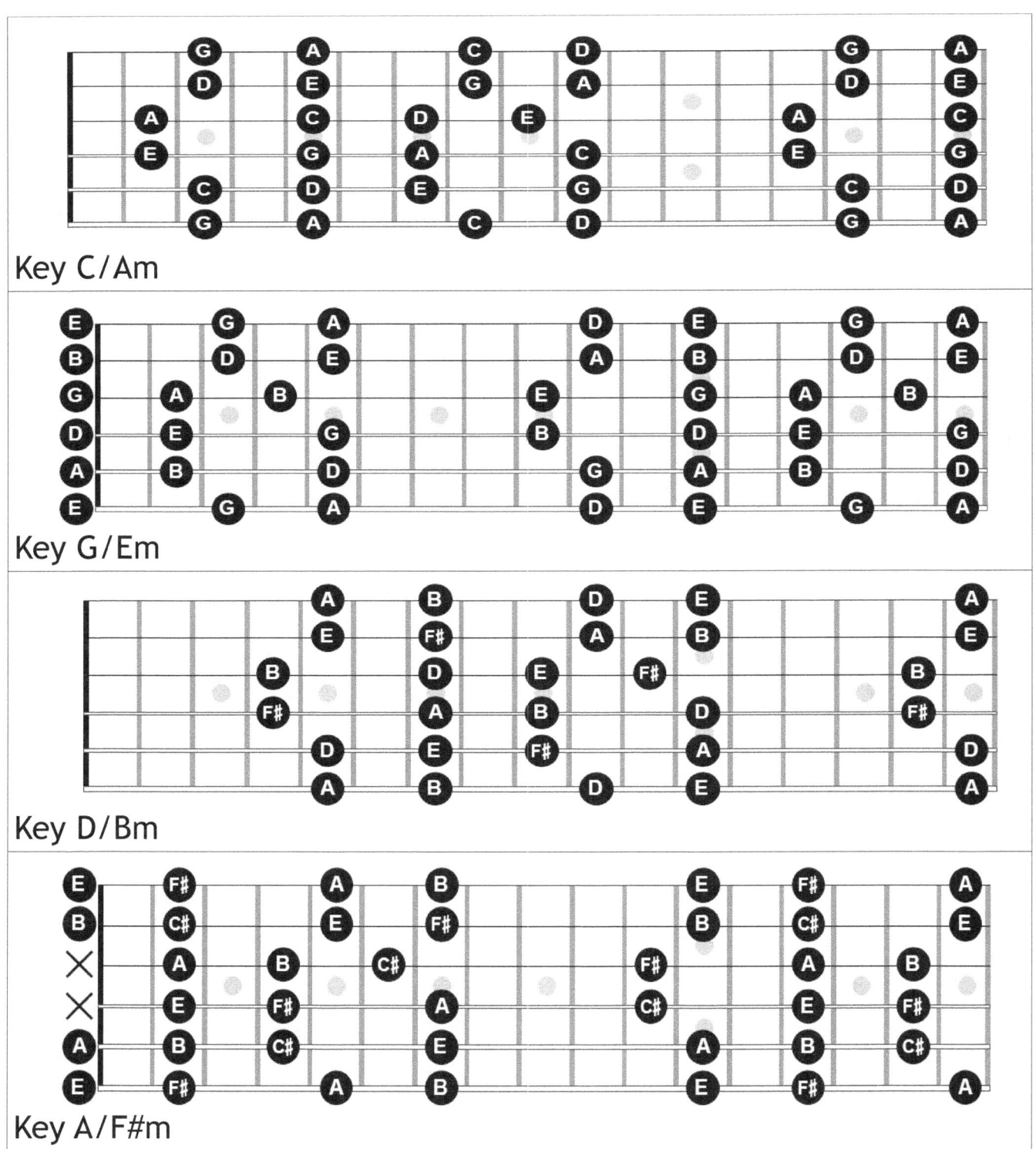

Key C/Am

Key G/Em

Key D/Bm

Key A/F#m

REVIEW

As a Musician:

- A Pentatonic scale is a five note scale.
- Naturally there are two types: Major and minor.
- Major chords get Major pentatonic and minor chords get minor pentatonic scales.
- For every Major Key/Chord/Scale there is a RELATIVE that shares the same notes/chords and Key.
- There are 12 notes is all of music.
- There are 12 RELATIVE relationships in music.
- We can induce a BLUES sound when playing a **minor pentatonic over a Major chord.**
- We can add a BLUE NOTE at anytime we want to add an extra sound to our solo/melodies. It's not supposed to work but does (most of the time).

As a Guitar Player:

- We learned the 12 notes on the LOW E string to help navigate our scales.
- Pattern #1 is the primary shape you will use and start navigating with.
- Pattern #1 connects the RELATIVE MAJOR and the RELATIVE MINOR. I call it the "ROCK AND ROLL RULE."
- Pattern #2 has the SAME notes as #1 and is ALWAYS ABOVE pattern #1 on the fretboard.
- Pattern #5 has the SAME notes as #1 (and #2) and is ALWAYS BEHIND pattern #1 on the fretboard.

NECK ANATOMY

Neck Anatomy is the name I gave the biggest revelation in my guitar life (of over 35 years). It has to do with how to look at octaves on the guitar and how to use them in many different ways. It was a way I had never seen before, and even today I still don't see a lot of players referencing it. It makes you look at the guitar in a much simpler and musical way, bypassing most of the pattern based learning.

Back in 1986 a movie called "Crossroads" came out about a classical guitar player who loves blues and eventually battles the devil's guitar player to win back the soul of an old bluesman. In this final scene, the devil's guitar player was played by Steve Vai (who also composed and performed all the crazy guitar stuff in the movie). I had just gotten his solo album "Flexable" so I was really excited to see him move and play. (Remember this was before the internet and MTV had only just begun. It wasn't easy to watch your heroes play unless it was live in concert or a pro shot video of the artist.) The end of the movie was crazy and I never saw/heard a guitar player play like that. I was blown away.

Soon after the movie came out Guitar World magazine had a transcription of this famous guitar battle. My goal in life was to try to learn it. I was way over my head. I had never seen anything like this. The very first bar was a nightmare. It was moving all around the fretboard in a way I didn't understand. Luckily, my teacher had me reading music at this time and not TAB. I looked at just the music and noticed it was just the notes A C E up and down for three octaves. I thought it was weird that Vai had played it like it was written. Every octave played different even thought they were the same notes. I decided if I was going to try to remotely figure out this piece of music I would have to re-tab it out in an easier way for me to play. So I decided to play the same shape for each octave because it was just easier to see and remember. Here is what I did. This is an **A minor arpeggio for 3 octaves in sixteenth-notes**. On the left is the original version from the magazine and on the right is my version. I circled the shape that is the same every time, just pick up your hand and move to the new octave.

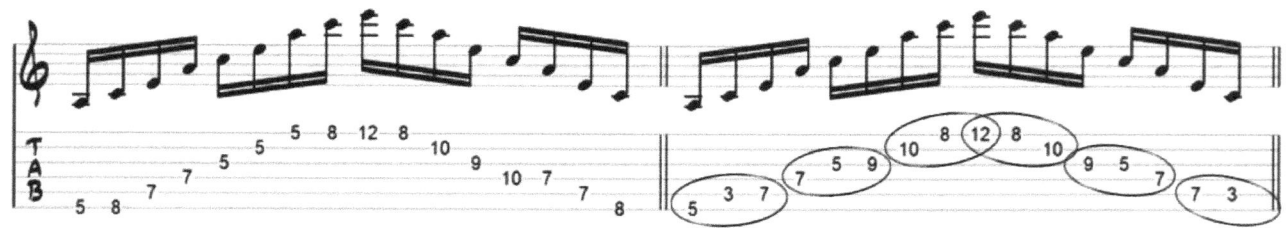

I worked through the piece and it helped me a lot to re-map out the notes so I could play it and remember it. A few years later I was in my first year at Berklee College of Music and I was supposed to be learning a whole-tone scale in position. I was having a hard time remembering it and it just felt weird to play. I went to class that day and afterwards I was talking to my teacher Bob Stanton. As I was walking out of class he said "don't forget the neck works at an angle." I quickly agreed, thinking about where the lowest note on the guitar was (low open E) and my highest note (the highest note on the high E string). But then it hit me while I was headed back up stairs to my dorm room. "Can I do the same thing with this whole tone scale that I did with that Steve Vai piece?" and YES! I could. I was blown away. Not only could I do it for 2 octaves but it worked for three! I got really excited that I saw this and started to think of all of the implications of this idea. (It's still going 30 years later!)

This is a totally new perspective of the guitar I had not seen. Once I started to play flute, sax and piano I started to see how similar it was to other instruments. Guitar players were making life really hard for themselves with this horizontal box approach, where every pattern looks and feels different even thought they are the SAME notes.

The first step is to navigate the OCTAVE SHAPES.

There are only two shapes, the short one for the thicker strings (E + A) and the long one for the thinner strings (D + G). These are the same on ANY FRET.

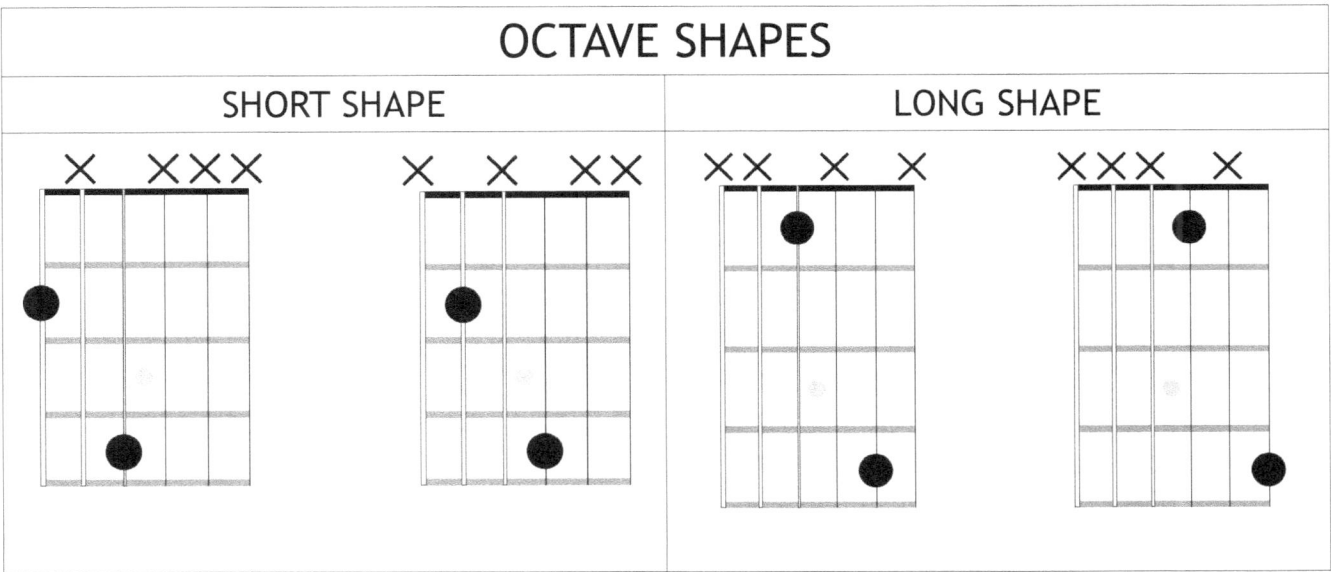

THE KEYSTONE

I was once asked, "How many G notes are on your guitar?" Whoa! I had no idea. How do I even begin? First you have to think a little mathematically. There are only 12 notes, therefore after 12 frets on the same string the notes start over (of course, the 12 fret). Each note gets represented once per 12 frets per string. We have 6 strings so there would be 6 G notes in the first 12 frets of our neck and then it repeats again above that. Let's focus on the first 12 frets.

THE KEYSTONE TO NECK ANATOMY IS:
SHORT OCTAVE TO LONG OCTAVE

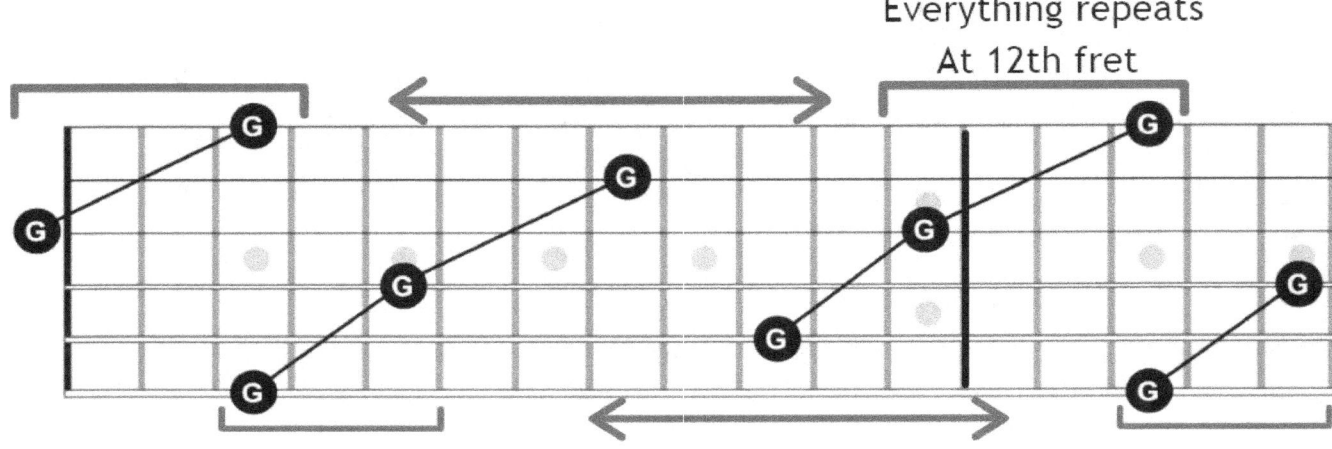

We use Neck Anatomy to help us:

- See the fretboard and get to know the notes.
- Find the ROOT note of our pentatonics.
- Find the BLUE NOTE in our scale patterns.

Once I learned all 5 pentatonic patterns I had the arduous task of re-memorizing each one to learn where the MAJOR Root note was. Then I had to re-re-learn them again to memorize where the MINOR Root note was. By the time I had to do it again for the BLUE NOTE I had had enough. I felt like I memorized dozens of shapes just to remember where one note was and I did! It's SO MUCH EASIER to just look for the one note (ROOT, BLUE NOTE or other) than to re-memorize tons of black dots in patterns with regard to some random string, finger, and fret combination.

PRACTICE

The first step to starting to navigate is to pick one of the 12 notes. (G)

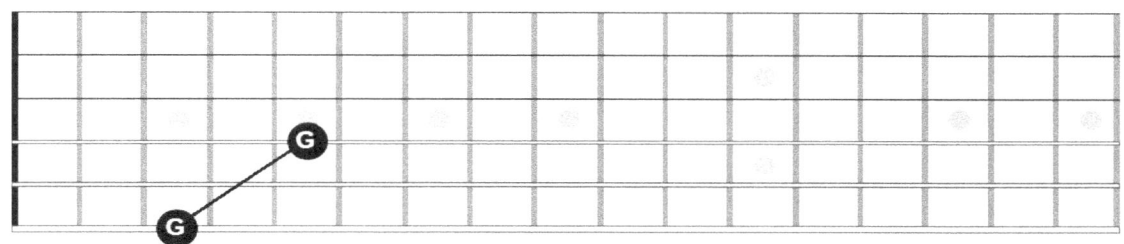

Find the NOTE on the LOW E string and make SHORT OCTAVE.

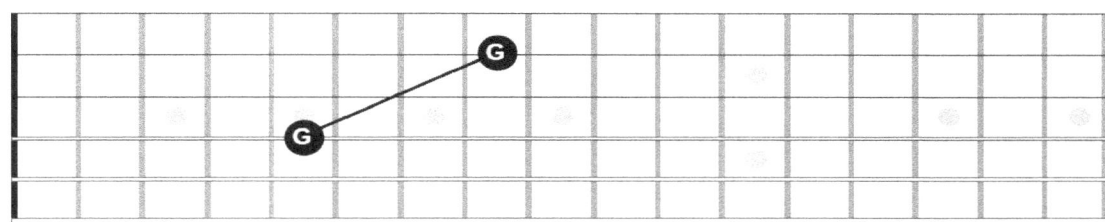

ADD LONG OCTAVE to the SHORT OCTAVE.

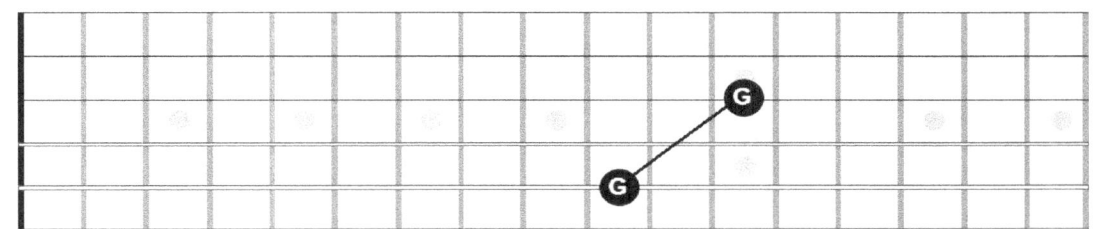

Start again on the A STRING. Find the note and make a SHORT OCTAVE.

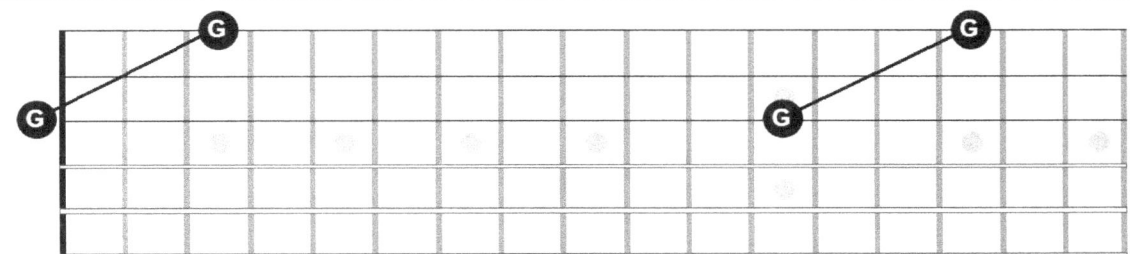

Add a LONG OCTAVE to that SHORT OCTAVE. Anything that touches the 12 fret or above will also repeat at the open strings (like a conveyor belt).

You will ALWAYS have a SHORT OCTAVE to LONG OCTAVE from the Low E string and a SECOND SHORT OCTAVE to LONG OCTAVE from the A string. I like to think of it like BAR CHORDS. There is one that is based on the E string and one on the A string.

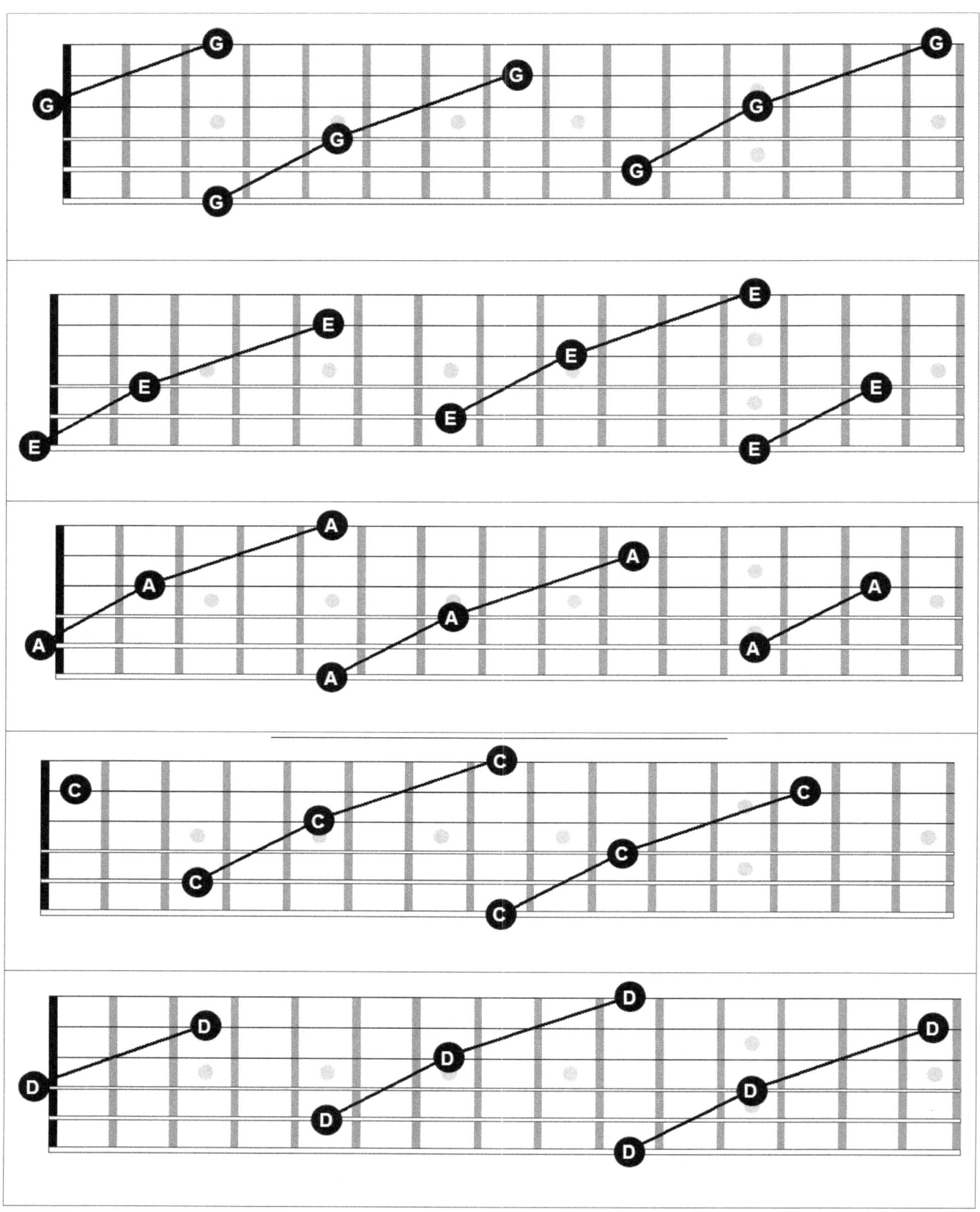

SUMMARY

We are musicians. We are guitar players.
We learn the language of music. Melody, Harmony, and Rhythm
We learn the craft of playing the guitar as an instrument.

We warm up with Muted String Ladders (MSL) and SHELLS.

RHYTHM is most important.

We EXERCISE our scales and licks. Round the Block is an easy and effective way to memorize and run the patterns.

We learn musical ideas (LICKS) to start to build "musical conversation" to learn to improvise.

AS A MUSICIAN:
- We decide on the "main" chord and base the scale upon that chord.
- MINOR chord gets a MINOR scale.
- MAJOR chord can get either the MAJOR pentatonic and/or the BLUES pentatonic.
- Add the Blue Note for extra color.
- Octaves are the landings in the staircase. Each octave starts the same and we build scale up and down from them.

AS A GUITAR PLAYER:
- Once we know the music scale we need to find the ROOT note on the low E string.
- Then we decide on the the FIRST FINGER for MINOR or BLUES or we use the PINKY for MAJOR.
- Once Pattern #1 is on the fretboard everything is relative to it.
- Add Pattern #2 and #5, always connected on either side of pattern #1 to extend the range of the scale further up and down the fretboard.
- SHORT OCTAVE and LONG OCTAVE shapes help us see the notes on the fretboard and help us navigate scales and so much more.

CHAPTER 5

TUNE IN

"I am a musician and a guitar player. Music is my language and my guitar is my voice. Music is Melody, Harmony and Rhythm. I develop my language skills and my instrument skills. They are two separate worlds working together to complete the circle of music."

Rhythm is the number one factor to sounding great as a musician.

WARM UP

MSL top 4 strings all gears.
Play ALL DOWN picked, ALL UP picked and ALL ALTERNATE picked, then change to next gear.
If limited by time (tempo, or literal) you can ALTERNATE pick all of it.

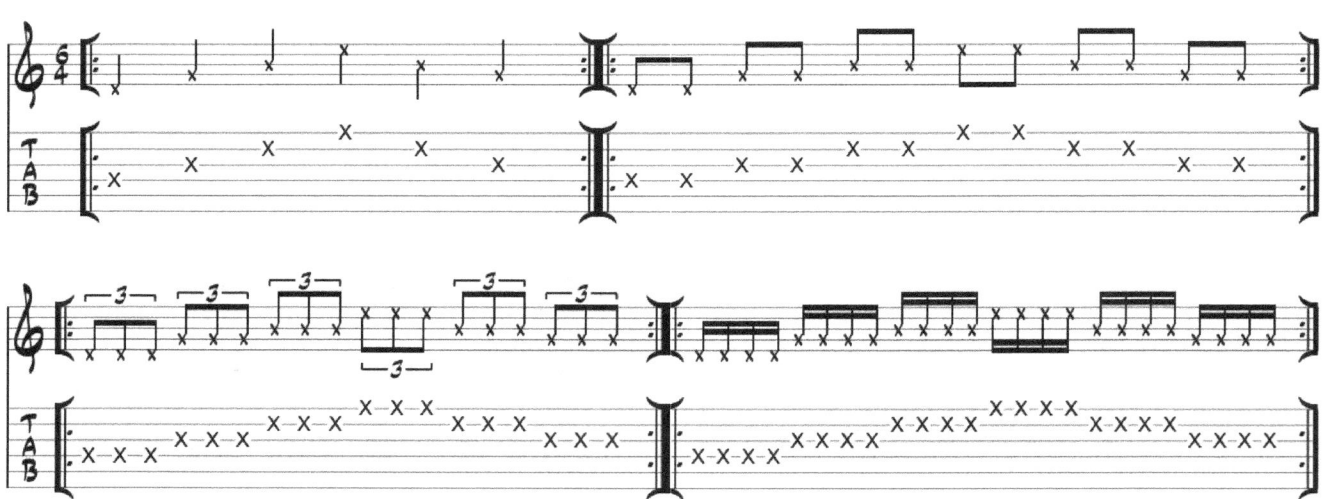

SHELLS
SHELL STRETCH *(2 whole steps)* 1 2 3 slide in Quarter-notes

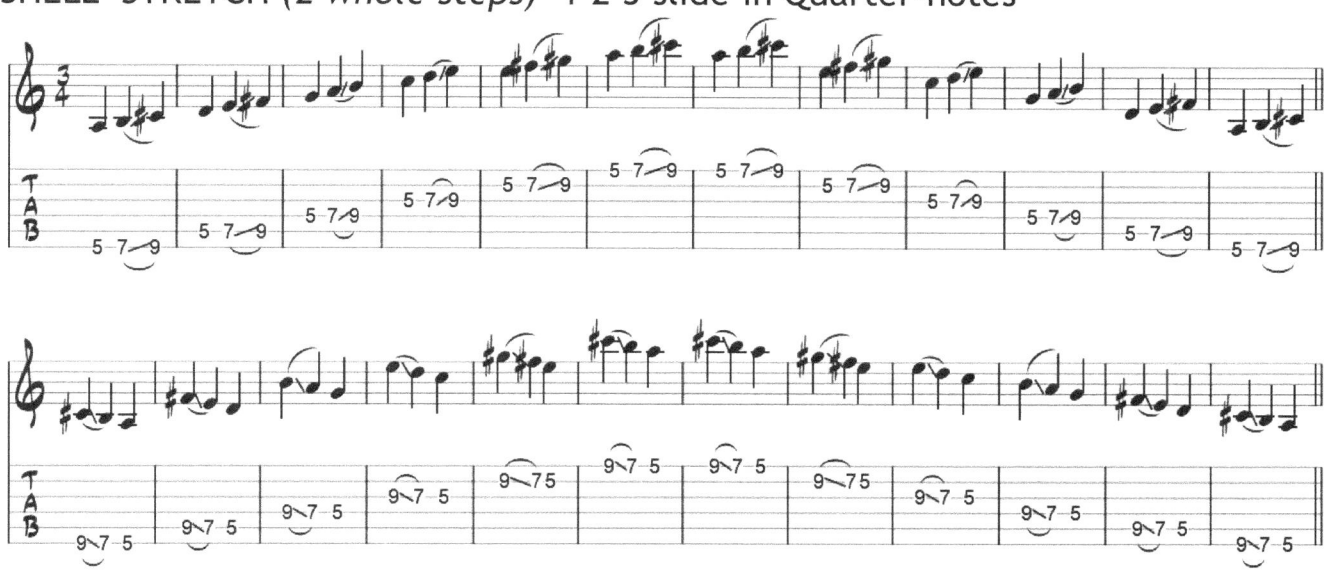

SHELL 1 3   up and down string in 8th notes

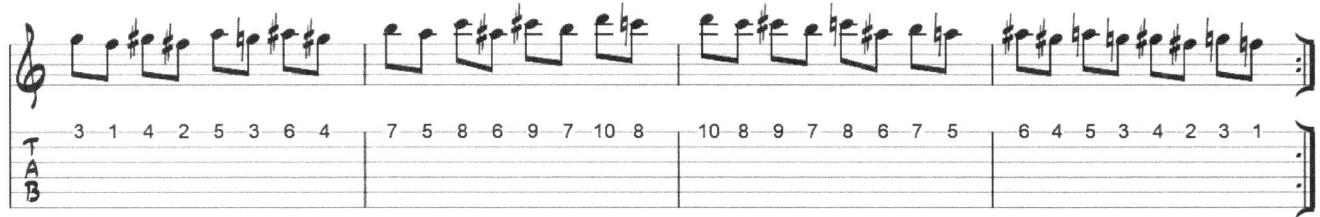

<u>TIPS:</u>

- When sliding make sure to adhere to the rhythm. Use the full beat.

- When moving up and down 1 string, move the hand as a whole
  for each fret. DON'T "inchworm."

EXERCISE

Patterns #5, #1, #2 up and down and Round the Block

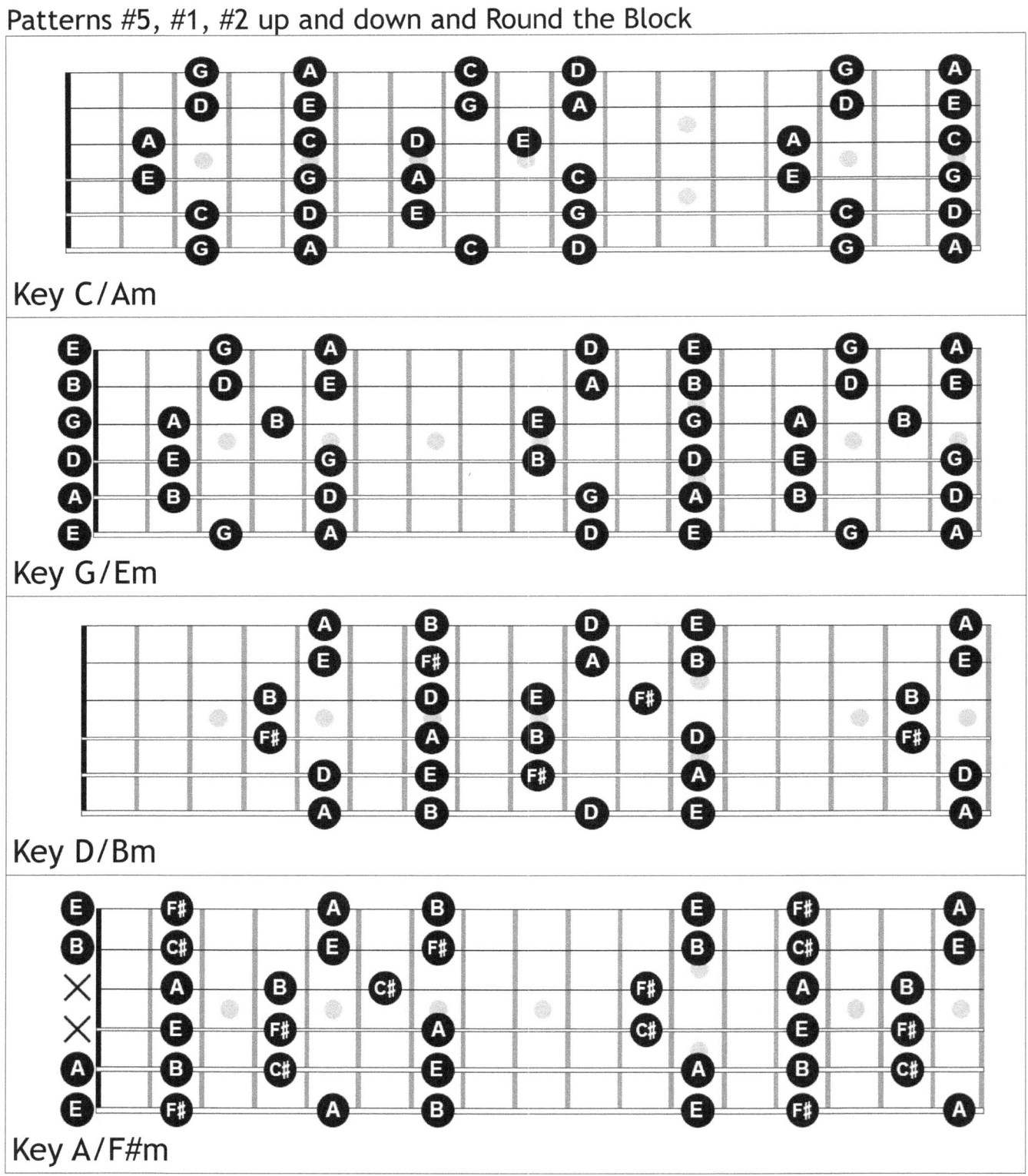

Key C/Am

Key G/Em

Key D/Bm

Key A/F#m

REVIEW

Neck anatomy is the name I gave the biggest revelation I had on the guitar. It was a way to use octaves to see the notes move on the neck in a natural way.

There are only 6 of any note on the first 12 frets of the fretboard, one per string for the six strings. If you start on the LOW E string you can build a SHORT OCTAVE to LONG OCTAVE to find the first three. Then go to the A STRING and do it again. Find the note, make a SHORT OCTAVE to LONG OCTAVE to find the remaining three.

You will use Neck Anatomy to the find the ROOT of ANY scale/chord/arpeggio.

THE KEYSTONE:
SHORT OCTAVE to LONG OCTAVE

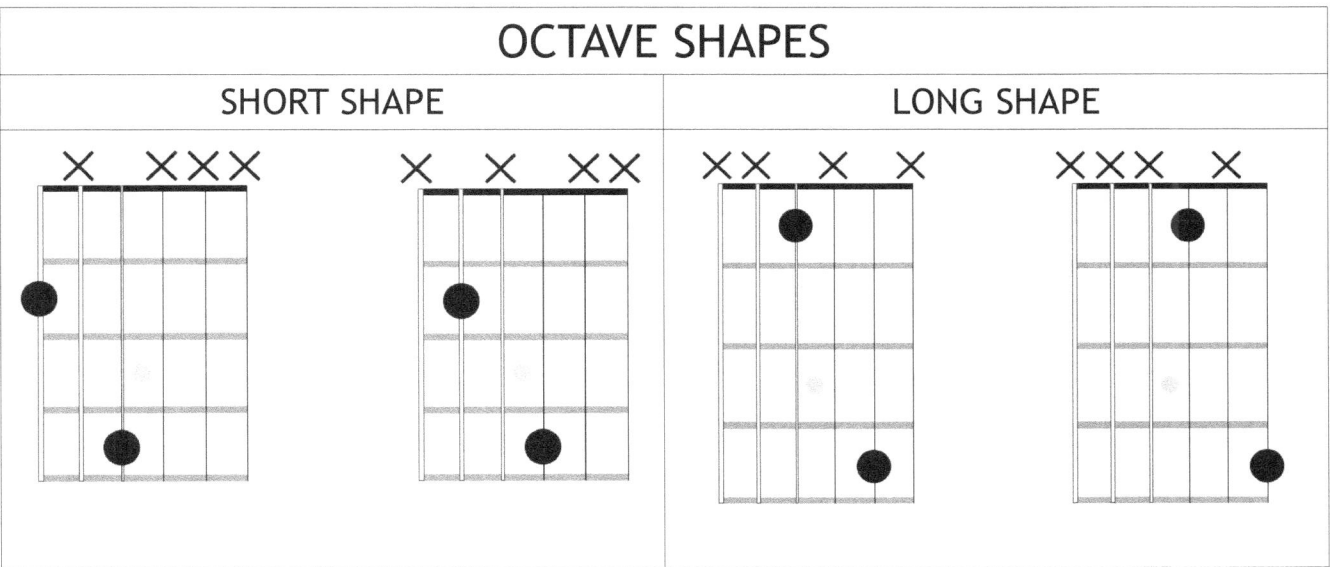

OCTAVE SHAPES	
SHORT SHAPE	LONG SHAPE

You should always view the guitar as short octave to long octave. If you know the E and A strings, then you will start to see that every note everywhere is SHORT OCTAVE to LONG OCTAVE. You will see the symmetry in scales and in music. The fog on your fretboard should disappear.

Patterns #1, #2, #5 with NECK ANATOMY ROOT NOTES (Key of G, C)

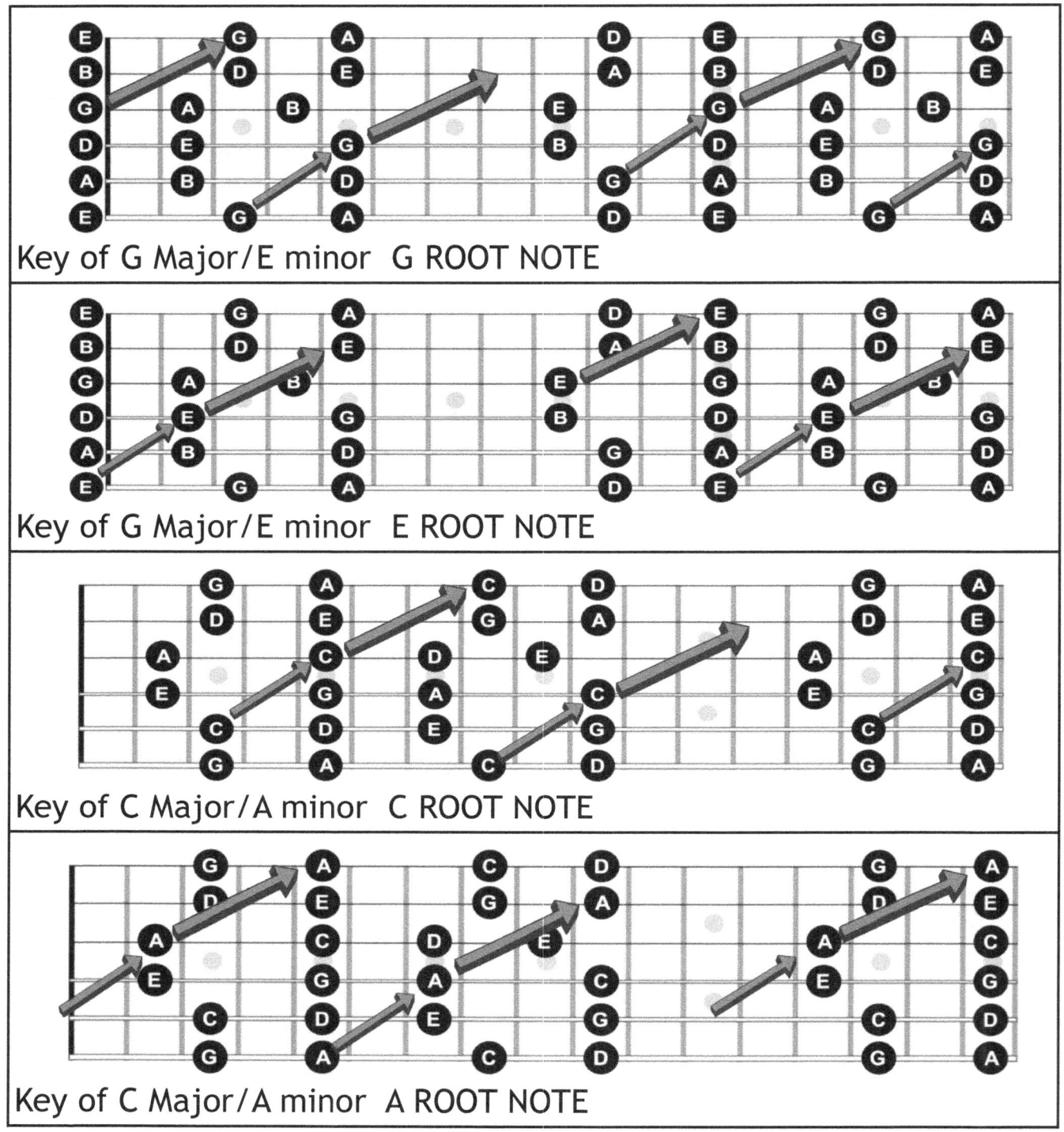

Key of G Major/E minor G ROOT NOTE

Key of G Major/E minor E ROOT NOTE

Key of C Major/A minor C ROOT NOTE

Key of C Major/A minor A ROOT NOTE

Even if you don't know a scale pattern you should ALWAYS see the SHORT to LONG OCTAVES happening.

BENDING

Bending is one the coolest things we do as guitar players to help us get in between the notes as we transition from one note to another. In level #1 we discussed the basics of bending. Here is a quick review on the technique of bending.

HOW TO BEND:

1. Use third finger to play the note (for example 5th fret on high E string).
2. Put middle finger on previous fret, same string, right behind third finger. This is there to help push/leverage the string.
3. Keep thumb on top of fretboard binding. This is the BLUES grip covered in Level #1.
4. Pluck note, *turn wrist to hook note* with curled fingers to push string up. You should hear the note go up. Don't expand/contract the fingers.
5. Use your EAR, and help it to check the bend by playing it first without the bend. Play a fret higher to listen, then go back and bend to that same note.

SETUP	BEND
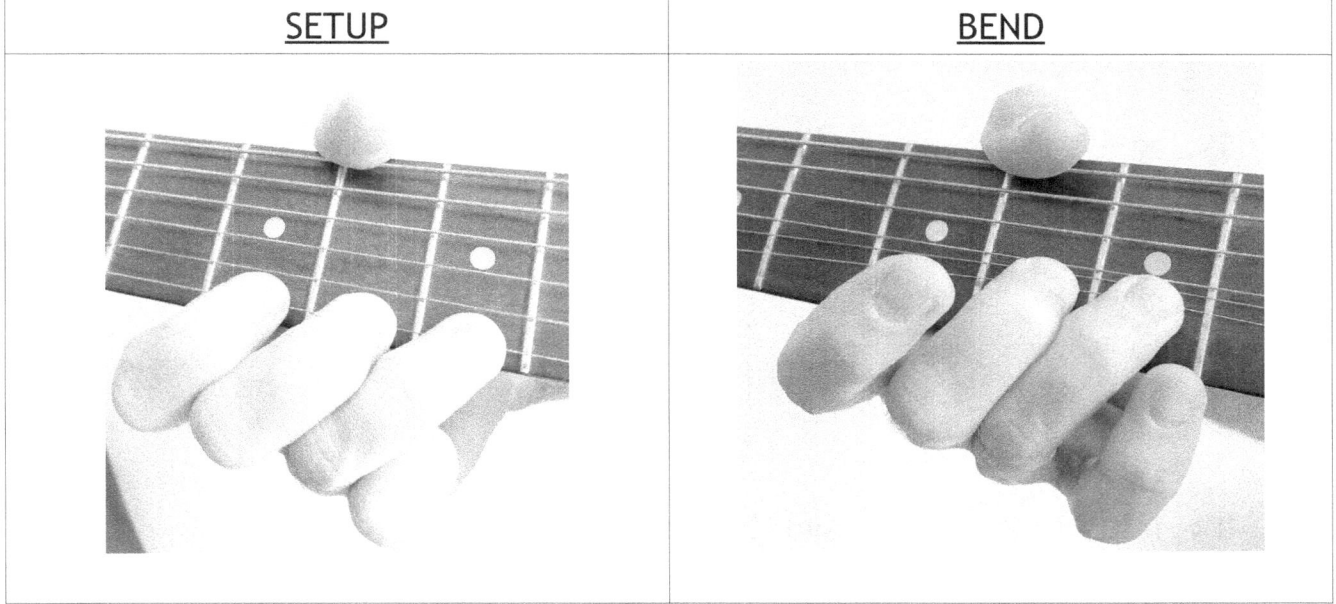	

- Usually there are one of two intervals that you bend to; a half-step and a whole-step bend. They are the equivalent of 1 or 2 frets respectively.
- The ONLY way to bend is by EAR.

UNISON and DOUBLE STOP BENDS

Once you are comfortable playing a **WHOLE-STEP bend** on the B and G strings you can play two of the coolest bends we have on guitar. The UNISON BEND and the DOUBLE-STOP BEND. These are tricky, two string style bends that require you to bend one string while holding the other stationary.

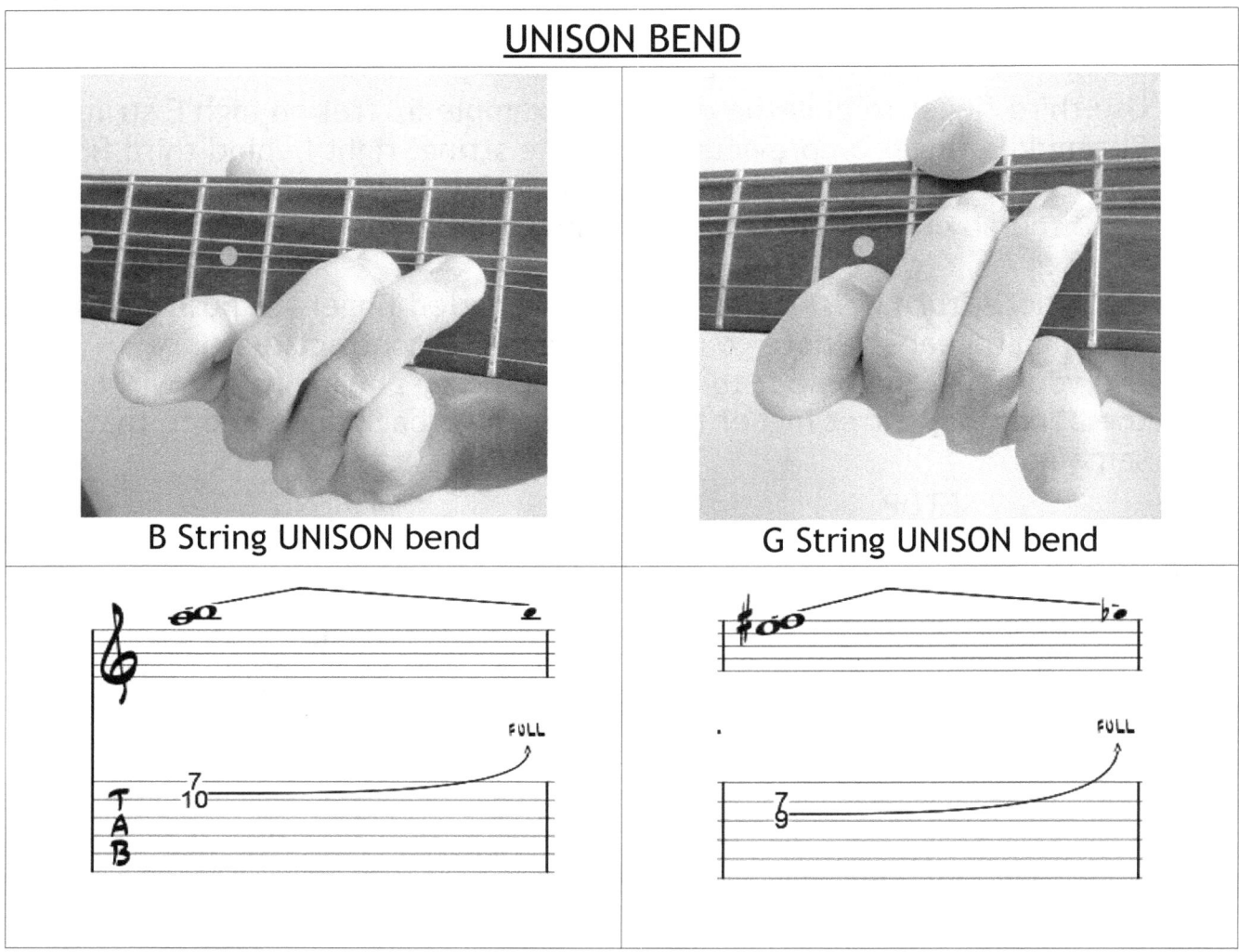

UNISON BEND

B String UNISON bend

G String UNISON bend

- It is important to keep two fingers behind bend for leverage.
- Practice just the whole-step bend first and then add the note on the higher string.
- Practice holding up the whole-step bend and keep it up.
- Bending leverage is in the wrist and is NOT finger "push-ups."
- Unison bends will be the SAME NOTE (doubled).

DOUBLE-STOP BEND

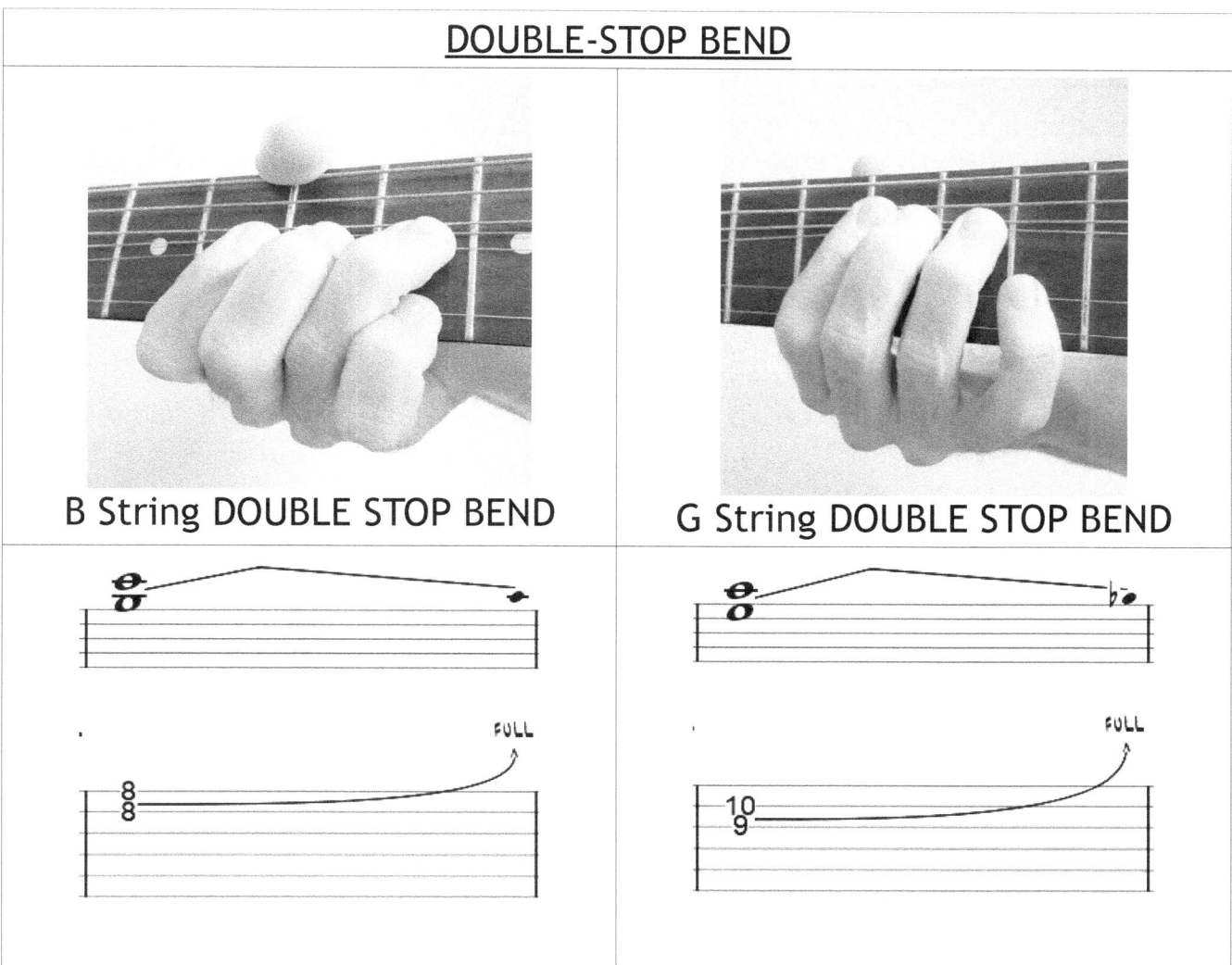

B String DOUBLE STOP BEND

G String DOUBLE STOP BEND

- It's important NOT to bend the note on the thinner string.

- These sound incredible with overdrive/distortion.

- They have to align with the pentatonics, and both of these work GREAT in PATTERN #1.

PICK BLOCKING

Pick blocking is a subtle but very powerful technique to stop a string from ringing by blocking the string with your pick. There is an UP and DOWN block. After you strike a string you come back in the opposite direction and land the pick on the string to stop it.

Pick DOWN then BLOCK UP

Pick UP then BLOCK DOWN

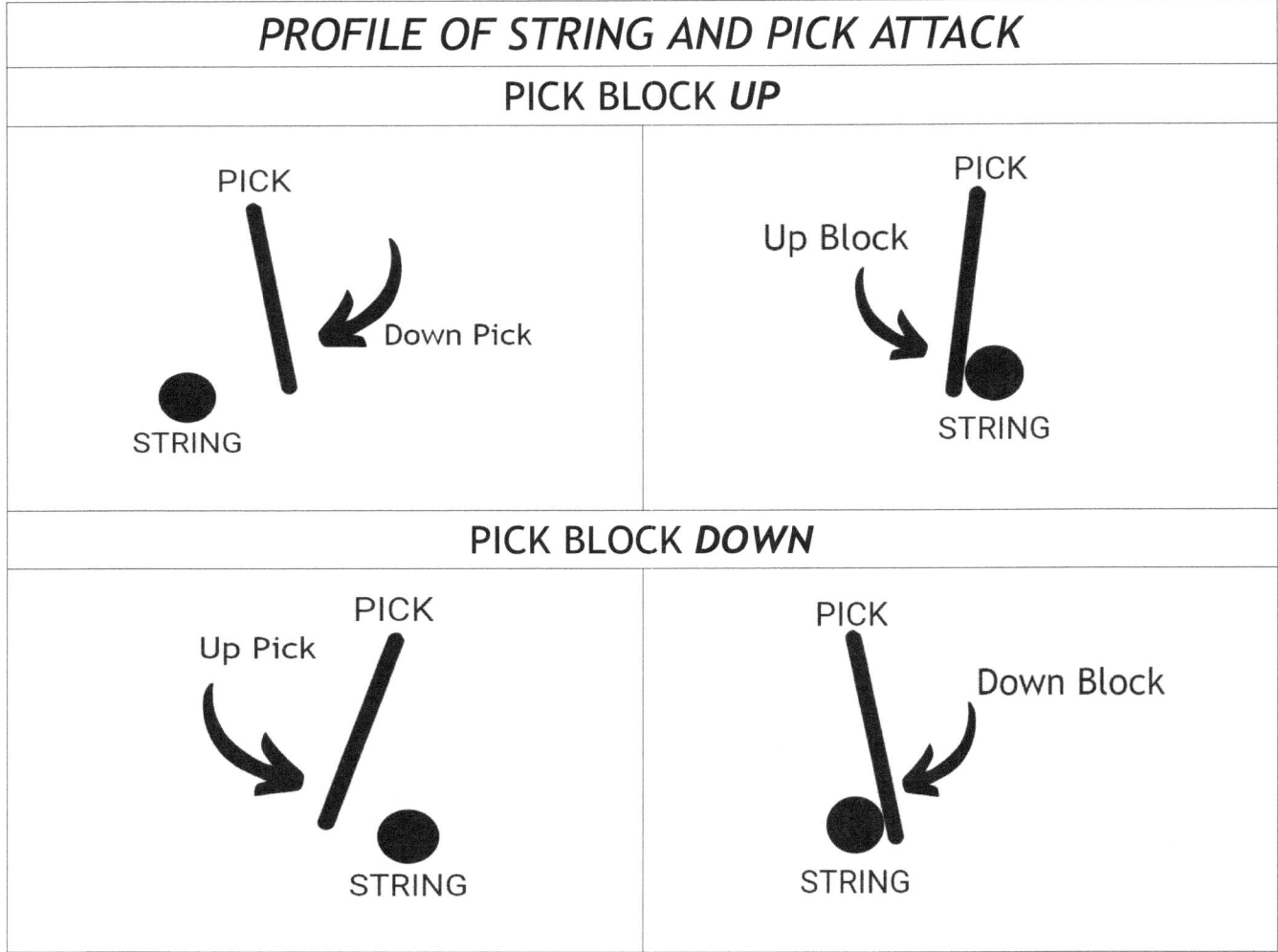

- Pick Blocking is PERFECT to stop bends at their peak without letting the note fall after bending.

- It adds a ton of percussive and rhythmic elements to your playing.

Watch "Secret Picking Technique" video at
www.LeadGuitarWorkshop.com

PRACTICE

Neck Anatomy Octaves SHORT to LONG
Navigate each octave in time (TAB). BONUS-use 1st finger only

E NECK ANATOMY OCTAVES

G NECK ANATOMY OCTAVES

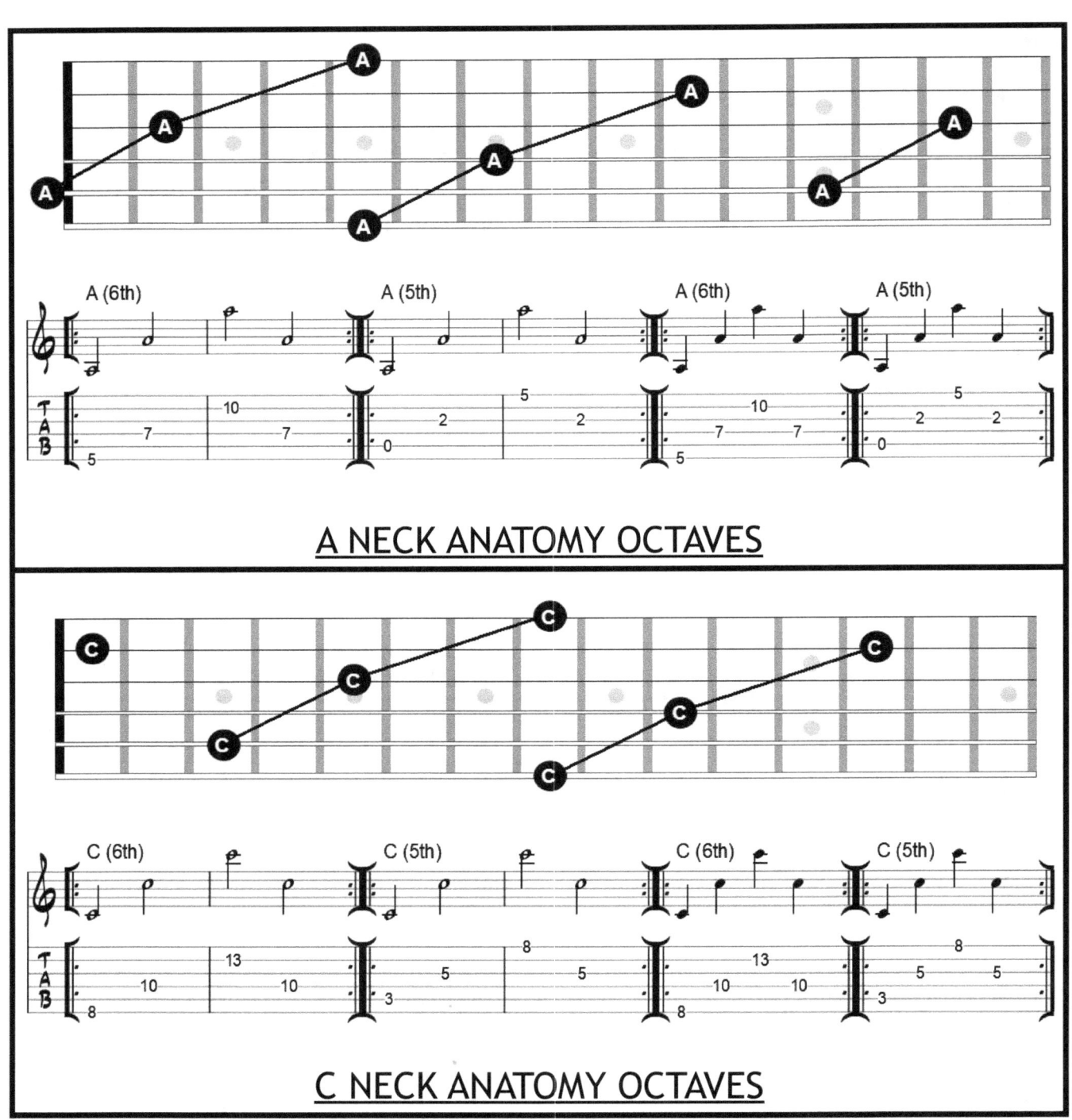

A NECK ANATOMY OCTAVES

C NECK ANATOMY OCTAVES

BENDING
UNISON Bends (E note) in E minor Self-Gen

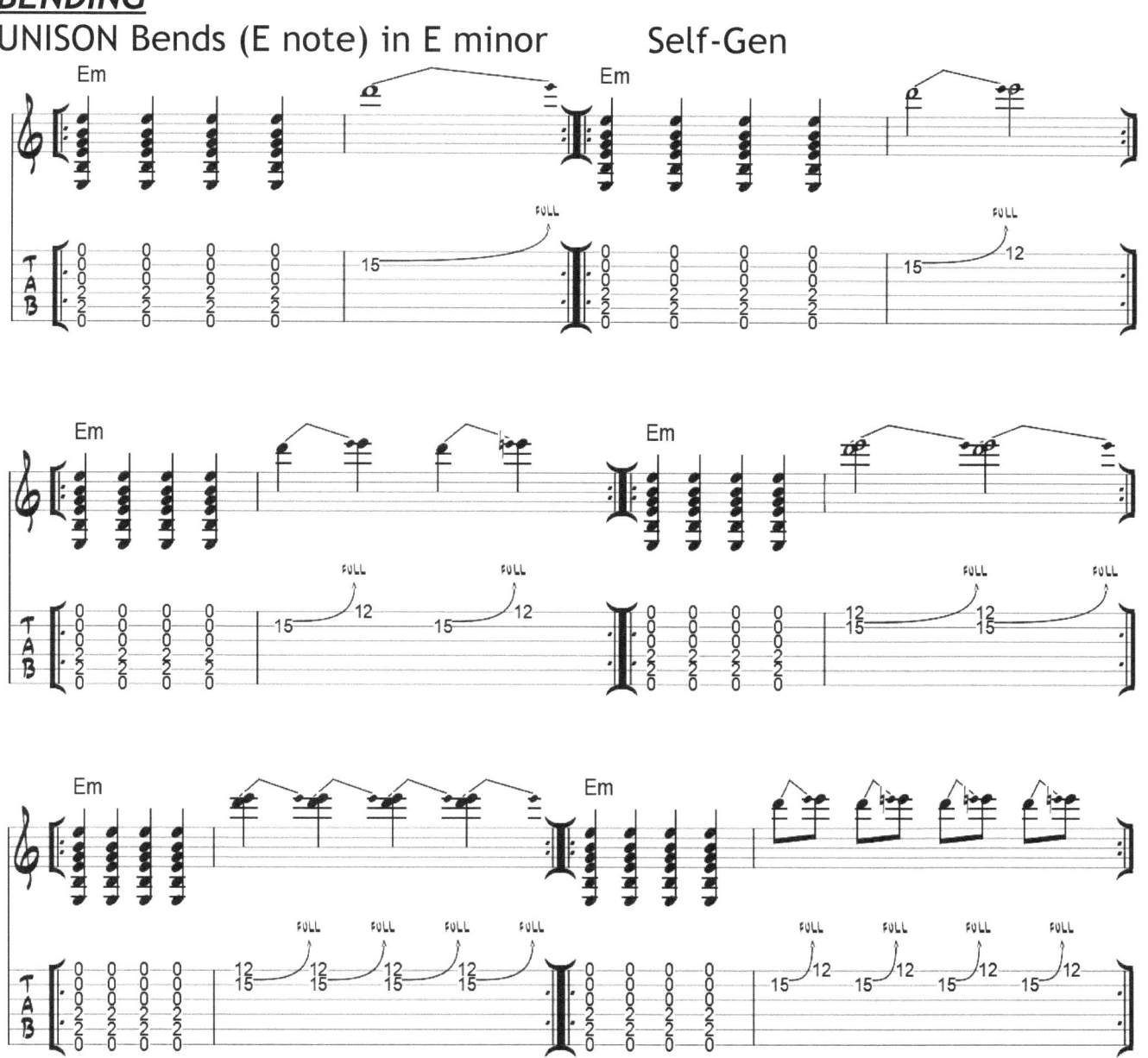

BENDING
DOUBLE STOP Bends (E note) in E minor   Self-Gen

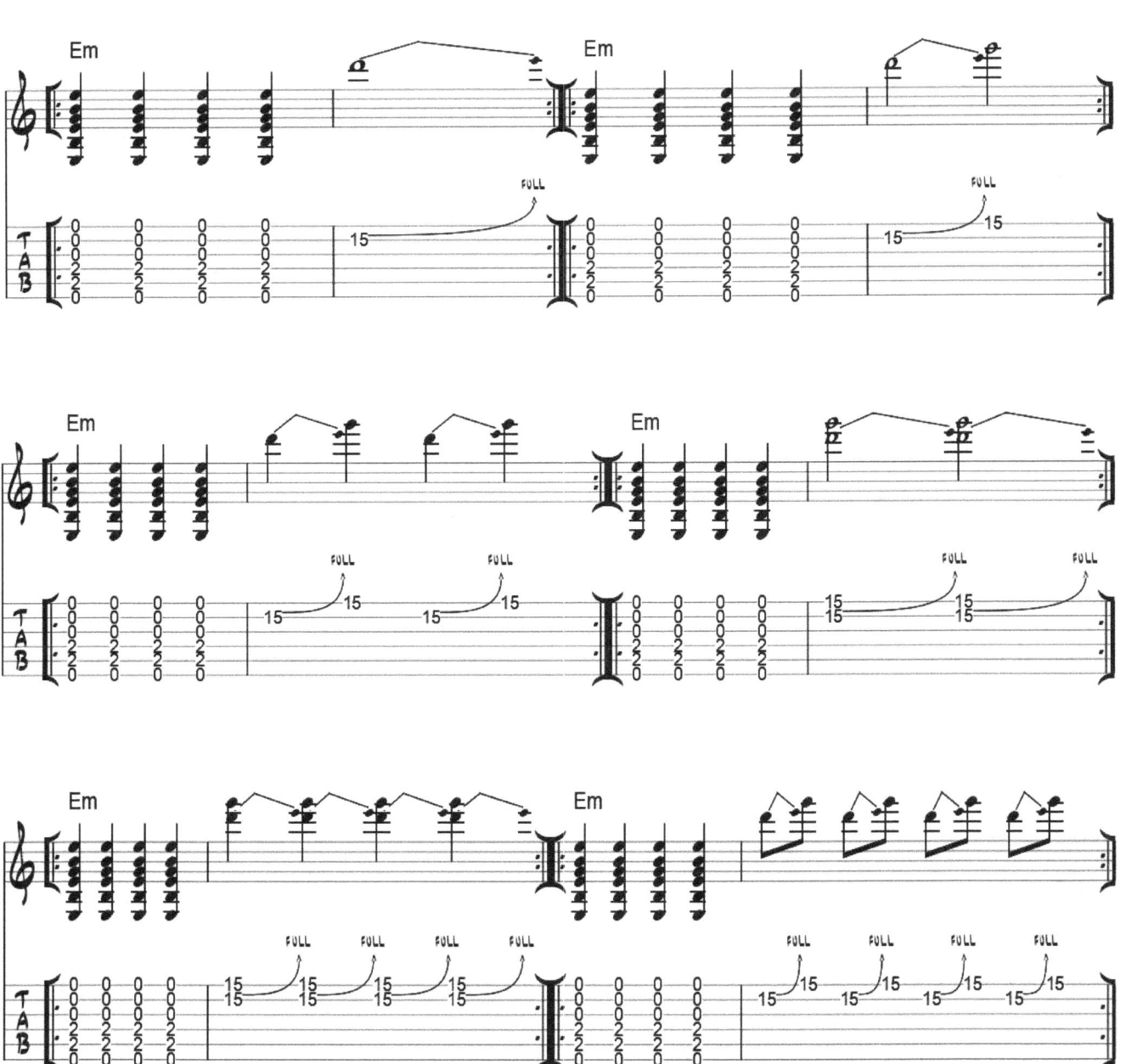

NOTE: The difference is the highest note. Instead of an (E) note for the unison, it is a (G) note on the 15th fret. This means the note on the B string (D) is being bent up a whole-step to (E). On the highest string you are adding a (G) note. This will create a minor third interval (E and G).

PICK BLOCKING

Pick blocking can happen on any note anywhere at anytime. An effective way to practice is with a pentatonic pattern.

Imagine the pick is a magnet and every time you pick the string the magnet pulls it back to the string. This happens in both directions.

Pick blocking can create a STACCATO effect. Staccato is when the notes are usually very short and separated in sound. Staccato is indicated as a little DOT above/below a note. Staccato can happen in many different ways, not just by pick blocking.

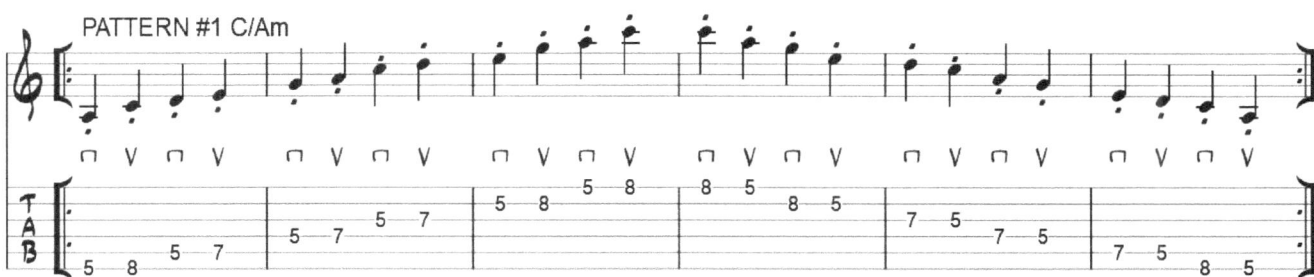

BENDING LICKS

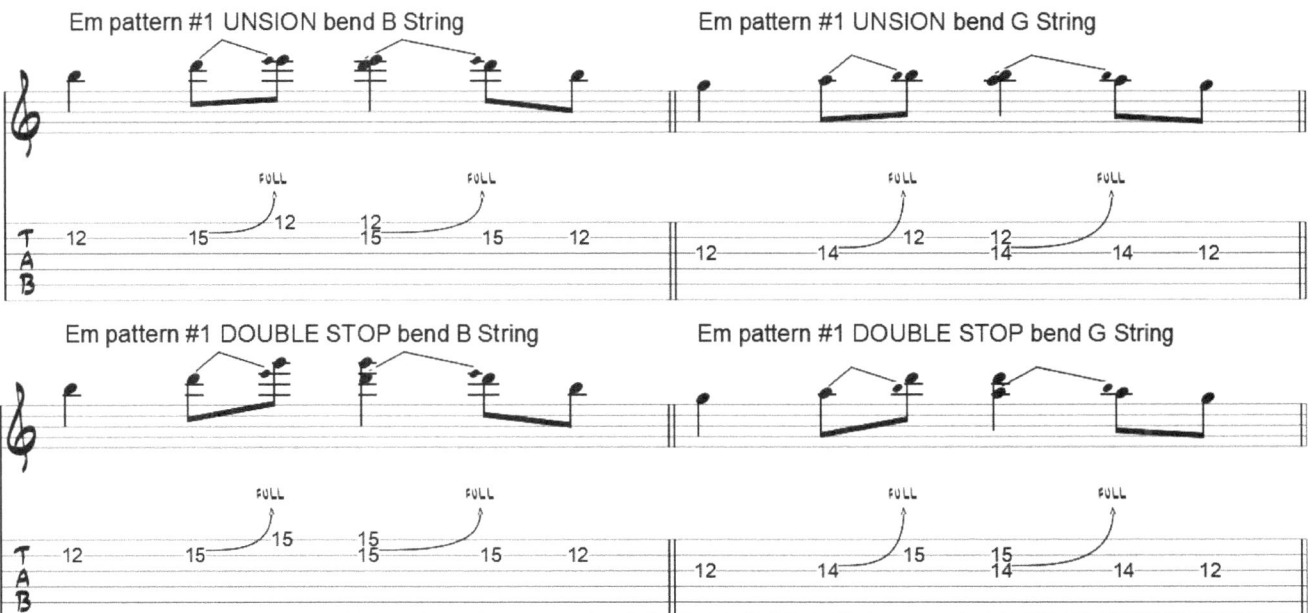

SUMMARY

We are musicians. We are guitar players.
We learn the language of music. Melody, Harmony, and Rhythm
We learn the craft of playing the guitar as an instrument.

We warm up with Muted String Ladders (MSL) and SHELLS.

RHYTHM is most important.

We EXERCISE our scales and licks. Round the Block is an easy and effective way to memorize and run the patterns.

We learn musical ideas (LICKS) to start to build "musical conversation" to learn to improvise.

AS A MUSICIAN:

- We decide on the "main" chord and base the scale upon that chord.
- MINOR chord gets a MINOR scale.
- MAJOR chord can get either the MAJOR pentatonic and/or the BLUES pentatonic.
- Add the Blue Note for extra color.
- Octaves are the landings in the staircase. Each octave starts the same and we build scale up and down from them.

AS A GUITAR PLAYER:

- Once we know the music scale we need to find the ROOT note on the low E string.
- Then we decide on the the FIRST FINGER for MINOR or BLUES or we use the PINKY for MAJOR.
- Once Pattern #1 is on the fretboard everything is relative to it.
- Add Pattern #2 and #5, always connected on either side of pattern #1 to extend the range of the scale further up and down the fretboard.
- SHORT OCTAVE and LONG OCTAVE shapes help us see the notes on the fretboard and help us navigate scales and so much more.

CHAPTER 6

TUNE IN

"I am a musician and a guitar player. Music is my language and my guitar is my voice. Music is Melody, Harmony and Rhythm. I develop my language skills and my instrument skills. They are two separate worlds working together to complete the circle of music."

Rhythm is the number one factor to sounding great as a musician.

WARM UP

MSL 4 strings ADGB

All DOWN pick
All UP pick
All ALTERNATE pick
Change to next Rhythm
Time permitting, only play ALTERNATE when necessary.

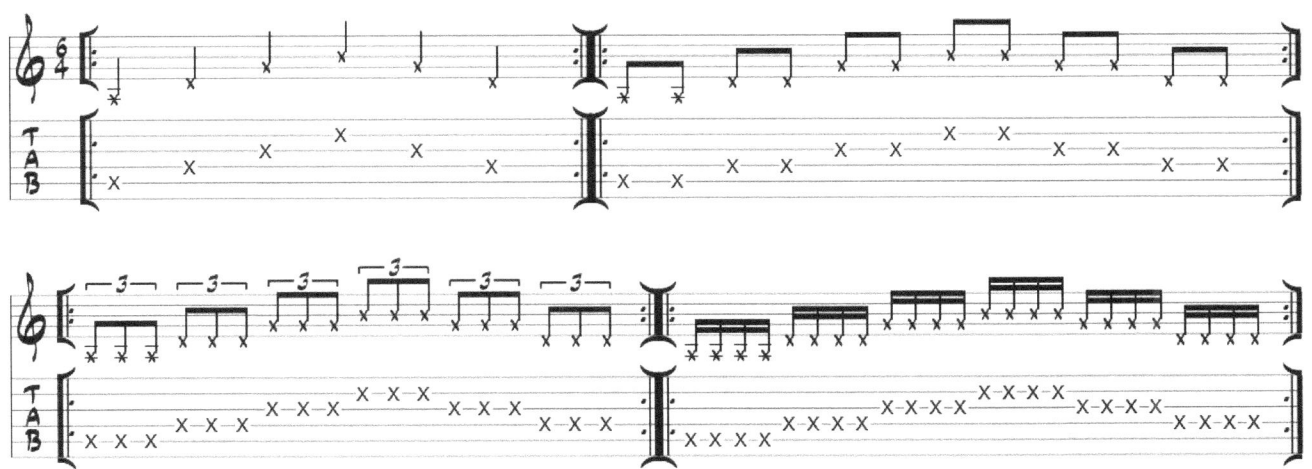

SHELL

SHELL 1 3 4 with ½ bends *(only first half of shell)*

Pull down bend on thicker strings, push up on thinner strings.
Hold each bend for two beats (half-note).

SHELL 1 4 single string as 8th notes

Move hand as a unit for each fret. Don't "inchworm."

EXERCISE

Patterns #5, #1, #2, up and down and Round the Block

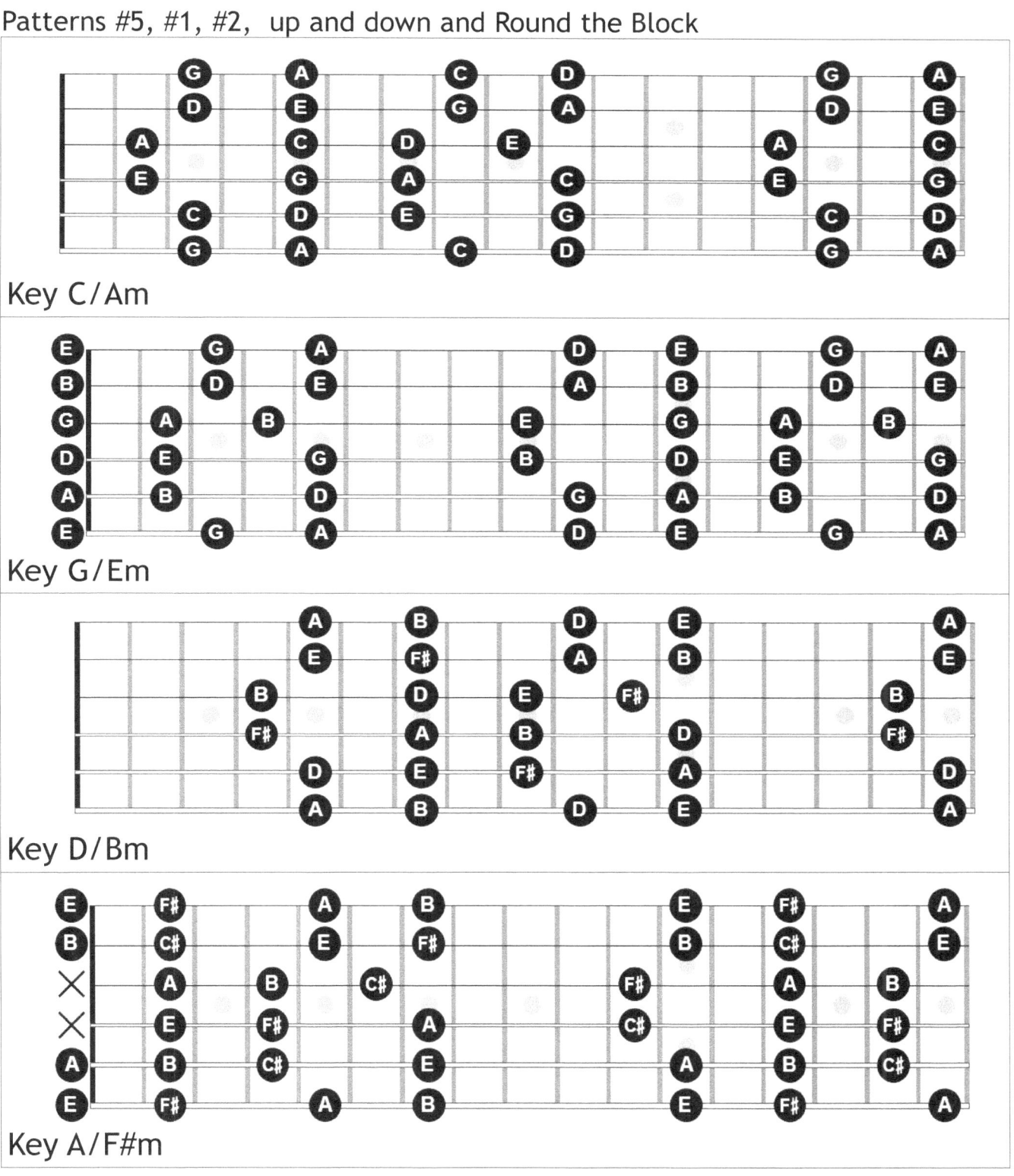

Key C/Am

Key G/Em

Key D/Bm

Key A/F#m

REVIEW

Musician

- We base our scale choice on the "main" chord of a progression.

- minor chords get minor pentatonic scales.

- Major chords have two options: Major pentatonic or Blues pentatonic

- Blues pentatonic scale is when you play the minor pentatonic over the Major chord. The mismatch sounds bluesy.

- There are only 12 notes. There are 12 Major pentatonic scales and 12 minor pentatonic scales.

- Relative Major/minor is a two-for-one deal.

Guitar Player

- Once we know the "main" chord we go to the E string and find the ROOT.

- We then use the "Rock and Roll Rule" to decide whether to put our first finger on the root for minor, or the pinky finger on the root for Major.

- We start with pattern #1 on the fretboard to get into the key correctly.

- Once we know where Pattern #1 is, we know that pattern #2 is right above #1 and pattern #5 is right behind #1, ALWAYS.

- We can add hammer-ons, pull-offs, slides and bends to add cool articulations to our solo to be more expressive.

RHYTHM - CHANGING GEARS

I started to play guitar when I was 12 years old. I played every day and took lessons from the beginning. I went through all of High School with a guitar teacher giving me lessons each and every week (bless my mom). I then went for four years to Berklee College of Music. After I graduated I still didn't sound like I envisioned. Something was still missing and I couldn't quite figure it out. I had done everything I was taught. I could see and name every note on my fretboard (as a guitarist) and I knew every note of every scale, chord and mode (as a musician). I knew every chord shape and scale shape I would ever use, yet I still didn't sound like I wanted to.

It wasn't until I met drummer Erik Egol and joined the band Schleigho that I began to understand why. He asked me to do things rhythmically that I had not done before (for example play 5 repeated notes in 16ths). He completely challenged how I thought about rhythm and how it worked with notes. Rhythm was the keystone to sounding great. I had finally realized after all these years of studying melody and harmony that the ultimate musical ability didn't deal with notes and chords. It was time itself and how I surrounded that time with my notes. It was having control over all the different types of rhythms to allow notes and chords to flow unrestrained and in a groove.

Rhythm first needs a pulse/beat. This is our tempo and what we tap our foot to (usually). Once that is established all rhythms are relative to it. One way to think of tempo is as a ratio. One clap to match every beat is 1:1 and that is our quarter-note. Two claps per beat (evenly) is 2:1 and that is eighth-notes. Three claps per beat (evenly) is 3:1. Four claps per beat (evenly) is 4:1.

I call these four rhythms (Quarter-notes, Eighth-notes, Triplets, and Sixteenth-notes) the GEARS. To me it is just like driving a 4 speed stick shift. These four GEARS make up most of the rhythmic basis of all of your playing. A great musician can effortlessly switch in and out of the GEARS and all of the inner combinations (rests/ties others).

In our band we lived and toured together usually playing between 150-200 shows per year for years. We learned and grew musically in ways that no College, University or teacher could ever teach someone.

One day when I came back to the band house (we lived upstairs and played downstairs in a farmhouse on 40 acres) Erik was practicing with his drum pad and a metronome. He seemed to be playing as fast as he could. I asked him why he was playing with a metronome if he was just playing as fast as he could. He said he was actually practicing 11 notes in a beat! I laughed and asked again, and he was serious. My jaw stayed open. He explained to me that with his certain combination of left and right sticking patterns he could remember where the eleventh stroke was and match that to the beat. He said if he did that evenly it would be 11's (yes, 11th GEAR, and jaw still open).

This really got me thinking. How well do I know the GEAR that I was playing? Could I really measure it like he did? Drummers spend a lot of time thinking and dealing with all of the ways they use their left (L) and right (R) hands. For example they have a combination called a PARADIDDLE and it is LRLLRLRR. The problem for us guitar players is that our DOWN and UP pick doesn't line up in the same way L and R does for a drummer. Meaning, if we are playing steady 8ths on a string we would alternate pick. It would be disadvantageous to play it like DUDDUDUU. I had to figure out a simple way to measure myself playing GEARS, and, I had to just start with the first four.

It's really important to understand that RHYTHM is its OWN LANGUAGE. It doesn't need notes or chords to exist. It's older than our spoken languages and it is the deepest thing we connect on as humans. Anything can play rhythms. You can clap your hands, knock on a door, or tap a pencil. It could be the blinker in a car or a car alarm. There is rhythm all around you every day and you are the instrument. You can ALWAYS play and practice RHYTHM at any time of day with anything, no instrument needed.

CHANGING GEARS

- Pick a tempo and start metronome (60 bpm).
- Your first finger will ALWAYS match the metronome. It is the note which we line up to make sure we are playing the gear correctly.
- Each NOTE/Finger adds to the GEAR.
- Only change gears when ready. You must play the current gear multiple times correctly before switching.
- Later, switch GEARS by BAR and eventually by the beat (advanced).

RHYTHMIC GEARS

NAME	FINGERING	TAB EXAMPLE
Quarter-note	1	
Eighth-note	1 3	
Triplet	1 3 4	
Sixteenth-note	1 3 4 3	

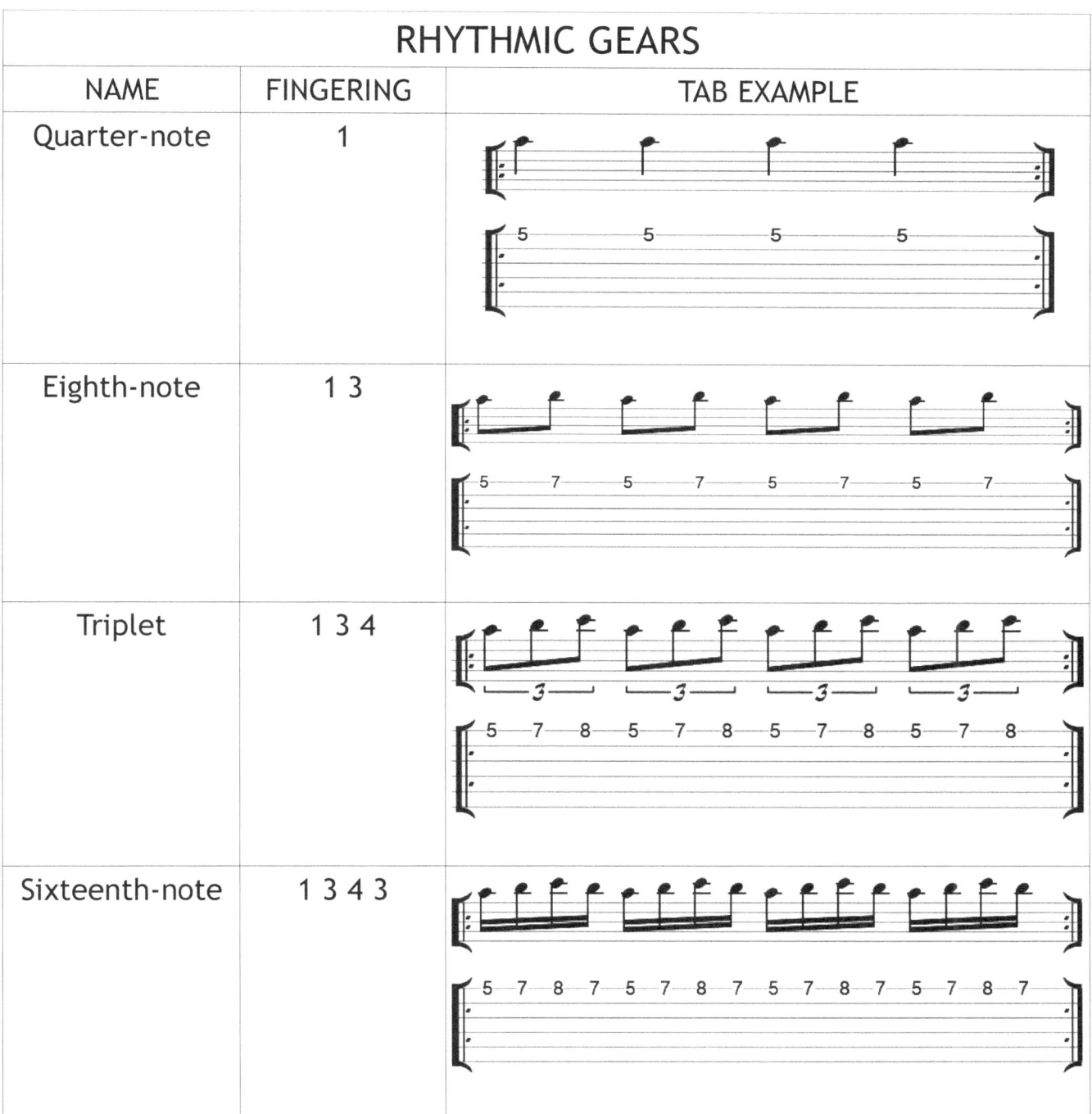

REMEMBER: This is just an exercise to make sure you can feel each gear and be able to measure yourself. ANY NOTE CAN BE IN ANY RHYTHM, meaning that triplets don't have to be three notes. There can be two or four. Sixteenth-notes can just have three notes, any mismatch. GEARS have nothing to do with notes. They are timings.

PATTERN #3

Once we have made our music decision (what chord and what scale) and we have properly placed pattern #1 down, the other four patterns just help you use the whole range of your instrument (whole fretboard on all strings) by showing you where the same FIVE notes are all over your instrument.

There are only five patterns in total that will connect the first 12 frets of your fretboard. Then the whole thing starts over again after the 12 fret. Remember the notes across the 12th fret are the same names as the open strings.

Keep in mind that the guitar is about a 3 octave instrument. Any one pattern of the pentatonic scales is 2 octaves (2/3rds) of your whole instrument!

Take time with the patterns. It is definitely QUALITY VS QUANTITY in terms of the number of patterns you know. It is much better to kick ass in the first 2 patterns than to half ass four or five of them.

Really get to know Patterns #1 and #2 first. They are career making. Hendrix and Stevie Ray Vaughn spent a significant amount of their musical time in the first two patterns. In George Orwell's Animal Farm, the pigs made a sign that said, **"All animals are equal but some animals are more equal than the others."** I like to think of it as, **"All 5 patterns are equal but patterns #1 and #2 are more equal than the others."**

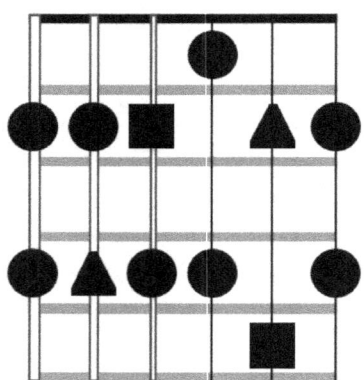

Pattern #3

Pattern #3 is the trickiest to get a good fingering. I use my FIRST and THIRD for ALL EXCEPT the B STRING (I use FIRST and PINKY).

Key of G/Em Patterns #1, #2, # 3 and #1, #2, #3, #5 combined

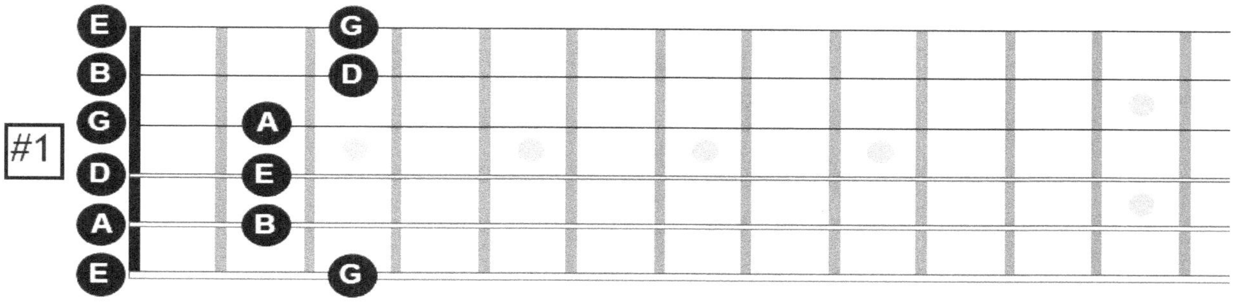

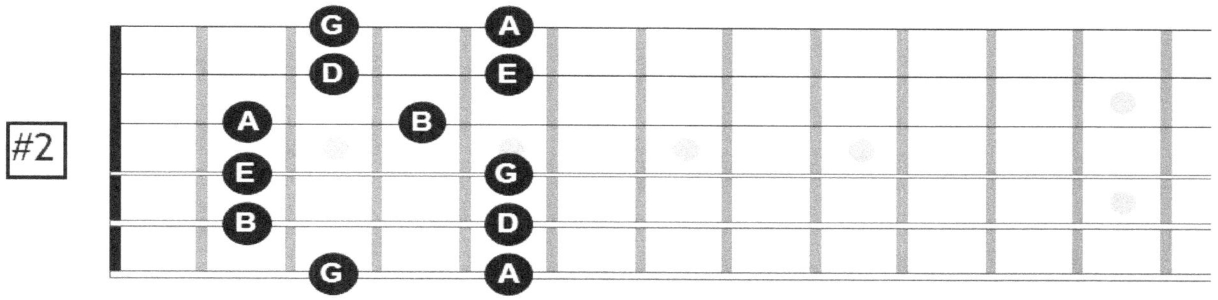

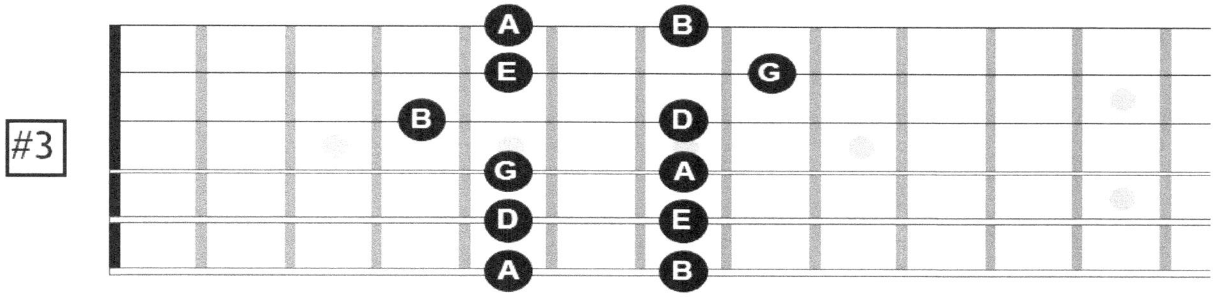

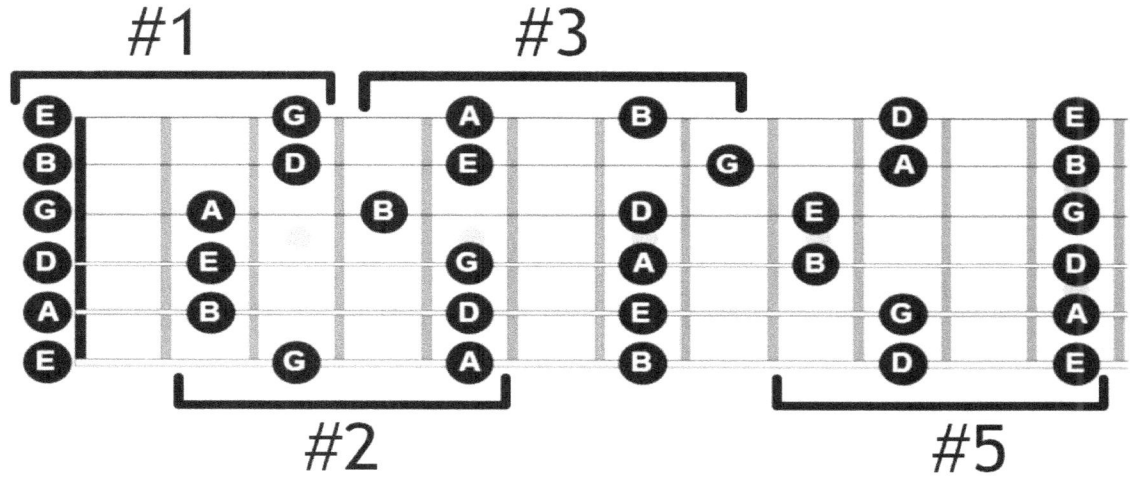

PRACTICE

Pattern #3

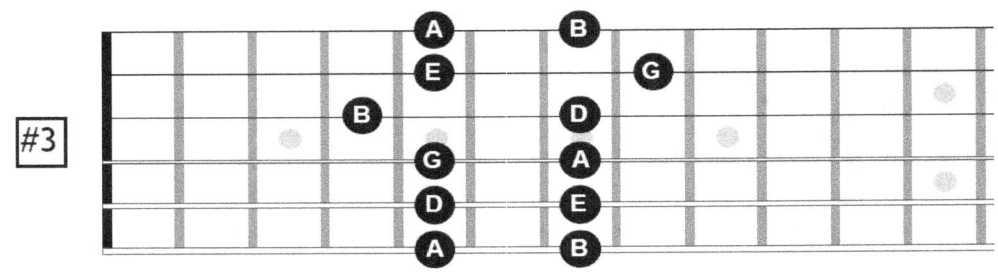

Pattern #1 G/Em   ALL FOUR GEARS

Pattern #1 G/Em Triplets

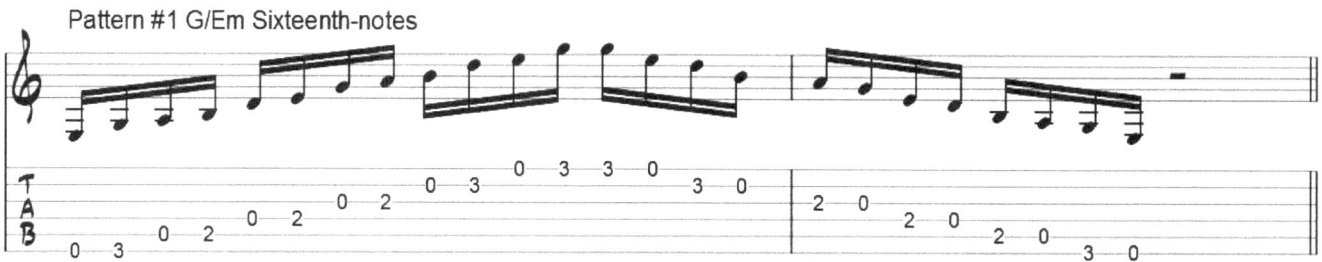

Pattern #1 G/Em Sixteenth-notes

LICKS

Pattern #1 Em Lick in four GEARS

Em LICK 1 in Quarter-notes   Eighth-notes   Triplets   Sixteenth-notes

Pattern #3 Em Lick with Blue Note in four GEARS

Pattern #3 Em LICK w Blue Note

Pattern #3 G Lick in four GEARS

Pattern #3 G Lick

SUMMARY

We are musicians. We are guitar players.
We learn the language of music. Melody, Harmony, and Rhythm
We learn the craft of playing the guitar as an instrument.

Music is Melody, Harmony and Rhythm.
RHYTHM is most important.

We warm up with Muted String Ladders (MSL) and SHELLS.
We EXERCISE our scales and licks. Round the Block is an easy and effective way to memorize and run the patterns.

We learn musical ideas (LICKS) to start to build "musical conversation" to learn to improvise.

AS A MUSICIAN:
- We decide on the "main" chord and base the scale upon that chord.
- MINOR chord gets a MINOR scale.
- MAJOR chord can get either the MAJOR pentatonic and/or the BLUES pentatonic.
- Add the Blue Note for extra color.
- Octaves are the landings in the staircase. Each octave starts the same and we build scale up and down from them.
- Rhythm is the ULTIMATE tool to connect to music and sound our best.

AS A GUITAR PLAYER:
- Once we know the music scale we need to find the ROOT note on the low E string.
- Then we decide on the the FIRST FINGER for MINOR or BLUES or we use the PINKY for MAJOR.
- Once Pattern #1 is on the fretboard everything is relative to it.
- Add Pattern #2, #3, and #5, always connected to each other in the same way to extend the range of the scale further up and down the fretboard.
- SHORT OCTAVE and LONG OCTAVE shapes help us see the notes on the fretboard and help us navigate scales and so much more.

CHAPTER 7

TUNE IN

"I am a musician and a guitar player. Music is my language and my guitar is my voice. Music is Melody, Harmony and Rhythm. I develop my language skills and my instrument skills. They are two separate worlds working together to complete the circle of music."

Rhythm is the number one factor to sounding great as a musician.

WARM UP

CHANGE GEARS

- Start with metronome at 60 bpm. It is really important to use a metronome for this exercise.
- Decide on which picking you will do for each gear.
- Only switch to next gear when you successfully played a few bars.
- Once you can confidently switch gears, set a limit on the number of bars, or even beats before you switch gears.
- You can also practice mixing and matching gears and switching in different orders.

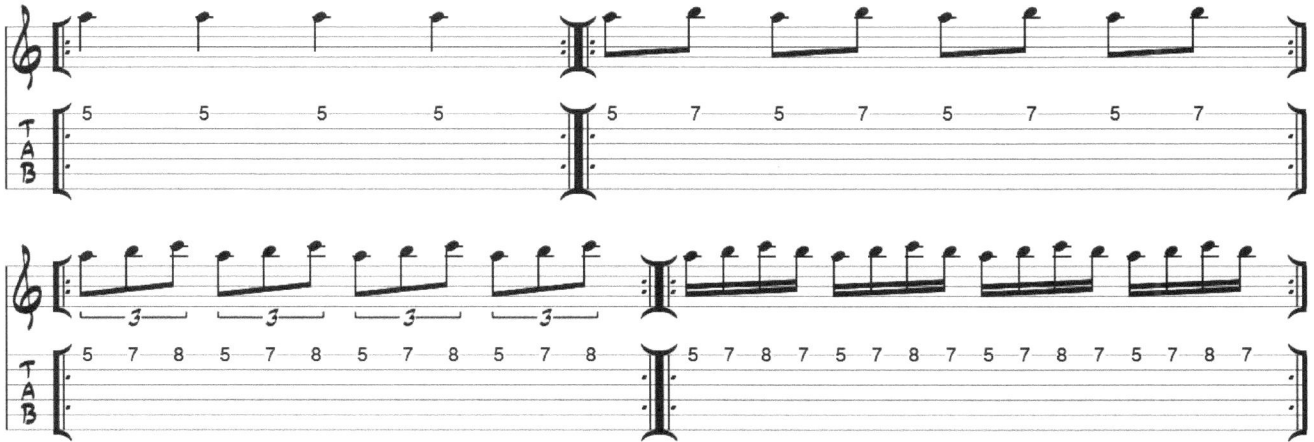

SHELL

SHELL 1 3 or 2 4 triplets

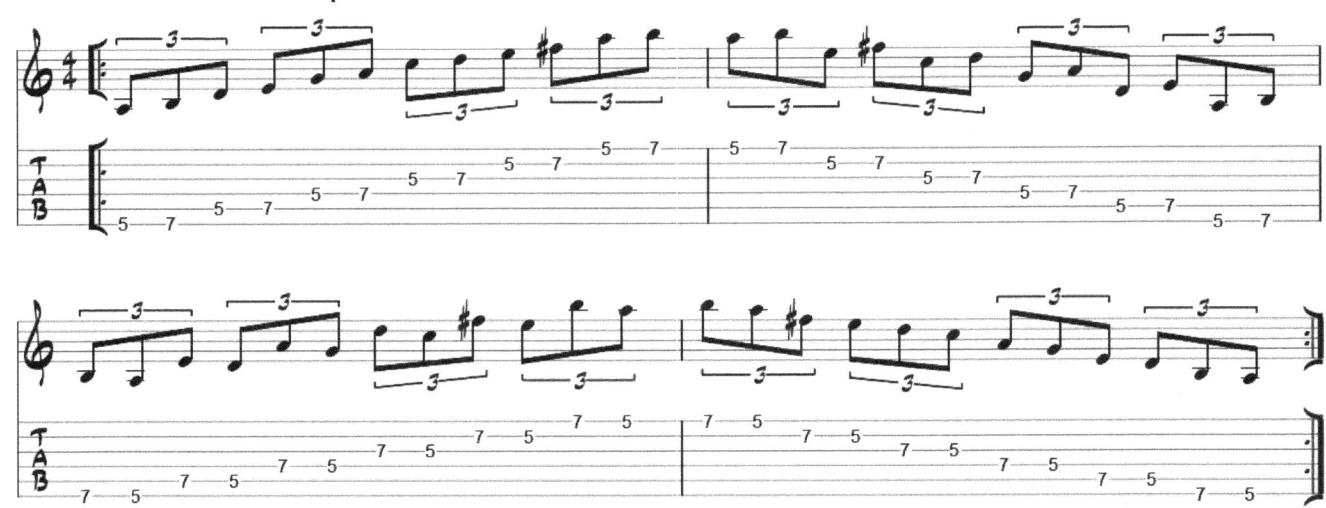

SHELL 1 3 or 2 4 sixteenth-notes

TIPS

Pentatonics only have two notes per string. This will create patterns when you are playing in the different gears.

In triplets you will feel you hand flip-flop between starting on the lower of the two notes and then the higher of the two notes.

Sixteenth-notes create a box, a two by two box that will repeat for each beat.

Having these expectations will help you know if you are truly playing triplets or sixteenths and not just faster than eighth-notes.

EXERCISE

Key G/Em Patterns #1, #2, #3, and #5   Ascend and descend   8ths 60 bpm

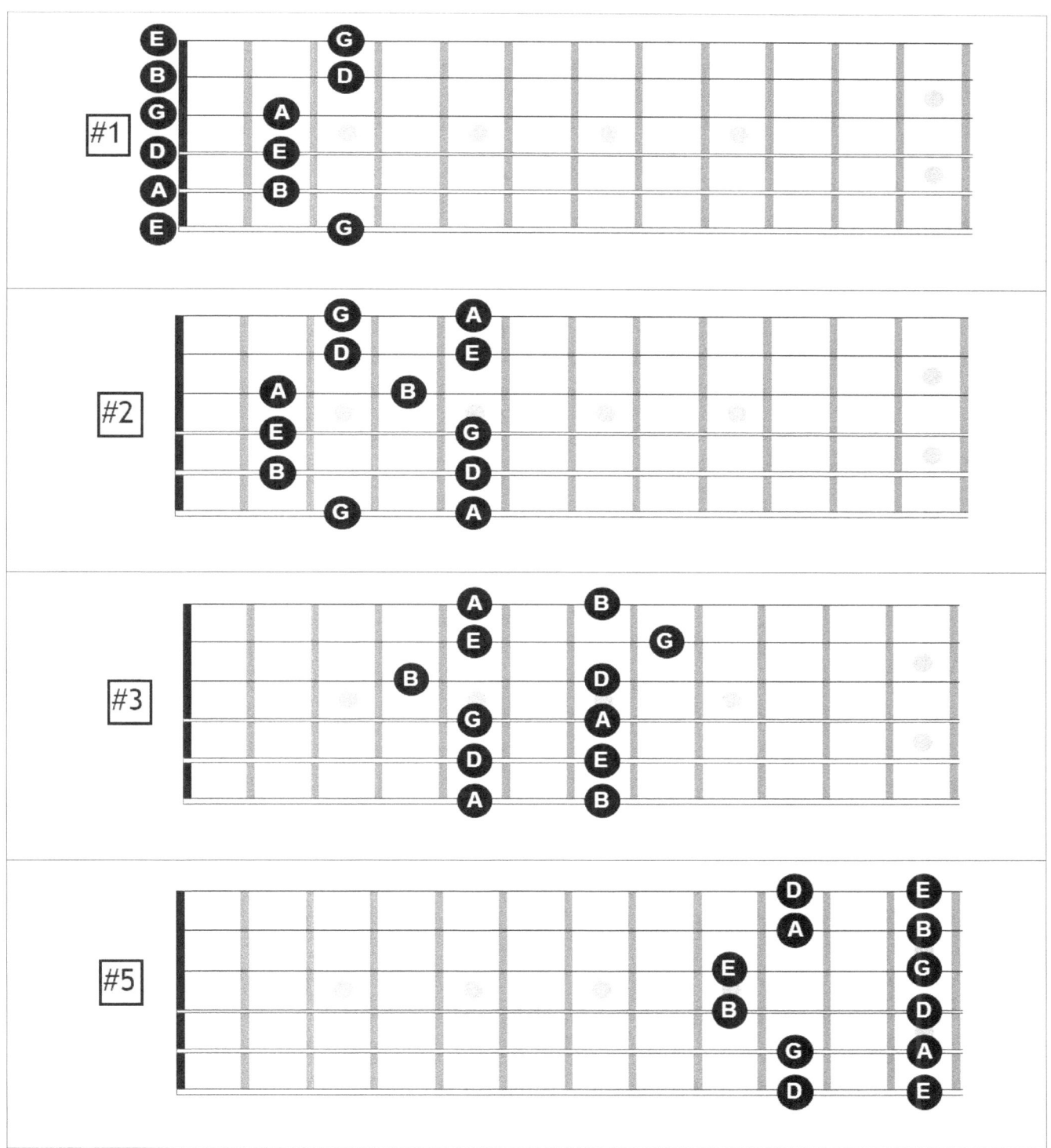

REVIEW

As I looked back at my guitar lessons throughout High School and even four years at Berklee College of Music, so much of my time was focused on notes and chords. It seemed like an endless ability to vary 12 notes and chords. Little attention was focused on the deeper level of rhythm. Rhythm seemed to be a utilitarian device, just to make sure I wasn't slowing down or speeding up, and rhythm was allocated to feel and groove. It was never the main thing to focus on. But I learned otherwise.

Rhythm is it's own language. It doesn't use notes, or chords or even need an instrument! Rhythm is time. Your heartbeat is rhythm. The sun rising and setting is rhythm. I once heard jazz composer George Russell say that a single note is just a super fast "beating" of a pulse. In essence, every note is a rhythm! Think of all the terms you use to describe how you feel when listening to music you like. "Music moves me." " I can feel it." When a concert starts and you see 10,000 people bobbing their heads, it's not that G chord that's doing it. It is the rhythm.

You are the ultimate rhythmic instrument. 24 hours a day you are capable of being rhythmic. When you walk or when you knock on a door you are being rhythmic. But, you can practice rhythms wherever and whenever. If your waiting in a lobby, you can tap your foot in quarter-notes and tap your hand on your thigh in eighth-notes. Change gears when you do this. Use two hands to spread out the rhythm, like you have two notes, or a down and up strum. If you're sitting down, you can use all four limbs. Tap 1 and 3 on the right foot and 2 and 4 on the left foot in quarter-notes. Play eighth-notes with the right hand and play on the 2 and 4 with the left hand. This is a basic drum beat.

When you want to sound better, focus on your rhythm. When you play a note, when you don't play a note, focus on your rhythm. Does everything you play groove in some way? It should. There are only 12 notes, only so many chords you will play and so many scales you will play. They will not change or improve. But how you put them into the world will improve. You will feel a better connection to the music because of your improved abilities in rhythm. If you play Do Re Me, does it sound like a halfhearted exercise or does it sound like music? Is every note, intended and deliberate, grooving in it's gear? Anytime you are playing you should make people bob their head and tap their foot. Then you know you are starting to connect together.

SEQUENCES

In music, a sequence is a tried and true method for building a melody and developing a musical idea. It involves a restatement of a phrase at a higher (or lower) pitch. Usually the phrase would restart on the next note of the scale after the first one. The technique is widely common to classical music and offers a wonderful alternative to the blues style "call and response" nature of music.

Whether it is purely a practice method or in a musical situation every musician, regardless of instrument, plays sequences. They are just as common in composition as they are in improvisation. They strengthen your ear, they increase your ability to hear on your instrument, and they get your hand skills together. The concept is simple, the possibilities are endless. When I started to play flute and sax the first thing I did immediately after learning how to play the notes was sequencing scales.

First, you need to understand a musical sequence as a concept before you bring it to your instrument. The most basic sequence I have ever heard is a 3 NOTE SEQUENCE. Usually, you play the first three notes of a scale. Then you play the next three notes starting from the second note. Then, from the third note play three more, and then again from the fourth note, play three more. This idea can ascend and descend and use any rhythm.

Another way to think of this is simple math, If you had

123 234 345 456

you would recognize a pattern. You were counting three numbers from each number. If you think of a scale you can do the same thing. Our E minor pentatonic scale is

E G A B D

If you follow through a three note sequence with this scale you get

EGA GAB ABD BDE DEG (repeats in next octave)

Any scale with any root can do this. Once we go to the guitar we have to visualize this process happening on the guitar. On the following page is a diagram using the numbers above. It's pattern #1 for E minor (starts on the E note) and for G Major (starts on the G note).

3 NOTE SEQUENCE

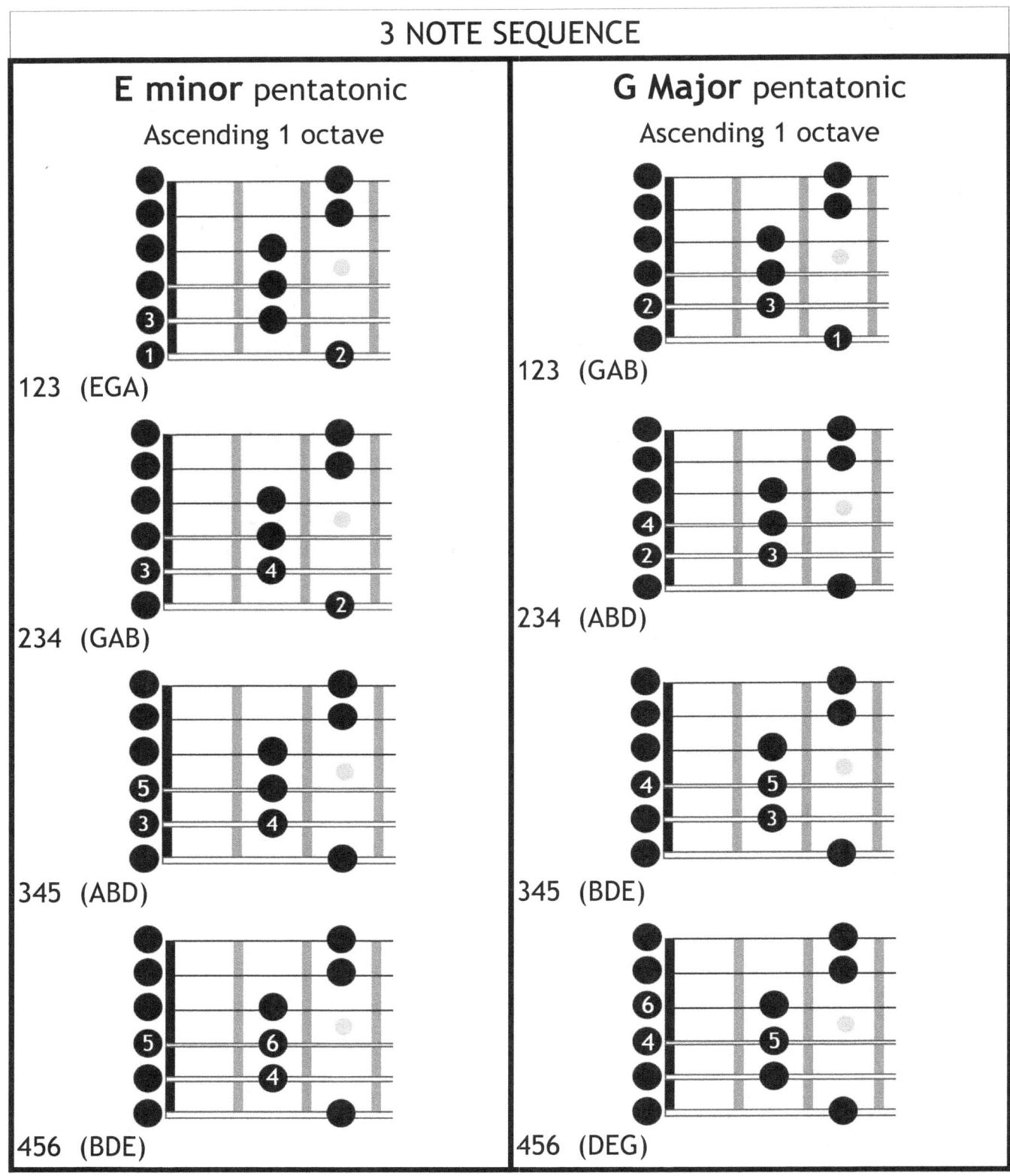

E minor pentatonic
Ascending 1 octave

123 (EGA)

234 (GAB)

345 (ABD)

456 (BDE)

G Major pentatonic
Ascending 1 octave

123 (GAB)

234 (ABD)

345 (BDE)

456 (DEG)

You will feel a 3 note sequence flip-flop between the lower and higher notes on a string.

HOW TO BUILD A SOLO with ABAC

When I used to solo, I always felt like I played the same solo every time, doing the same things. I learned to realize that I didn't need to know more (scales, licks, alien codes). I needed to ask more of what I already knew. I realized that I had tons of cool, simple ideas. But I would blow past them in search of new ones, I needed to nurture the ones I had. I didn't know how to do that. In reality I didn't know how to build a melody.

At some point I came across a really simple way to build on my ideas. It's basically a super call and response. Call and response is an old gospel and blues idea of a question and answer. "Can you feel me?" "We can feel you!"

I call this idea ABAC. Simply put, you have a small idea, 3-5 notes and we call this A. You play a related phrase, maybe start the same but end on a lower note, and we call this B. Play the first A phrase again. Lastly, play another response phrase, different than B. This is our C phrase.

"A" phrase   Key of E minor   Pentatonic pattern #1

Here is an example of ABAC with our A phrase. There are no rules as to how many notes to use or how much of a variation there is. It's just a simple guide to control and nurture an idea. It's a really natural sound. This concept really showed me how to build melodies and momentum.

PRACTICE

SEQUENCES

Start with pattern #1 in G/Em. You can exercise the whole pattern. Starting the sequence on the E note or the G note would help establish the scale but here we can just exercise the whole pattern.

It's *really important* to see the sequence starting from each note of the scale. Do not relate it to how it starts over (or goes back one). Although it is true for just this sequence it will not be true for most every other sequence.

Pattern #1 Ascending quarter-notes with REST

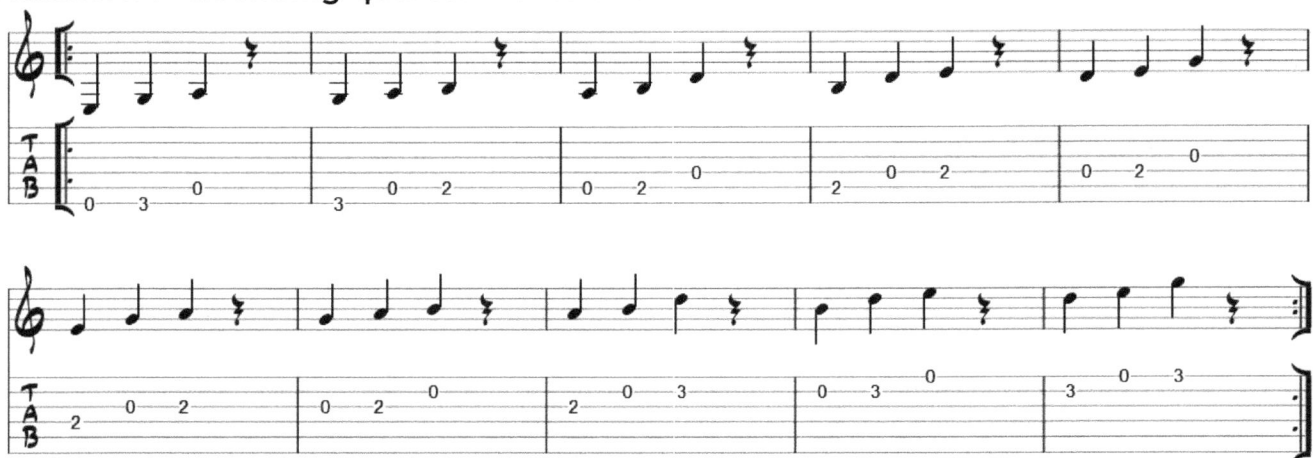

Pattern #1 Descending quarter-notes with REST

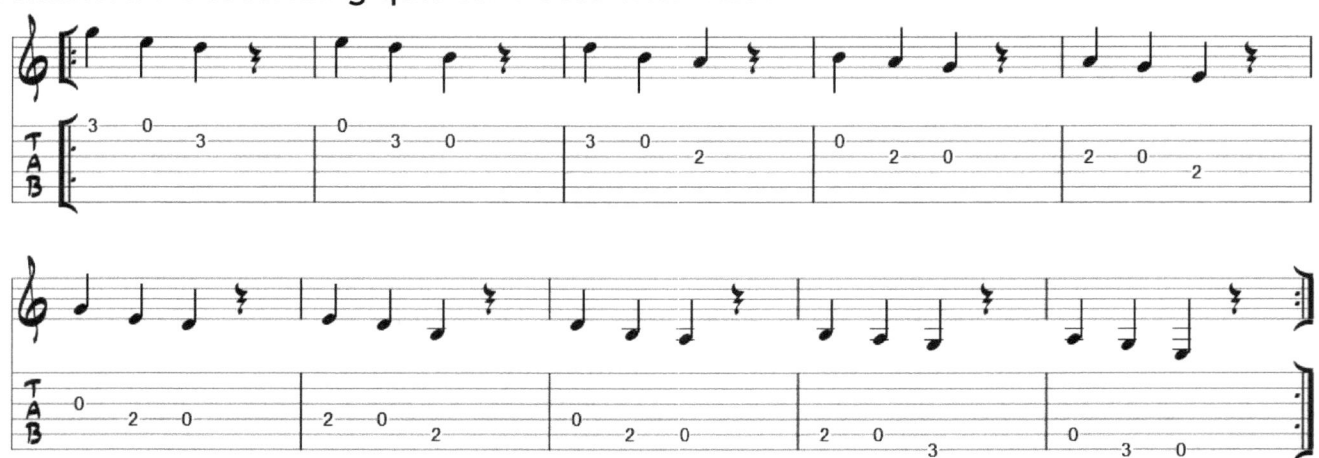

Pattern #1   Ascending and descending in quarter-notes

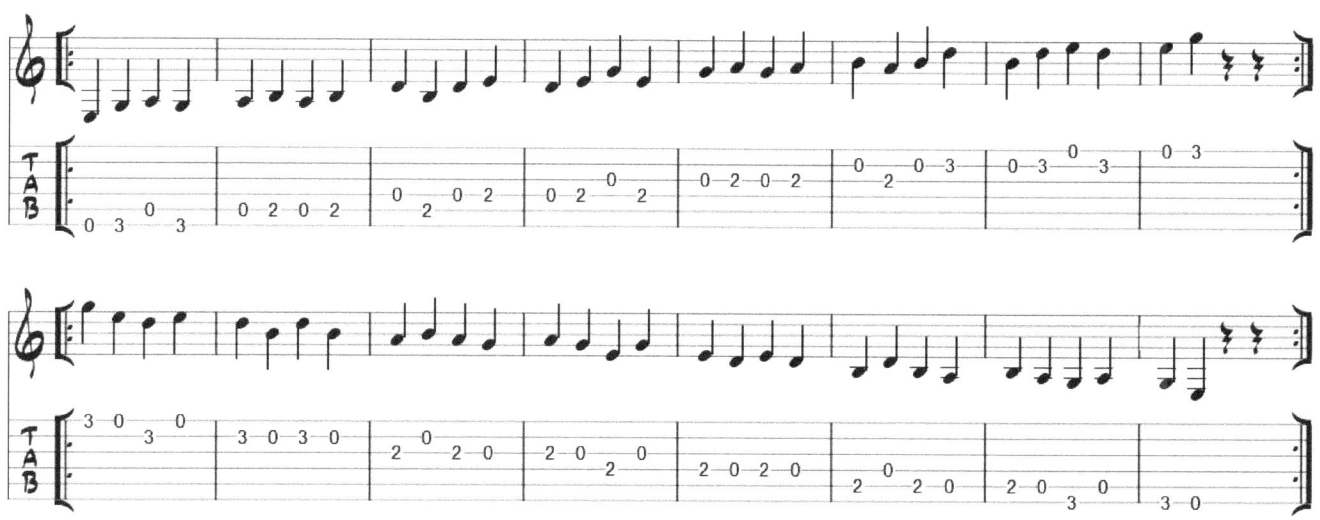

You can see how our ear would start to hear the 3 note phrase differently because of the four beats per bar. The sequence is crossing the bar line and seems to obscure the 3 notes, but they are still there.

This gets more involved when we change gears to eighth-notes.

Pattern #1 G/Em   Ascending and descending in eighth-notes.

ABAC

Self generate   E minor   Pattern #1   ABAC

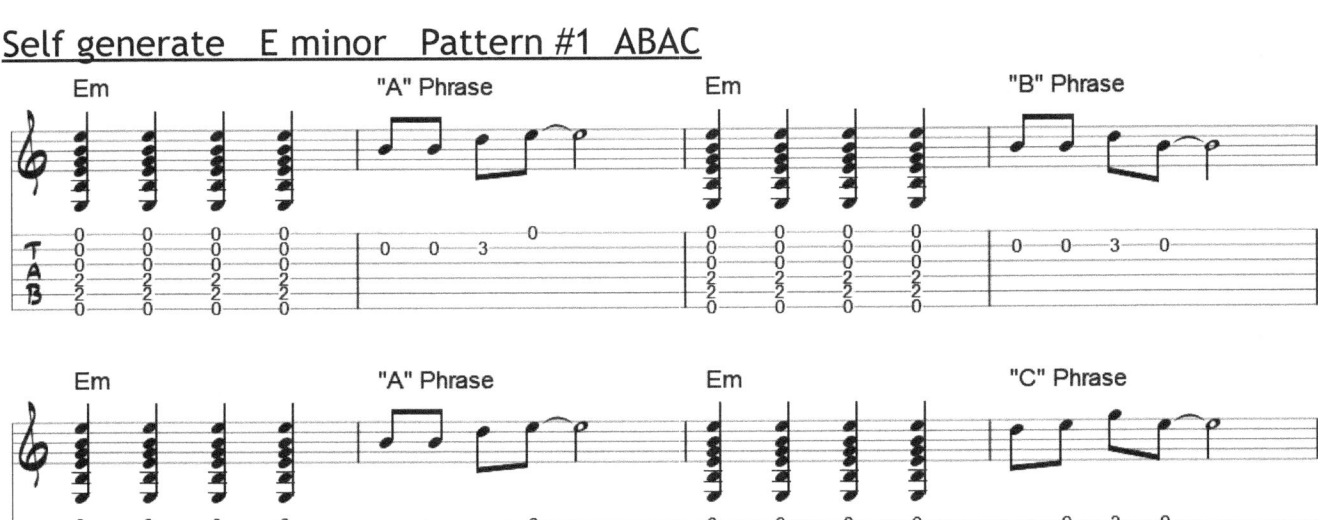

Self generate   G Major   Pattern #2   ABAC

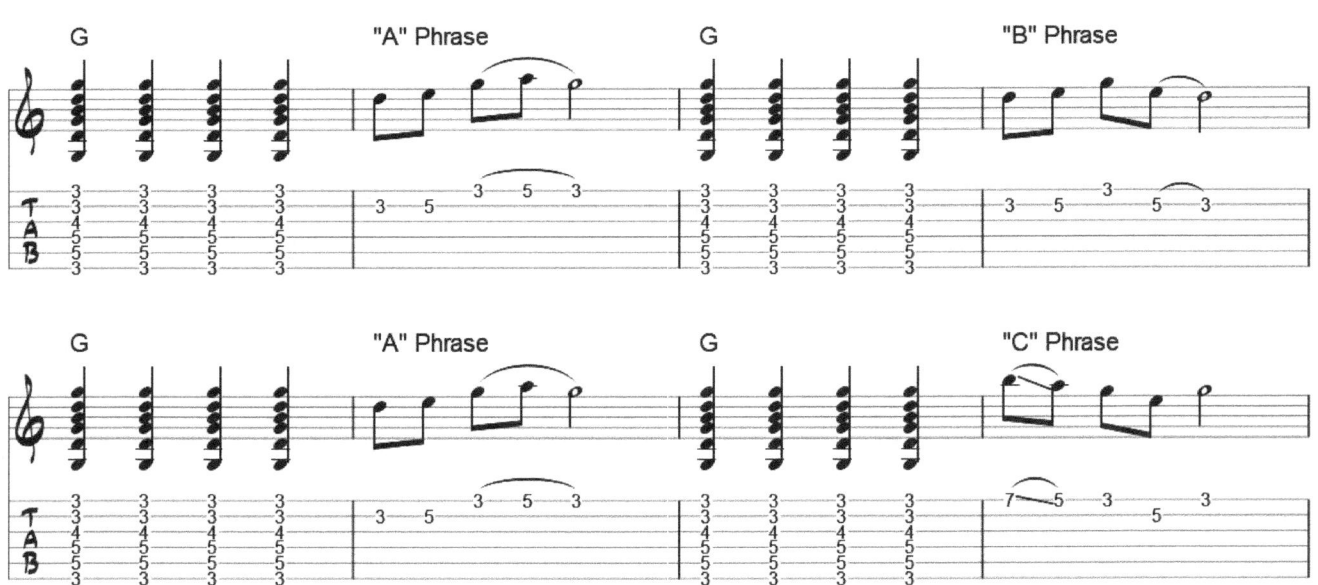

SUMMARY

We are musicians. We are guitar players.
We learn the language of music. Melody, Harmony, and Rhythm
We learn the craft of playing the guitar as an instrument.

Music is Melody, Harmony and Rhythm.
RHYTHM is most important.

We warm up with Muted String Ladders (MSL), Changing GEARS, and SHELLS.
We EXERCISE our scales and licks. Round the Block is an easy and effective way to memorize and run the patterns. Changing Gears helps us build rhythm, confidence and accountability.

AS A MUSICIAN:

- We decide on the "main" chord and base the scale upon that chord.
- MINOR chord gets a MINOR scale.
- MAJOR chord can get either the MAJOR pentatonic and/or the BLUES pentatonic.
- Add the Blue Note for extra color.
- Octaves are the landings in the staircase. Each octave starts the same and we build scale up and down from them.
- **Rhythm** is the ULTIMATE tool to connect to music and sound our best.
- ABAC is an ultra simple and extremely powerful tool to help build melodies and nurture ideas.

AS A GUITAR PLAYER:

- Once we know the music scale we need to find the ROOT note on the low E string.
- Then we decide on the the FIRST FINGER for MINOR or BLUES or we use the PINKY for MAJOR.
- Once Pattern #1 is on the fretboard everything is relative to it.
- Add Pattern #2, #3, and #5, always connected to each other in the same way to extend the range of the scale further up and down the fretboard.
- SHORT OCTAVE and LONG OCTAVE shapes help us see the notes on the fretboard and help us navigate scales and so much more.
- Sequences are great for solos and improvising. They help us hear and "build our chops." They are essential on any instrument.

CHAPTER 8

TUNE IN

"I am a musician and a guitar player. Music is my language and my guitar is my voice. Music is Melody, Harmony and Rhythm. I develop my language skills and my instrument skills. They are two separate worlds working together to complete the circle of music."

Rhythm is the number one factor to sounding great as a musician.

WARM UP

MSL 6 strings all gears. ALL DOWN picked, ALL UP picked, ALL ALTERNATE. Then change gears.

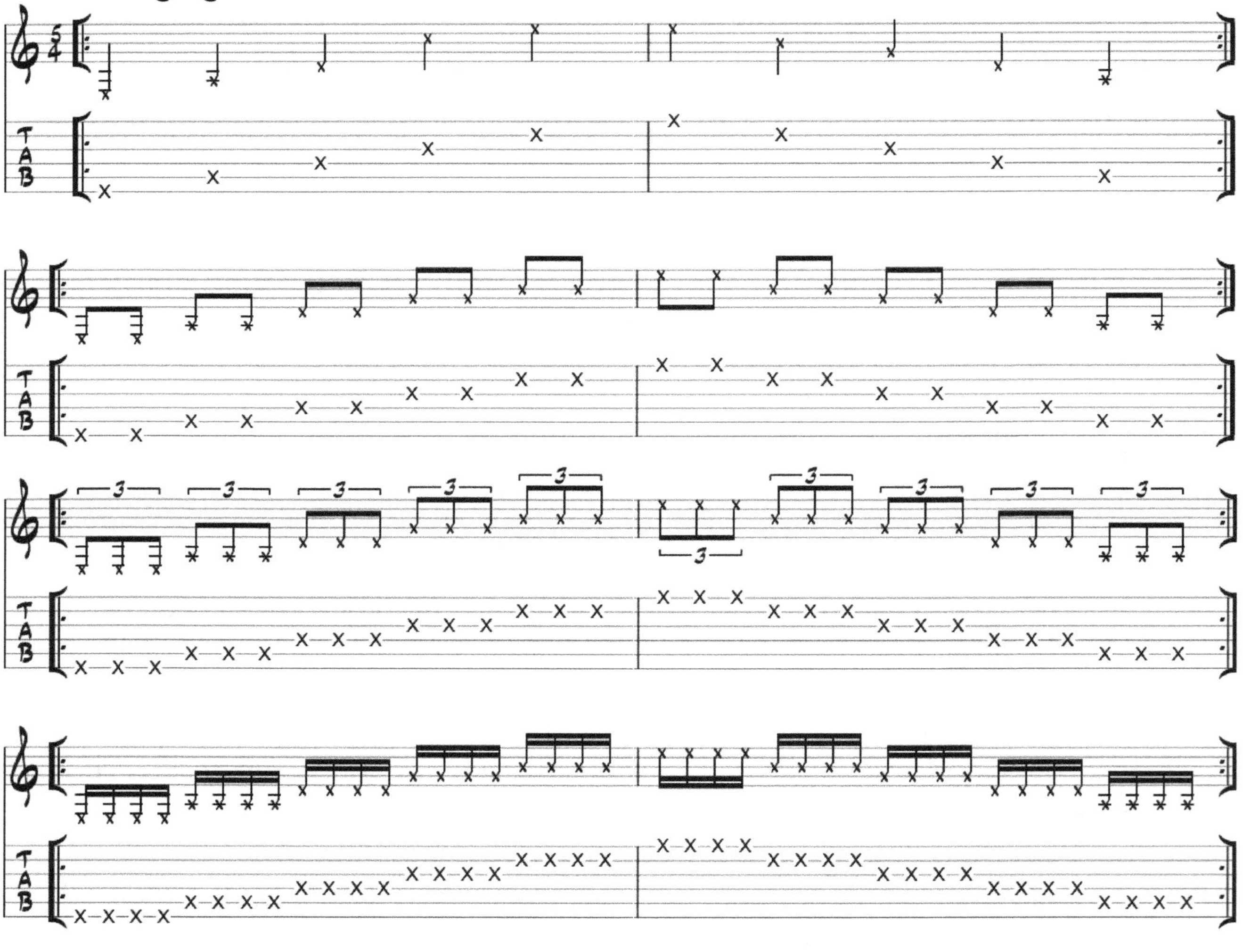

CHANGE GEARS

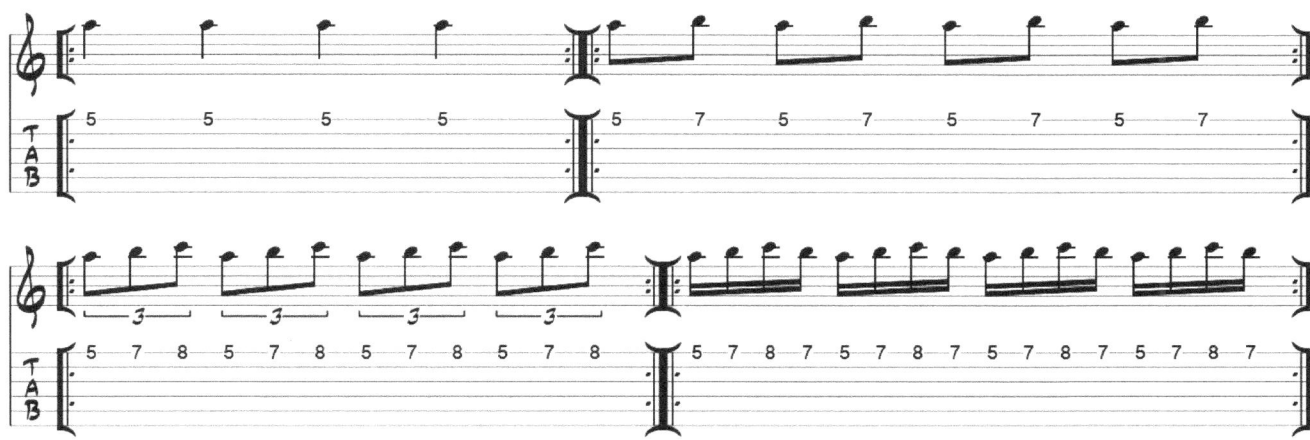

SHELLS

SHELL 1 3   skip 1 fret   quarter-notes

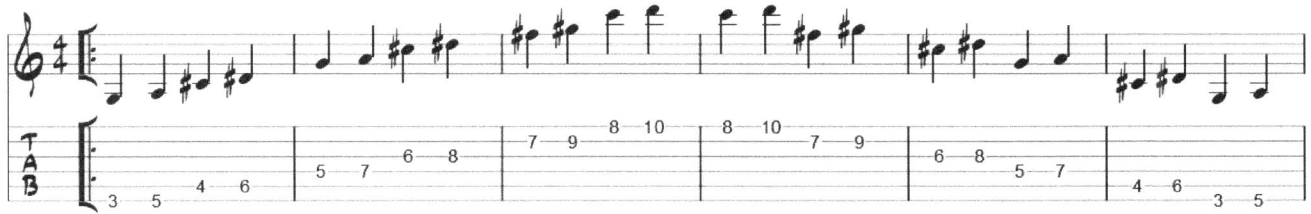

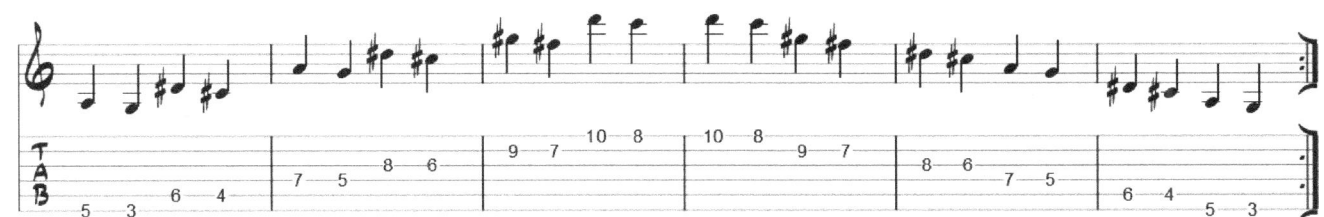

SHELL 1 3   skip 1 fret   eighth-notes

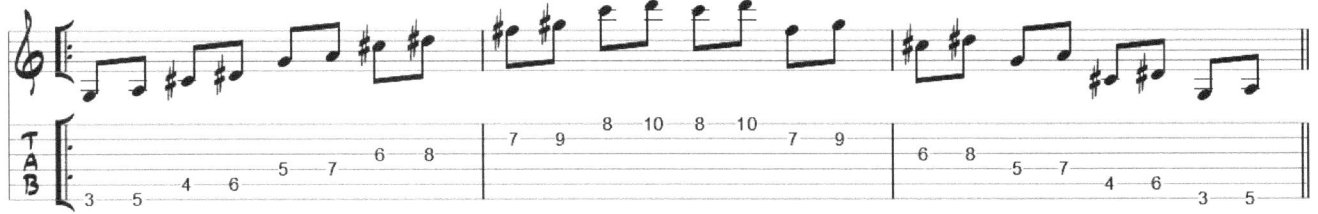

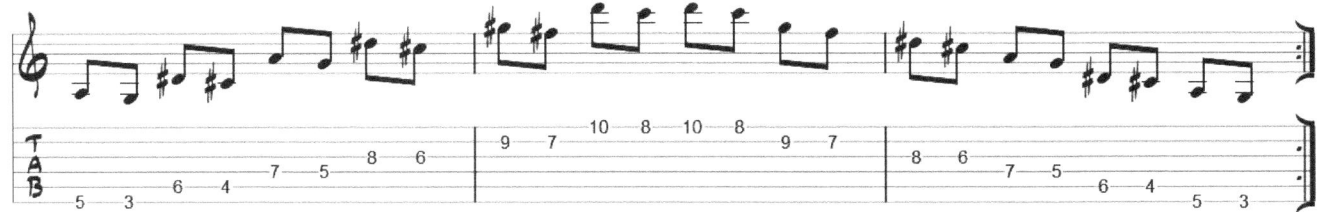

EXERCISE

Sequence Pattern #1

Pattern #1   G/Em   Ascending quarter-notes with REST

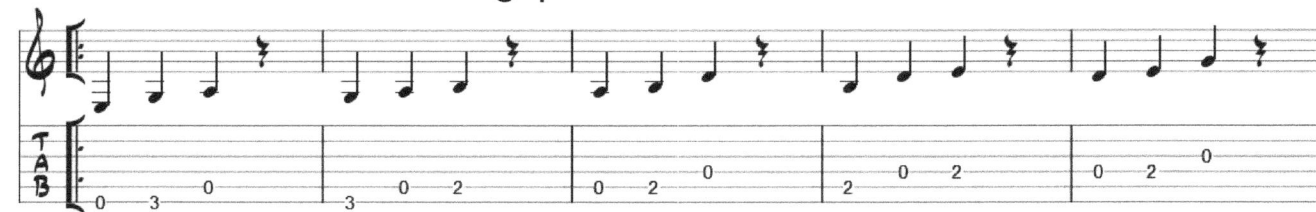

Pattern #1   G/Em   Descending quarter-notes with REST

Pattern #1   G/Em   Ascending and descending in quarter-notes

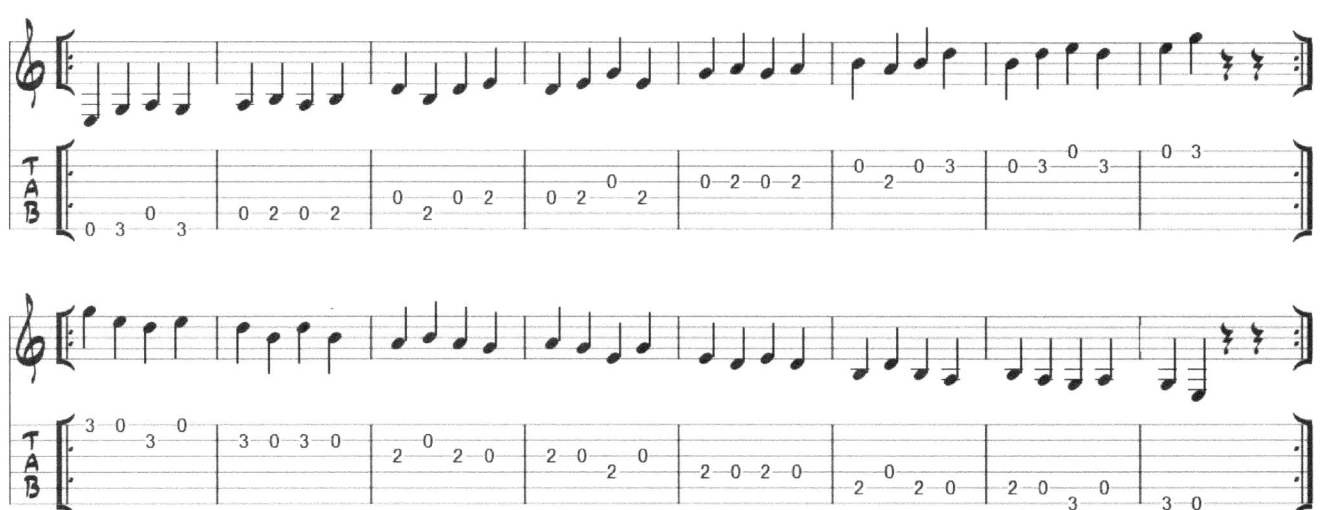

Pattern #1   G/Em   Ascending and descending in eighth-notes

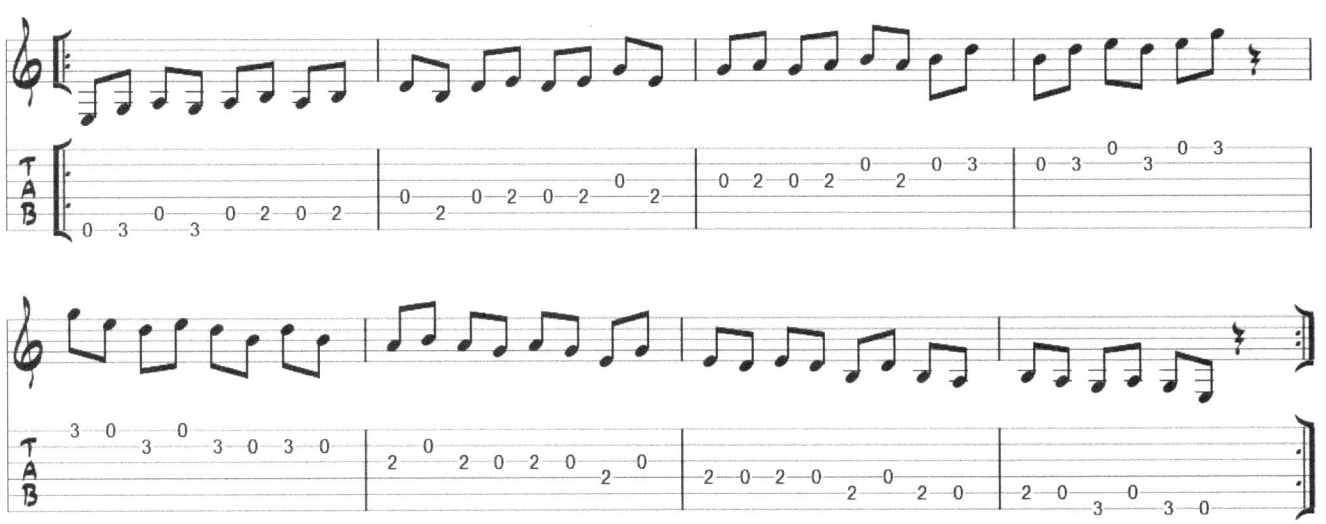

REVIEW

3 Note Sequence   G Major backing track

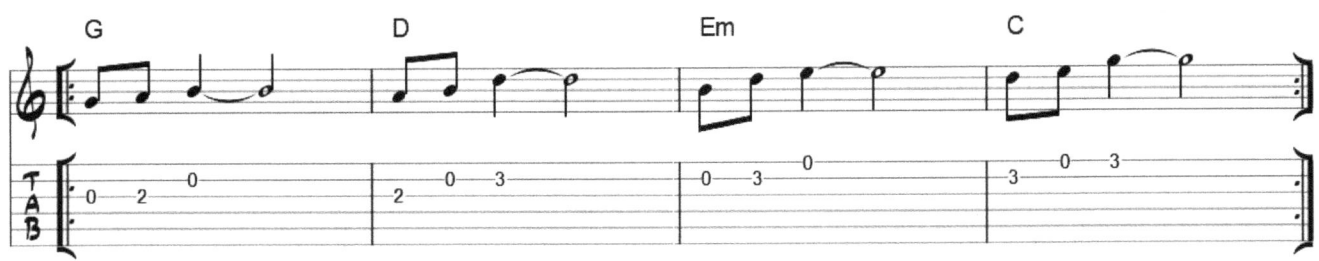

ABAC   G Major backing track

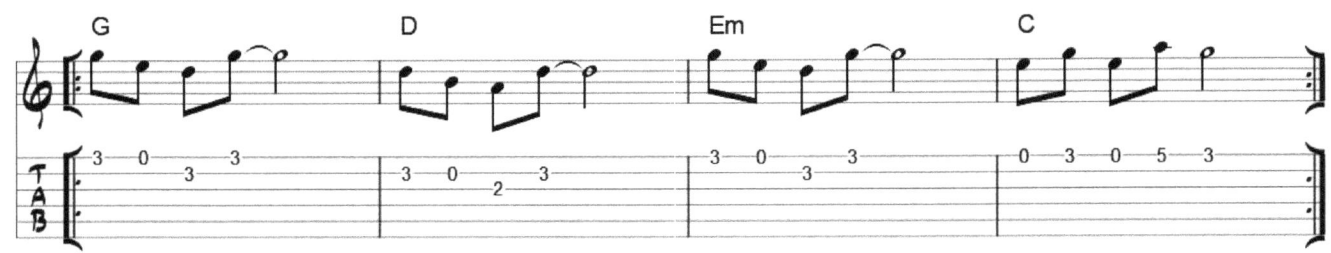

Combination ABAC and 3 note sequence   G Major backing track
Bars with G and Em have ABAC and bars with D and C use 3 note sequences.

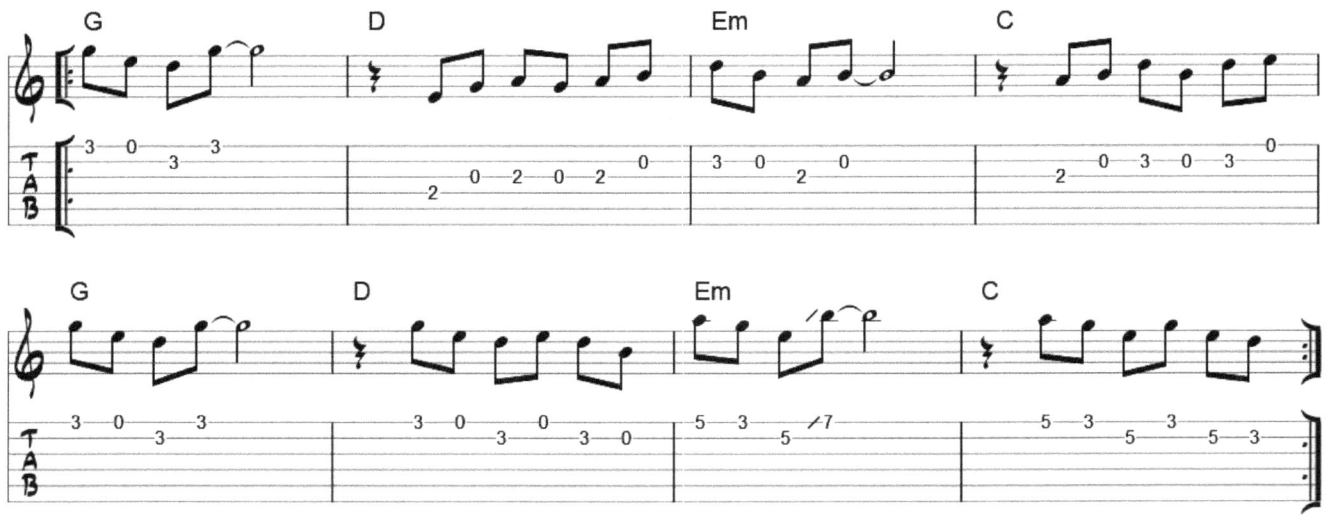

PATTERN #4

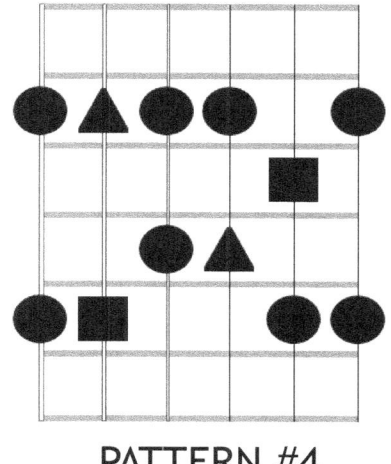

PATTERN #4

Although this is the last pattern we are learning to connect our entire fretboard it is not the least important. Pattern #4 is one of my favorites and is probably the third most often used after #1 and #2.

Pattern #4 is like the "A string" version of pattern #1, with similar thinking to bar chord shapes. If you are in the key of E minor, then you see that pattern #1 is on top of the open E minor chord. If you play Em as a bar chord on the 7th fret (A shape) then you will see pattern #4 on top of that bar chord. Chords and scales are the same information. The chord shapes can be seen directly in the pattern.

You will notice the "Rock and Roll Rule" can be seen on the "A String." The TRIANGLE is the *minor root* and the SQUARE is the *Major root*.

Pattern #4 is also home to the **C form chord** in the **CAGED** system. This means it feels like an old school open C chord but you have to bar the top three strings. This shape is extremely important to get comfortable with. We will cover this in detail in the Lead Chords and Arpeggios book.

WATCH A VIDEO ABOUT CAGED at
www.LeadGuitarWorkshop.com

Key of G/Em

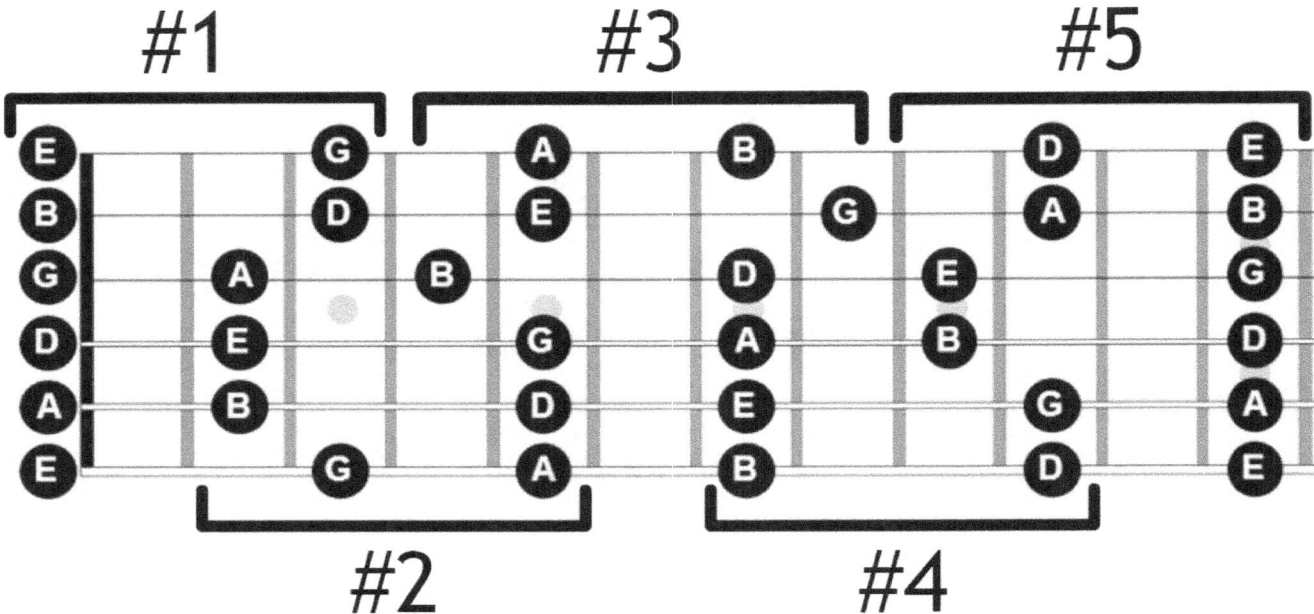

This is the entire pentatonic world to a guitar player. Our fretboard is multi-dimensional. You can move notes up a string or the same notes across strings on the same frets. There is a lot of redundancy that other instruments don't have to deal with.

- The 5 patterns are ALWAYS in the same order, just depends of which one is in the open position (which key).

- The 5 patterns are the SAME 5 NOTES, so the patterns themselves don't sound different.

- The patterns start over at the 12th fret and keep repeating.

- All the patterns overlap. The top of #1 is the bottom of #2 (speaking in terms of pitch/sound).

- The 5 patterns allow us to use the entire fretboard for our scale choice.

- As a musician, the 5 note pentatonic scale has 3 uses/sounds: Major, minor and blues.

- Get to know the key of G/Em first. It is the key you will play in the most.

PLAYING THE CHANGES

One of the first solos I learned where I recognized the pentatonic pattern #1 was "Stairway to Heaven." It was A minor pentatonic pattern #1 on the 5th fret. The first bend and bunch of notes seemed just like what I expected until the lead guitar player landed on the 8th fret of the A string. That note (F) was not in the pentatonic scale. I didn't understand why it was there, but it sounded great. I later heard about seven note scales called modes. I figured it must have been one of them because this new note didn't sound like (or look like) a blue note.

It wasn't till some time later that I learned what the chords were that Jimmy Page was soloing over. The band starts on an A minor chord (that makes sense) but then they go to an F chord! And sure enough, it was at the exact time that Page plays the F note. He did it on purpose. He knew if he stayed in the scale shape he would have landed on an E note, and that would have sounded dissonant and unresolved over the F chord. I was blown away. How did he know to do that?

I soon came to realize that some people play a pentatonic scale and just kick some butt on it. But others were adding notes, moving notes at certain times, and even playing different scales. Every time it was to match the chord at that moment. This is called **"Playing the Changes."** It's a slang term but a universal one.

When you Play the Changes, you are talking to each chord directly and not just globally. Instead of saying "Hi Everybody" you are saying "Hey Ted, Judy and John." It sounds connected and is a wonderful goal to attain as a musician.

One of the hardest parts is keeping track of the chords in your head as you solo. This is the most important part. If you don't know what chord you are playing over at a moments notice then there is no way you will be able to directly speak to it.

WATCH A VIDEO on HOW TO PLAY THE CHANGES

www.LeadGuitarWorkshop.com

| Am | D |

Here is a typical chord progression that you solo over (think "Oye Como Va" by Santana). Remind yourselves to ask the music questions first and then go to the guitar. There are two chords (*A minor and D Major*) and they last for one bar each (*harmonic rhythm*). If you played the chords a few times it would sound natural to end on the Am chord when you finish the song. **A minor is the main chord.**

As a musician we have a few options as to how to solo over this chord progression. When you think musically it supercedes all of the instruments. This is all language that happens before we need a physical object (instrument) to translate this language into sound.

BASIC SOLO METHODS

- **GLOBAL PENTATONIC**: Use the pentatonic scale of the *main chord* for everything (Am pentatonic). This is the easiest and most effective way to get right into a great solo.

- **PLAY THE CHANGES - PENTATONIC**: Use a pentatonic scale for *every chord* in the progression. Am pentatonic when the Am chord is playing and D Major pentatonic for when the D Major chord is playing. You must keep track of the chords in your head/ear to properly match the scale and its chord.

The A minor pentatonic (ACDEG) has all three notes of the Am chord in it (ACE), as well as the relative C chord (CEG). But it doesn't have all of the notes of the D chord (DF#A). When you play the changes you are accessing the notes of the chord you are in, not just the global scale. This is true of any pentatonic scale and its chord.

	Am	D	
A minor pentatonic *(global)*			
A minor pentatonic *(play the changes)*		D Major pentatonic *(play the changes)*	

PRACTICE

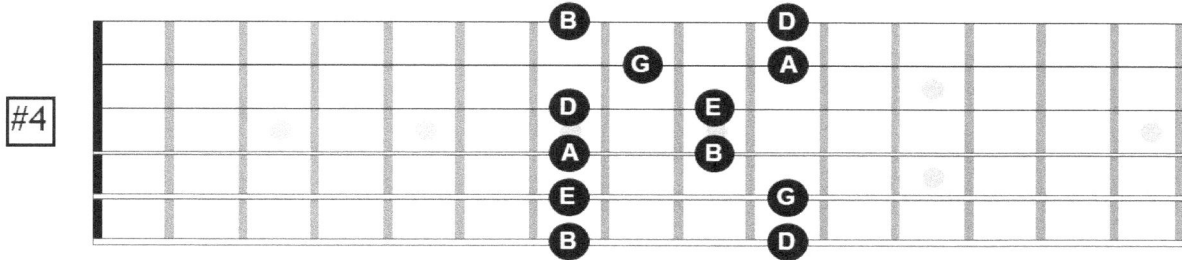

Pattern #4   ascend and descend

Self-GEN Pattern #4

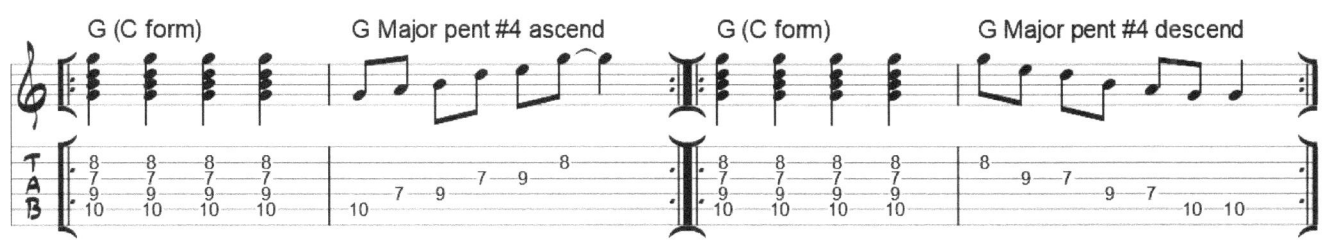

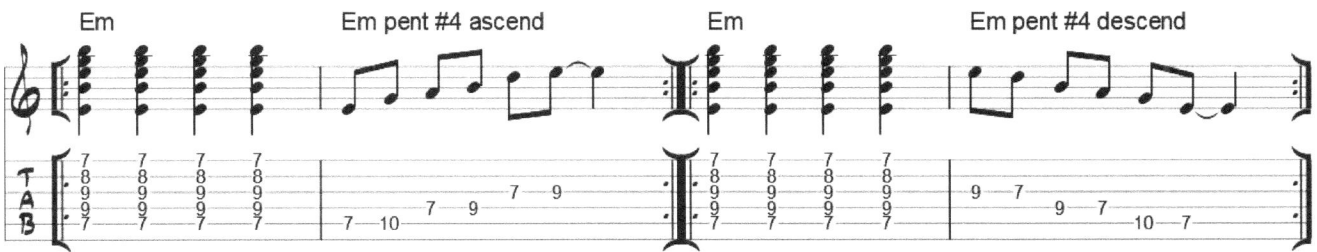

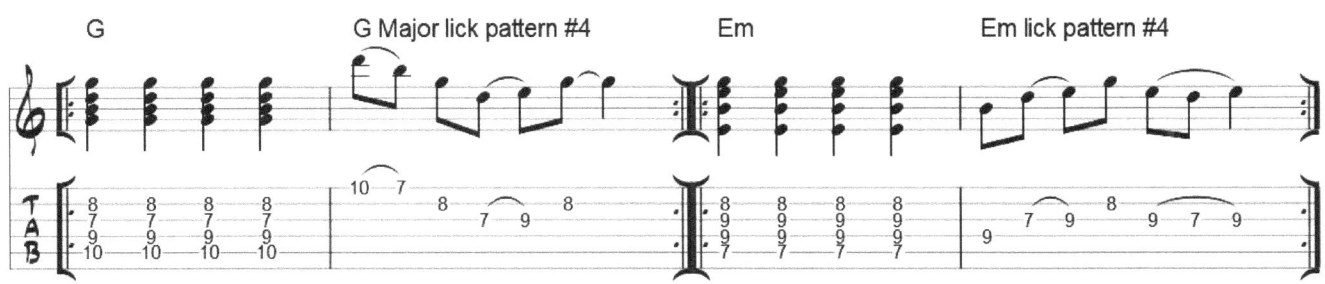

PLAYING THE CHANGES

|Am |D |

Play the changes with pattern #1 scales

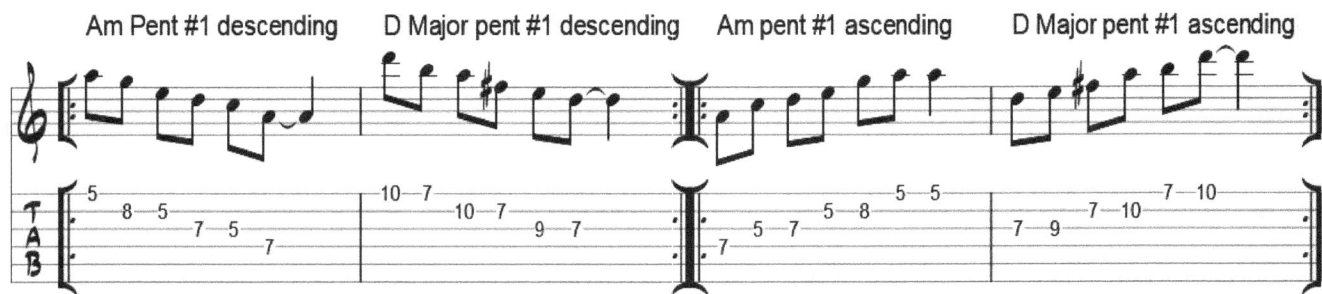

Play the changes with pattern #1 licks

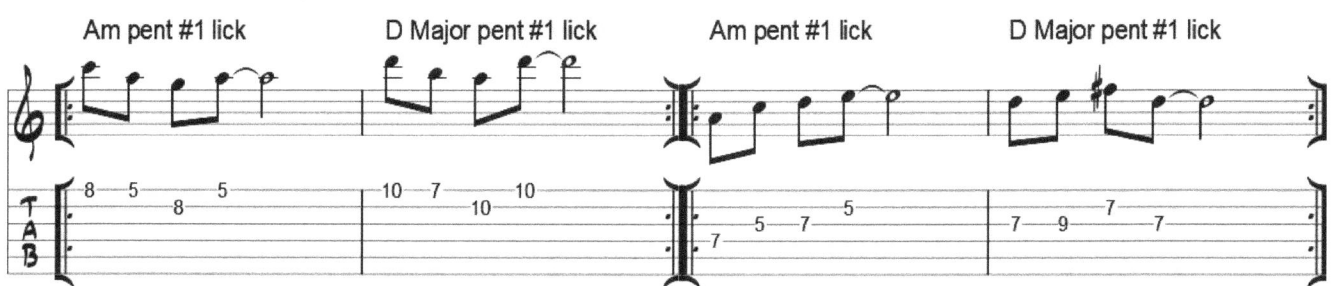

Play the changes with Pattern #1 and #5 licks for D

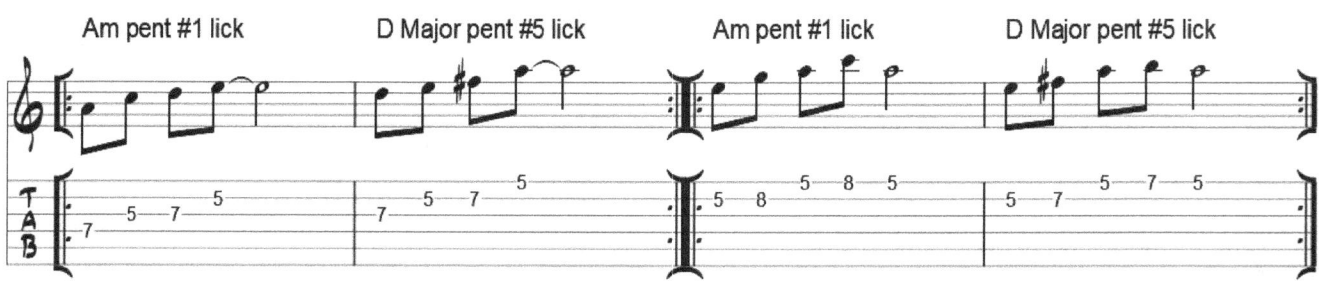

SUMMARY

We are musicians. We are guitar players.
We learn the language of music. Melody, Harmony, and Rhythm
We learn the craft of playing the guitar as an instrument.

Music is Melody, Harmony and Rhythm.
RHYTHM is most important.

We warm up with Muted String Ladders (MSL), Changing GEARS, and SHELLS.
We EXERCISE our scales and licks.

AS A MUSICIAN:
- We decide on the "main" chord and base the scale upon that chord.
- MINOR chord gets a MINOR scale.
- MAJOR chord can get either the MAJOR pentatonic and/or the BLUES pentatonic.
- Add the Blue Note for extra color.
- Octaves are the landings in the staircase. Each octave starts the same and we build scale up and down from them.
- **Rhythm** is the ULTIMATE tool to connect to music and sound our best.
- ABAC is an ultra simple and extremely powerful tool to help build melodies and nurture ideas.
- Playing the Changes versus playing globally is one of the two main methods for soloing. Playing the changes really ups the game in terms of sound.

AS A GUITAR PLAYER:
- Once we know the music scale we need to find the ROOT note on the low E string.
- Then we decide on the the FIRST FINGER for MINOR or BLUES or we use the PINKY for MAJOR.
- Once Pattern #1 is on the fretboard everything is relative to it.
- Add Pattern #2, #3,#4, #5, always connected to each other in the same way to extend the scale further up and down the fretboard.
- SHORT OCTAVE and LONG OCTAVE shapes help us see the notes on the fretboard and help us navigate scales and so much more.
- Sequences are great for solos and improvising. They help us hear and "build our chops." They are essential on any instrument.

CHAPTER 9

TUNE IN

"I am a musician and a guitar player. Music is my language and my guitar is my voice. Music is Melody, Harmony and Rhythm. I develop my language skills and my instrument skills. They are two separate worlds working together to complete the circle of music."

Rhythm is the number one factor to sounding great as a musician.

WARM UP

MSL 1 strings   all gears faster tempo   70 BPM-120BPM

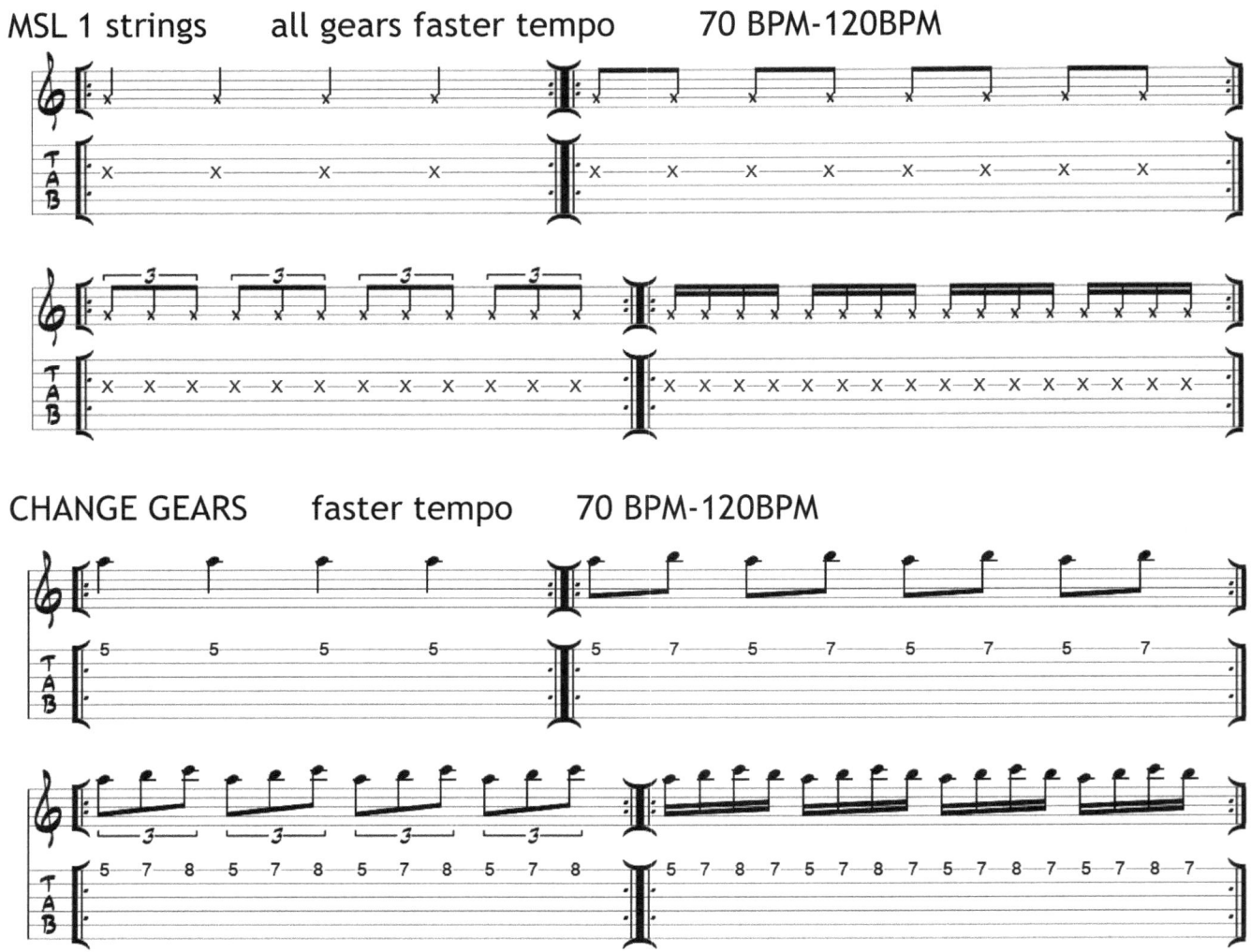

CHANGE GEARS   faster tempo   70 BPM-120BPM

SHELL

SHELL 1 2 3 4 is for speed and endurance. Every time you finish move up (or down) by a fret. Do as many as you can. Alternate pick and use a metronome. You can also do this as sixteenth-notes.

EXERCISE

Patterns #1, #2, #3 #4, #5 up and down and Round the Block

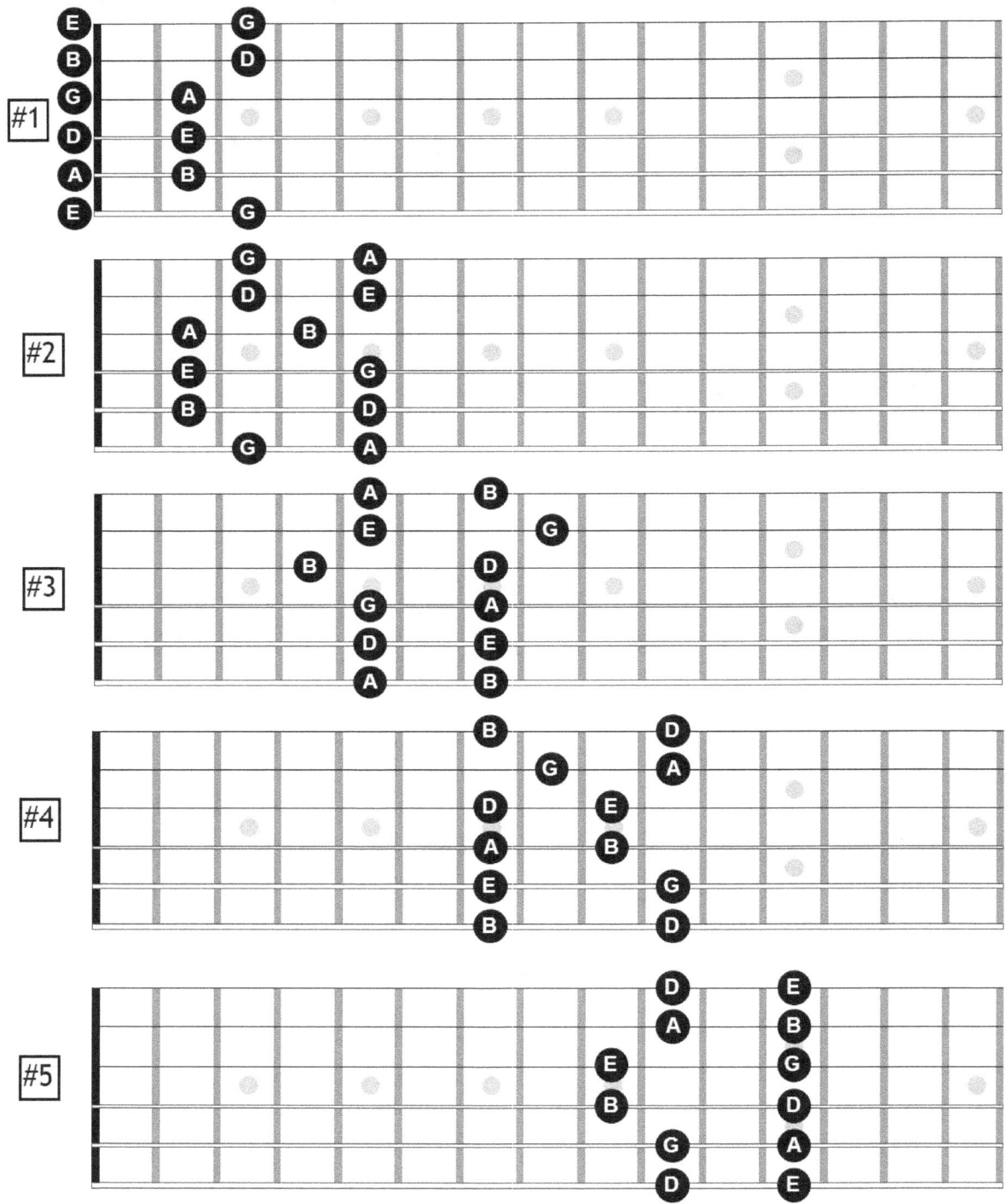

REVIEW

When playing the changes, you use notes and scales that directly relate to each chord and not just the "global" key.

Here is a 12 bar blues in A. There are 3 chords, A7, D7, and E7. They are all Major chords and get their respective pentatonic scale: A Major pentatonic for the A7 chord, D Major pentatonic for the D7 chord, and E Major pentatonic for the E7 chord. There is a one bar phrase. (Musician)

The one bar lick is in Pattern #2 (King Box). Rock and Role Rule says for an A Major pentatonic scale, pinky finger on the A note 5th fret for pattern #1 (which starts on 2nd). Pattern #2 is right above #1 and on top of the E form bar chord. It is easy to move this up and down to play changes....like a bar chord. (Guitarist)

WATCH A VIDEO on HOW TO SOLO OVER THE BLUES
www.LeadGuitarWorkshop.com

NECK ANATOMY SCALES

Neck Anatomy is the ultimate way to look at the octaves on your neck to truly see the notes and scale on your neck in a very musical and consistent way. Other instruments can move through octaves with the same fingers on the same notes, and we can too if we use Neck Anatomy.

There are only 12 notes in all of music, and we see them on the first 12 frets of any one string. We have six strings so we will expect six of any note on the first 12 frets of our guitar. We learned the keystone to Neck Anatomy is SHORT OCTAVE to LONG OCTAVE. If you locate a note on the low E string you build a SHORT to LONG OCTAVE and you can do it again from the A string. Here are the E notes. The 12th fret on the High E string is and octave higher than the open string. Then the entire process starts again at the 12th fret on the sixth string.

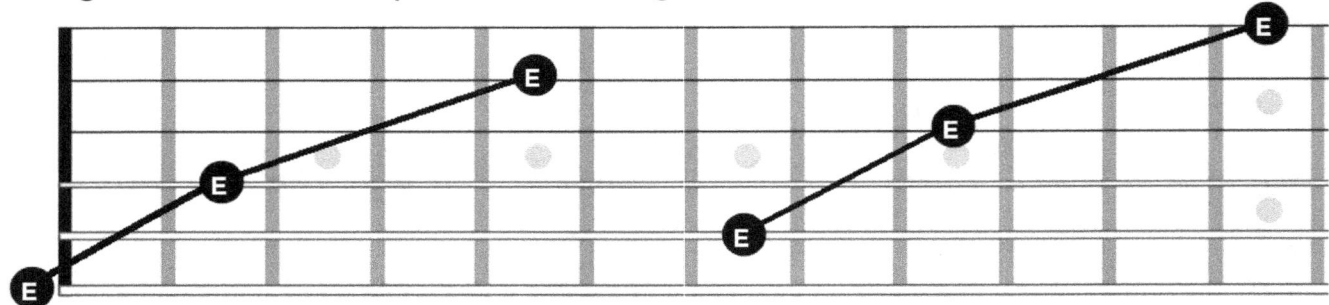

The guitar is about THREE full octaves worth of usable notes. (In the key of E you can hit the fourth octave in we can get to the 24th fret on the High E string.)

In reality, starting the SHORT OCTAVE to LONG OCTAVE on the Low E string will give you access to the three octaves.

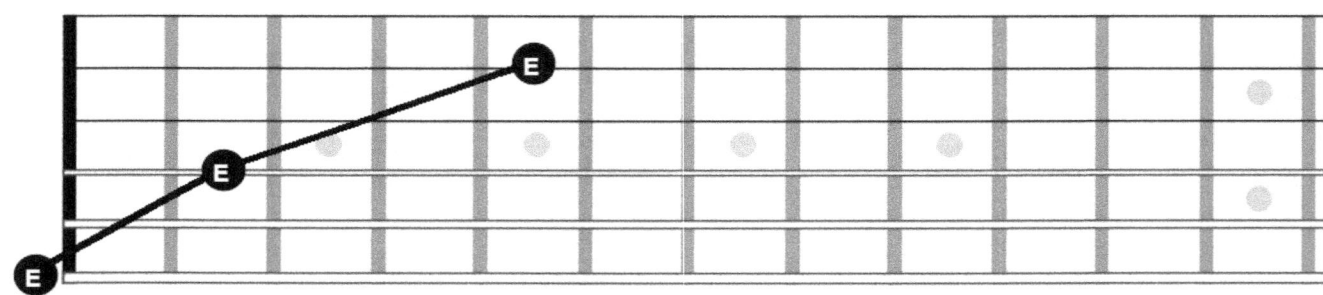

Once you navigate the first SHORT to LONG OCTAVE you can use it to help find the ROOT note of a scale. Then you can find the Blue Note, or any note. You can also BUILD SCALES!

First, add a note above the ROOT on the same string (E and G).

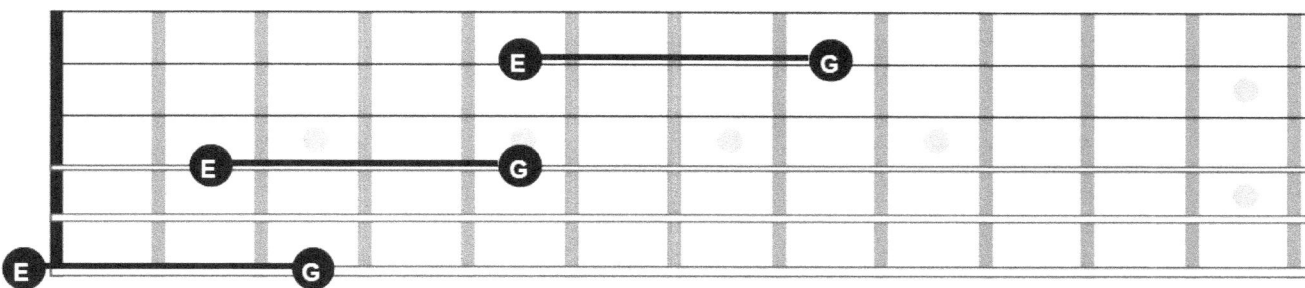

Next, add 2 more notes on the next string. This will be FOUR of the FIVE pentatonic notes. It is really easy to look at the four notes, as they are the same in all three octaves.

They will be the same shape, with the same fingers on the same notes.

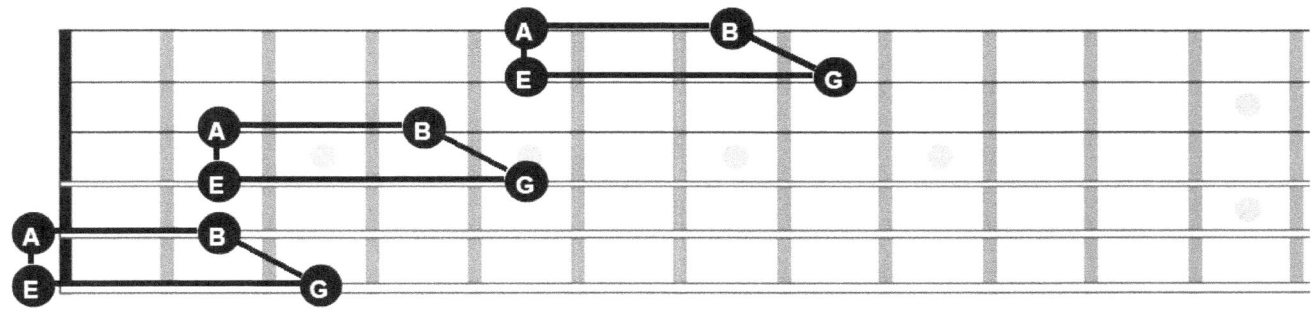

Finally, when adding the FIFTH note, look at it in relation to the ROOT (it is a whole-step below the next root).

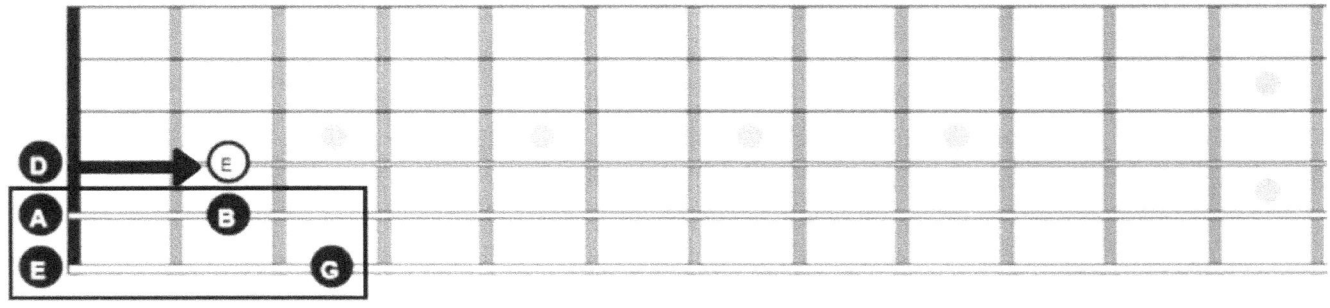

On the middle octave you have to compensate for the B string by 1 fret for the fifth note.

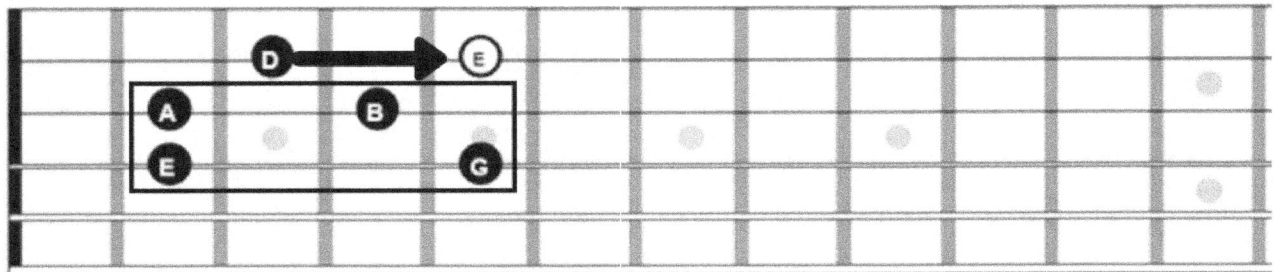

For the THIRD octave you will run out of strings. You just need to see the next ROOT again on the 12th fret and know that the last note of the scale is a whole-step below it.

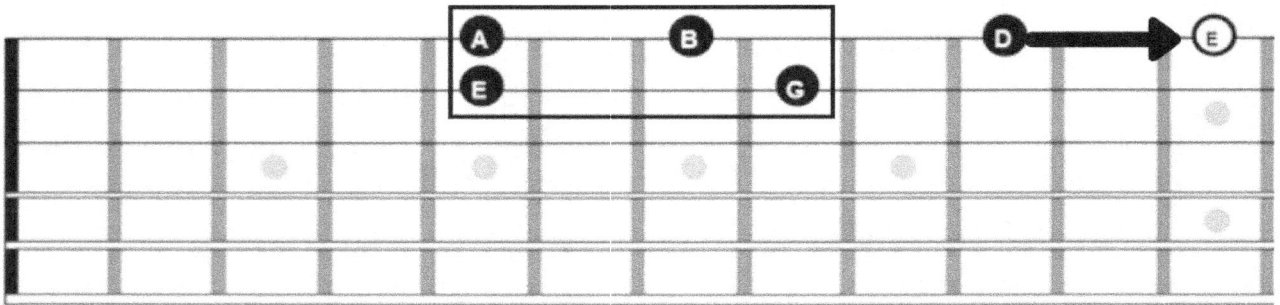

Aside from the B string and running our of strings the scale is almost identical in all three octaves for a minor pentatonic scale. This is not just for E, but any minor pentatonic scale starting on the low E string. In fact, you can move almost any shape or scale like this. I was not joking that this idea was the greatest guitar revelation I have ever had in over 35 years of playing.

Using Neck Anatomy for MAJOR Pentatonic scale is even easier if you use a new shape. The beauty is that the five note scale stays exactly the same for all three octaves. Same fingers, under the same notes for each octave.

G Major Pentatonic

First, locate all the G notes using SHORT to LONG OCTAVE.

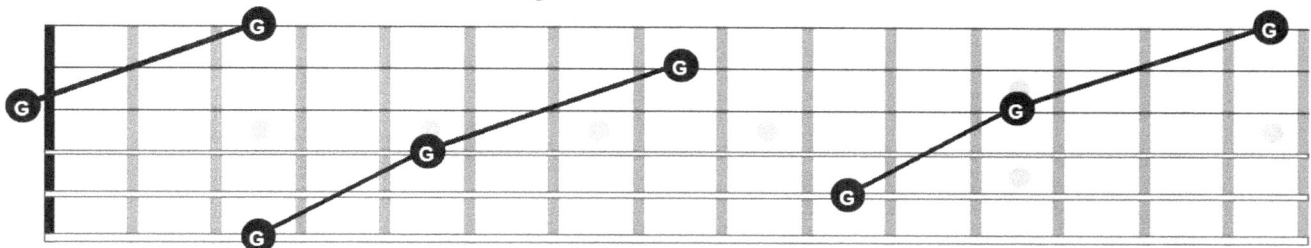

Second, isolate the 3 Octaves just from the Low E string.

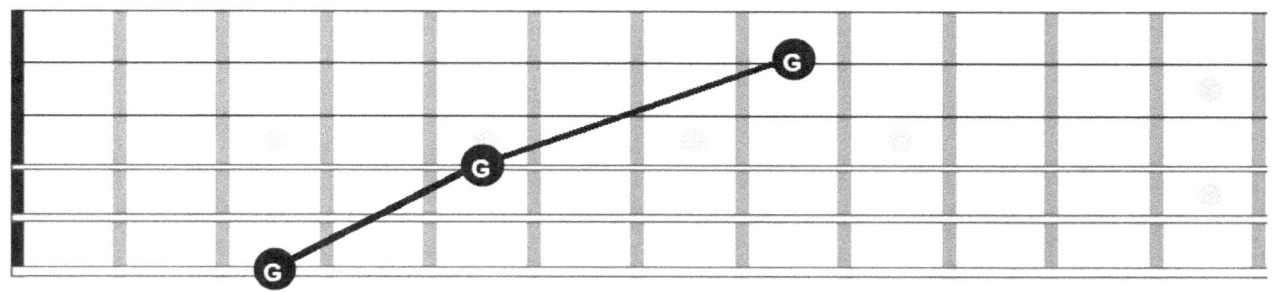

Third, add the next note in the scale (A) a whole-step above the ROOT (G)

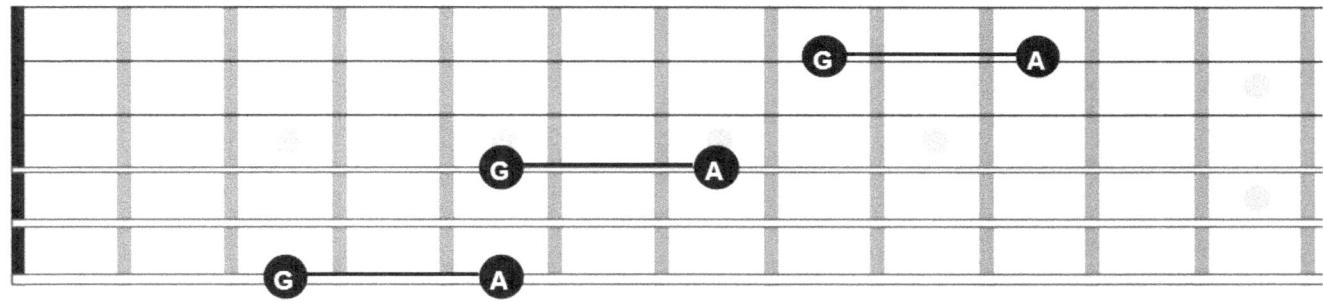

REMEMBER to play the SAME notes with the SAME fingers.

Fourth, add the THIRD note of the scale above the second note on the same string. This will be the 1-2-3 of the scale. The beauty is that you can play the first two notes with Index and ring finger and then SLIDE up the 3rd of the scale.

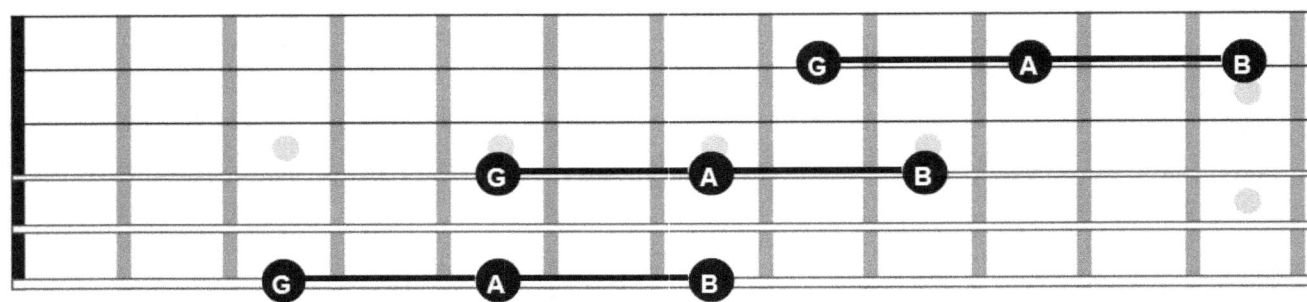

Finally, we add the remaining two notes of the scale (the 5 and 6 of the scale). Easy enough, play these notes with the Index and ring fingers that just finished the 2nd and 3rd of the scale on the previous string, same frets.

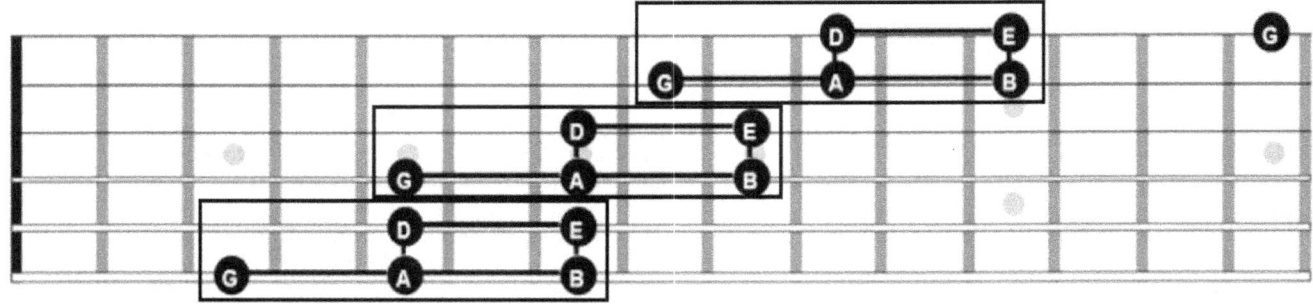

You can clearly see this box shape that is the same for all three octaves. You can play a three octave Major pentatonic scale with just two fingers and your Neck Anatomy knowledge. Each octave the same finger plays the same note in the same way. This makes it very easy to "feel" the scale as it moves through the three octaves.

PRACTICE

E minor Pentatonic Neck Anatomy "Build up"

ROOT FIRST

ROOT and SECOND NOTE

FIRST FOUR NOTES

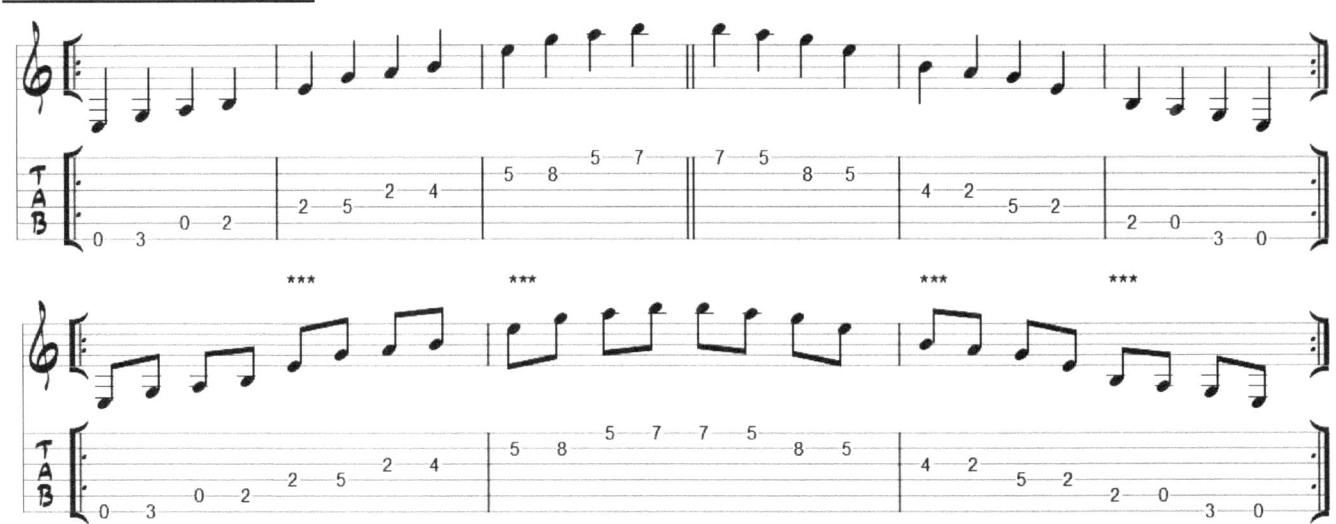

E minor Pentatonic 3 Octaves Neck Anatomy

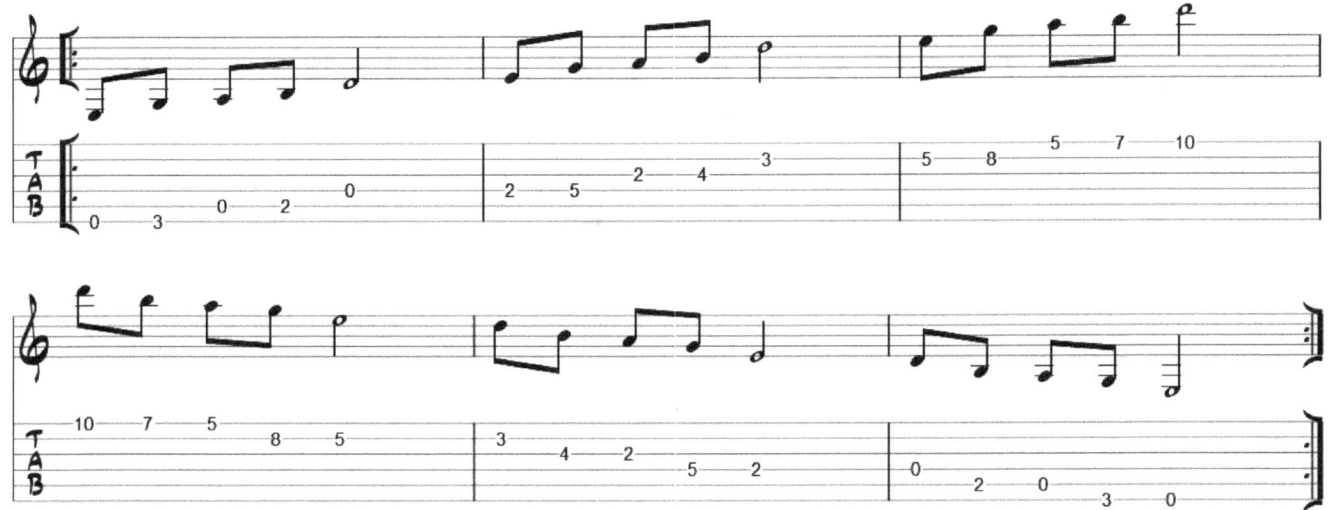

G Major Pentatonic Neck Anatomy "Build up"

ROOT FIRST

ROOT and SECOND NOTE

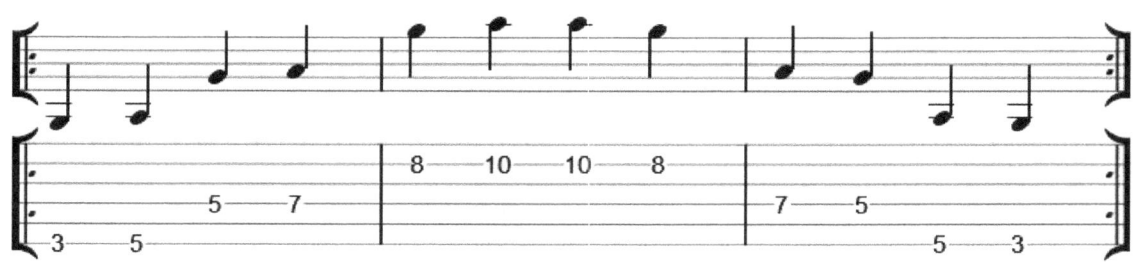

FIRST THREE NOTES 1 2 3

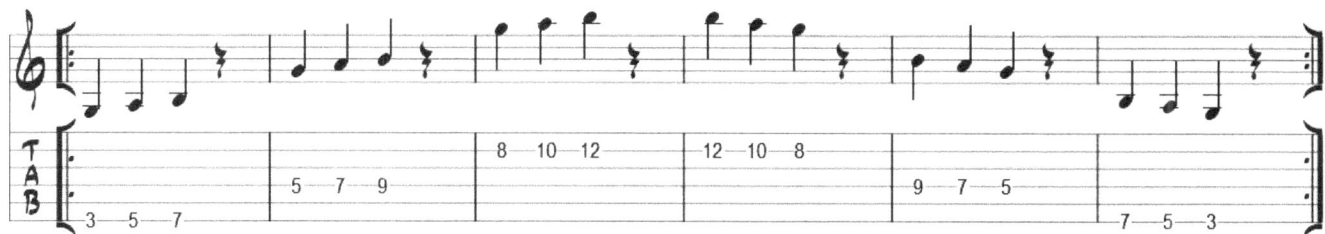

FIRST THREE NOTES 1 2 3 with SLIDES

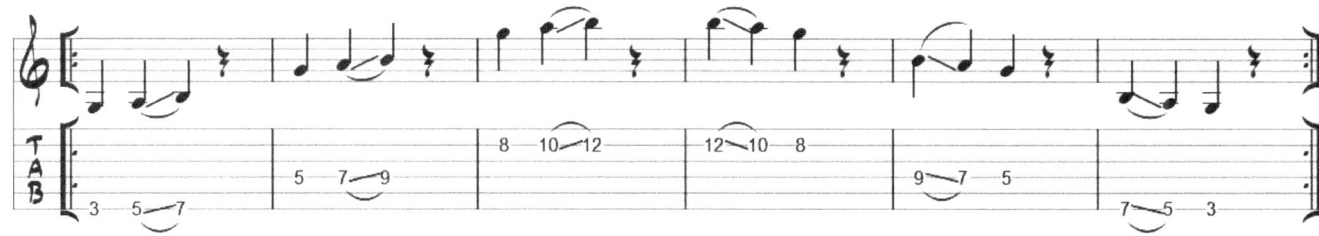

G Major Pentatonic 3 Octaves Neck Anatomy

SUMMARY

We are musicians. We are guitar players.
We learn the language of music. Melody, Harmony, and Rhythm
We learn the craft of playing the guitar as an instrument.

We warm up with Muted String Ladders (MSL), Changing GEARS, and SHELLS.
We EXERCISE our scales and licks.

AS A MUSICIAN:
- We decide on the "main" chord and base the scale upon that chord.
- MINOR chord gets a MINOR scale.
- MAJOR chord can get either the MAJOR pentatonic and/or the BLUES pentatonic.
- Add the Blue Note for extra color.
- Octaves are the landings in the staircase. Each octave starts the same and we build scale up and down from them.
- **Rhythm** is the most essential skill to connect to music and sound your best.
- ABAC is an ultra simple and extremely powerful tool to help build melodies and nurture ideas.

AS A GUITAR PLAYER:
- Once we know the music scale we need to find the ROOT note on the low E string.
- Then we decide on the the FIRST FINGER for MINOR or BLUES or we use the PINKY for MAJOR.
- Once Pattern #1 is on the fretboard everything is relative to it.
- Add Pattern #2, #3, and #5, always connected to each other in the same way to extend the scale further up and down the fretboard.
- SHORT OCTAVE and LONG OCTAVE shapes help us see the notes on the fretboard and help us navigate scales and so much more.
- Sequences are great for solos and improvising. They help us hear and "build our chops." They are essential on any instrument.
- Neck Anatomy is the ultimate tool to unlock your whole fretboard, from Root notes to Blue Notes and SCALES.

CHAPTER 10

TUNE IN

"I am a musician and a guitar player. Music is my language and my guitar is my voice. Music is Melody, Harmony and Rhythm. I develop my language skills and my instrument skills. They are two separate worlds working together to complete the circle of music."

Rhythm is the number one factor to sounding great as a musician.

WARM UP

MSL 2 strings all gears faster tempo 70 - 120 BPM

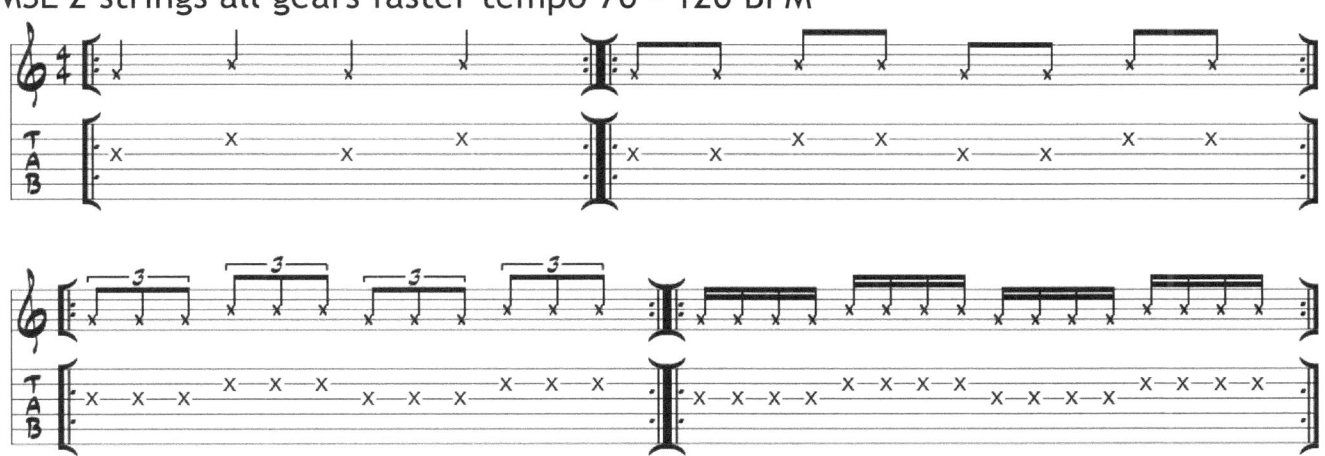

CHANGE GEARS

SHELL
SHELL 1 3 4 quarter-notes

SHELL 1 3 4 eighth-notes

EXERCISE

Patterns #1 #2 #3 #4 #5   up and down and Round the Block

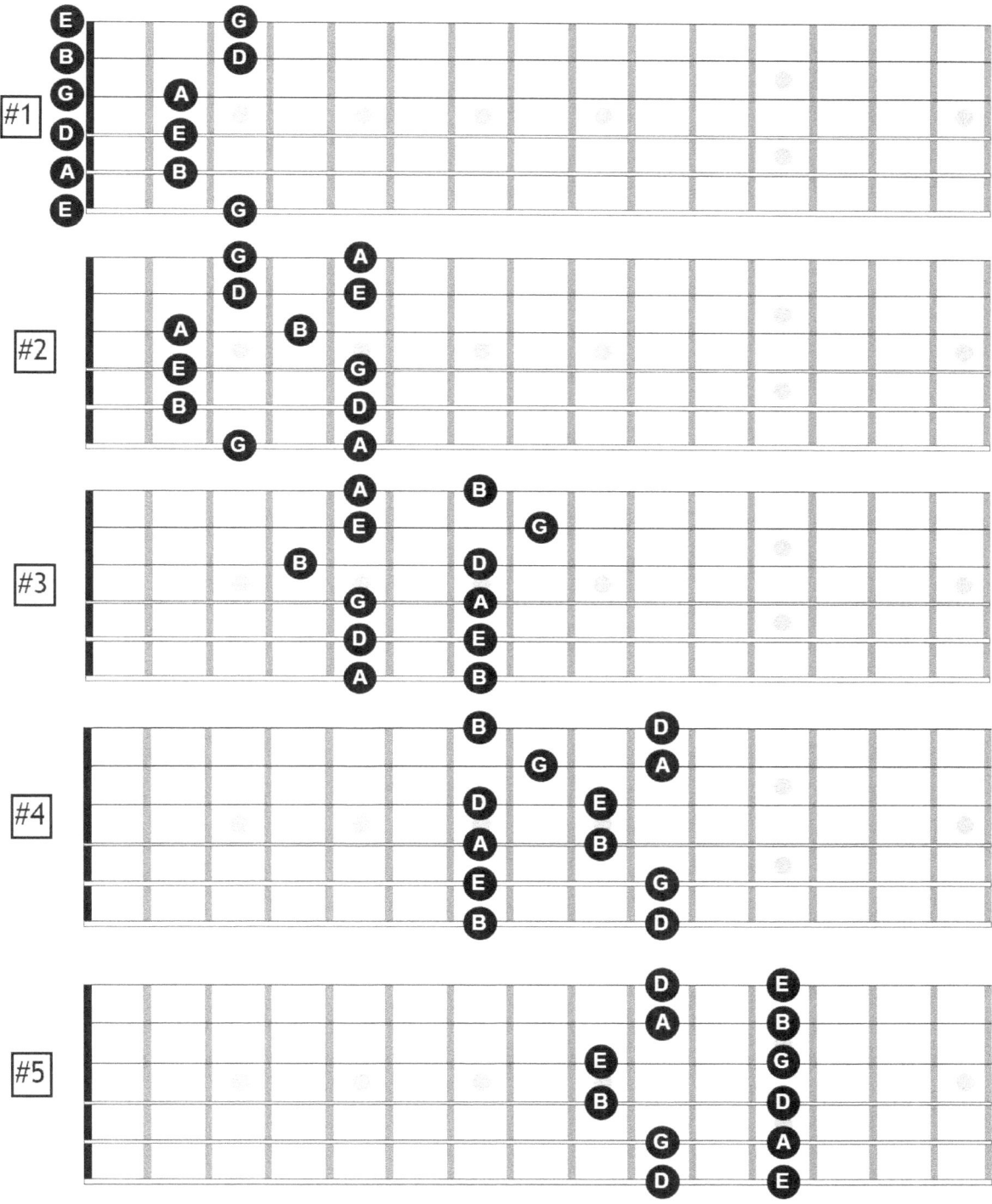

OVERVIEW

MUSICAL TRUTHS

- **There are only 12 notes**, 7 Natural notes (ABCDEFG) and 5 Accidentals. (# = sharp = raise ½ step)(*b* = flat = lower ½ step)
- There are 12 Major chords and 12 minor chords (one for each note).
- There are only 12 Keys in music. (Key=7 note scale and its 7 chords)
- There are 12 Major pentatonic scales and 12 minor pentatonic scales (5 note scale, no half-steps).
- For every *Key*, *Chord*, and *Scale* there is a **RELATIVE** (two-for-one). There are 12 of these relationships.
- Relative minor is ALWAYS 3 half-steps *below* Relative MAJOR and vice-versa.

MUSICAL IDEAS

- Soloing **Globally** we base our scale on the "main chord" of the progression.
- Use **Major pentatonic** for a Major chord.
- Use **minor pentatonic** for a minor chord.
- A **Blues scale** is a *minor* pentatonic over a *Major* chord.
- **Playing the Changes** we base our scale choice on *each* chord.
- The **Blue Note** is an "artificial note" that works great but is not originally part of the key.
- Use **ABAC** as a glorified call and response (call and response x2) to build phrases and develop ideas.
- **Sequences** help us hear, play and develop very natural sounding phrases.
- **Self Generate**: play one bar of chord, one bar of scale/lick/solo. Great way to be musical while playing.

It's really important to think like a musician first and act like a guitar player second. Keep your musical mindset in check. It is so easy on the guitar to go down a rabbit hole for some technique or idea and completely lose sight of what it is your actually trying to accomplish musically.

Once you know the language of music, the notes, the chords and the keys, that is it. It doesn't change or grow. It is the same on every instrument. You will be musical and can play any instrument once you physically adapt to it. Focus on the music, the language and the rhythm.

AS A GUITARIST

We have covered a lot of material in these first two books regarding guitar and fretboard information. It's important to keep things in check musically as to what you are really benefiting from when you add more guitar based learning.

- Know the **12 notes on the Low E string** to help navigate scales.

- Once you know the scale you need, use **Pattern #1** to get on the fretboard with the **"Rock and Roll Rule"** (first finger on the relative minor and pinky on the relative Major).

- Pattern #2 is Always above pattern #1 and pattern #5 is always behind pattern #1. They are bookends to our favorite pattern.

- There are **5 total pentatonic patterns** and they are _always_ in the same order, starting over again at the 12th fret.

- **All five patterns have the same 5 notes**, so they sound _exactly_ the same.

- We use **Hammer-ons**, **pull-offs**, **slides** and **bends** to make our solos sound more natural and voice like.

- **Pick blocking** is a tremendous tool to help you sound tight and clean.

- **Neck Anatomy** is the single greatest way to look at and unlock your whole fretboard. You use the octaves to navigate the notes instead of black dots in positions. Neck Anatomy unveils the symmetry in music and the ease of seeing it on your neck for the full 3 octaves. It can be used for locating notes, arpeggios, and scales.

BLUES SOLO EXAMPLE

Here are two choruses of a 12 bar blues in A. It builds off the example from the previous chapter and incorporates many elements covered in the first two books. Most of the solo is playing the changes, and therefore play:

A Major pentatonic for the A7 chord,

D Major pentatonic for the D7 chord and

E Major pentatonic for the E7 chord.

BLUES SOLO #2

This solo moves around a little more and gets a little more complicated. There are more bends and other patterns, and still plays the changes throughout.

BACKING TRACKS
www.LeadGuitarWorkshop.com

HOW TO PRACTICE

Time is valuable, and every single person is given the same 24 hour day to live and get things done. The biggest movers and shakers have had the exact same amount of time as you and I. Therefore, it is really important to dedicate your whole attention and mind to music when you are playing. TV off, phone face down and muted. You can get so much done in a focused period of time. So often my students say, "How much can you really get done in just 15 minutes?" I usually reply with, "Lets sit here and stare at each other for 15 minutes and see how long it feels."

Always stay musical when you practice. Treat it as a mini performance. Take the same effort and care that you would if you were playing in front of somebody. Make sure every note sounds as good as possible. You should focus on playing cleanly and smoothly. Always play and practice in time! It is so important. Music is *never* played without time so why in the world would you ever practice or play without time?

It is really helpful to "stack" your practicing. Why practice one thing at a time when you can practice multiple. For example, if you are practicing a new scale, self generate it. Not only are you playing a scale in time, you are hearing it in context with its chord (one bar chord followed by one bar scale/riff/lick). Not only that, you can add a new chord shape (maybe C form bar for example). On top of that, play the scale in a new pattern. Being creative and focused, you can practice many things at once and really accelerate your growth.

For some folks it helps to track your progress. Keep track of date, tempos, keys, exercises and other important factors. It was in doing this that I realized that music is melody, harmony, and rhythm.

You probably have noticed a similar flow to each chapter of these books. Each chapter represents a basic guide to how to practice. Each chapter is a complete session in and of itself.

The following percentage is shown as a basic guideline, so don't get too caught up in the timing part. If you are hot on something, stay with it and devour it.

Tune in - 5%
Take a few minutes to clear your head. Turn off your devices and do what you need before you dig in and play. Remind yourself that you are a musician and a guitar player. Everything you play should be rhythmically based, always.

Warm up - 10%
Muted String Ladders, Shells, and Changing Gears are some of the best warm ups. They simply get your fingers, hands, and internal clock all synchronized. Muted String ladders focus on rhythm and pick control. Changing Gears really harnesses the ability to feel and play rhythms. The Shells are best of both worlds and are like "wax on, wax off." Practice real world moves and patterns.

Exercise - 15%
This is where you run scales and patterns. This is a great opportunity to play through the five patterns. Always play them in time and play them ascending and descending or as "Round the Block" zigzag the patterns.

Review - 15%
Just as important as learning something new, make sure you're understanding something you have recently learned. It's essential to build your growth by reviewing past topics and understanding them deeper.

New Topic - 15%
Learn something new. However easy or small, it is growth. Every little bit moves you towards your goal of sounding great as a musician. Maybe it's learning the names of the notes in a scale, or a lick, a chord, anything that helps you sound better. You can learn as a musician, as a guitar player, and as a rhythmist.

"Practice" - 40%
The best way to practice is not to practice, but to play! It's true. Every one of our heroes played music more than anything else. Practicing refers to some future date that you are preparing for. Playing is now. Play in time, carry the song, the beat, the groove, all of it. Self Generating is the best way to play and get your practicing in. If you are practicing a turnaround in a blues, then you play the 12 bar blues and at the end you play the turnaround. If you miss it, keep playing and get it the next time around. This is what you would do onstage. Keep playing and you will get better, as you would if you "practiced."

THOUGHTS

The learning path in music is circular. You will learn something and come back around to it and get to know it better. Every time you do this you will gain more confidence and experience. There is only so much actual information you will need to learn. It is all about how to use and manipulate that material that makes the magic of music start. Learning music is not a linear path but a circular one.

Music is Melody (notes), Harmony (chords), and Rhythm.
Rhythm is the number one factor to sounding great.

Where attention goes, energy flows. So much of being a better musician is all about your mind set and what you focus your time and energy on.

"The process of learning consists not in what is brought to the learner, but what is drawn out of him." (Plato)

"The Student as a boxer, not a fencer. The Fencer's weapon is picked up and put down again. The Boxer's is part of him, all he has to do is clench his fist." (Marcus Aurelius-Meditations)

"The Student as a musician, not a guitarist. The guitarist's instrument is picked up and put down. The musician's is part of him. All he has to do is tap, clap, and sing." (Suke Cerulo)

You can play music without melody (just chords) and you can play music without chords (just melody, like your voice), but you can *never* play music without rhythm, it's impossible. As soon as you tap your foot or pluck a note, rhythm happens.

The language of music hasn't really changed in hundreds of years. It is much older than the guitar. Once you know the language, that's it. Now you can learn as many instruments as you want. You just have to adapt to the physical part of the instrument.

The instrument is silent without you. You are music!

ALL 12 KEYS - PENTATONIC PATTERNS

- Each of the 12 keys has it's own page and are ordered in the circle of 5ths.

- Each key is written starting with Pattern #1 at the top.

- The patterns are listed #1 down to pattern #5.

- At the bottom is summation of the 5 patterns.

- Each key has the 5 notes of the scale in all of the diagrams. Get to know the notes in a key/scale.

- When jamming or practicing in a key look at the full pattern at the bottom of the page to really take advantage of the whole fretboard. Follow the notes.

- When looking at the full fretboard think Neck Anatomy to see all of the short to long octaves for all of the notes.

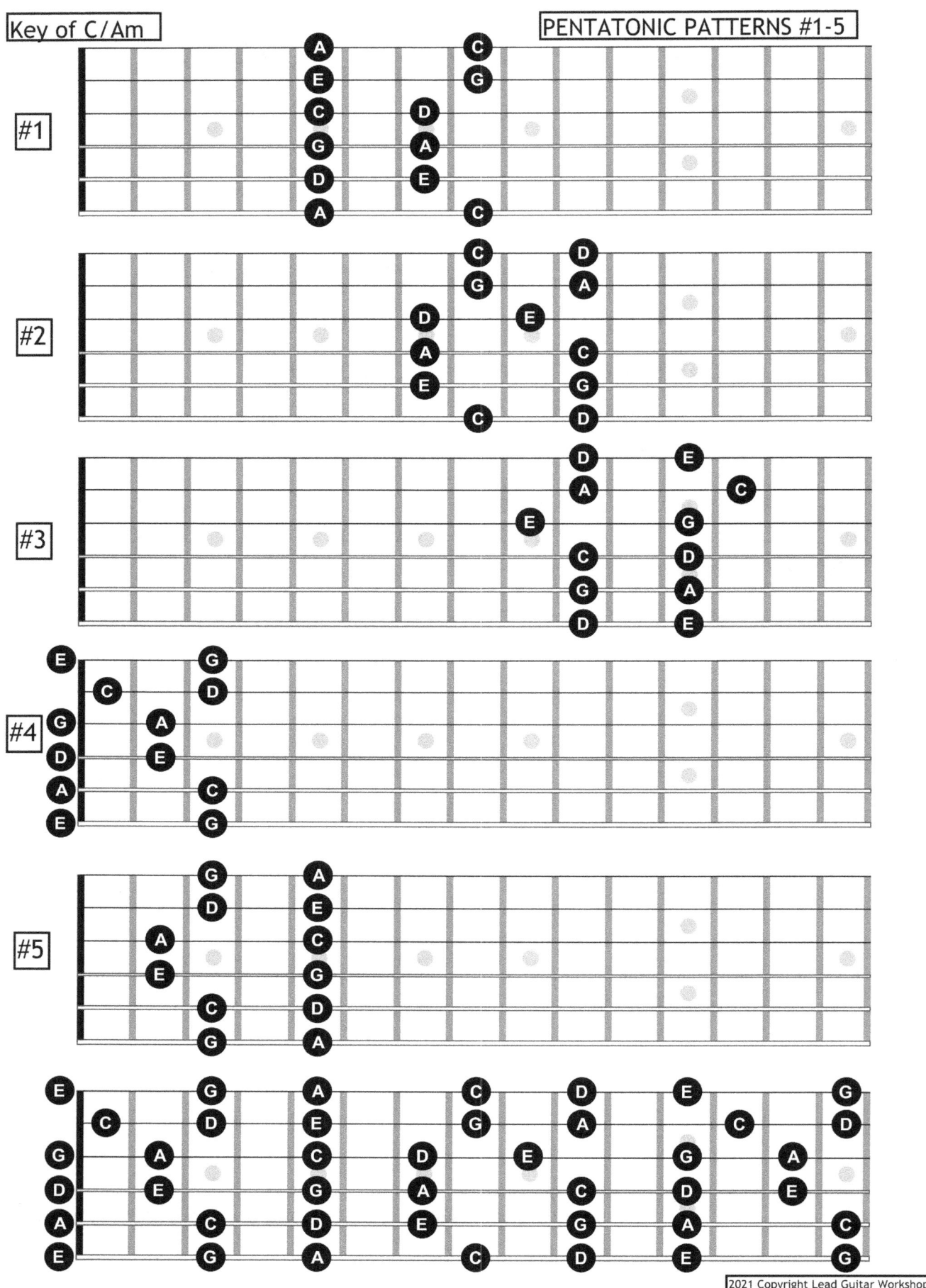

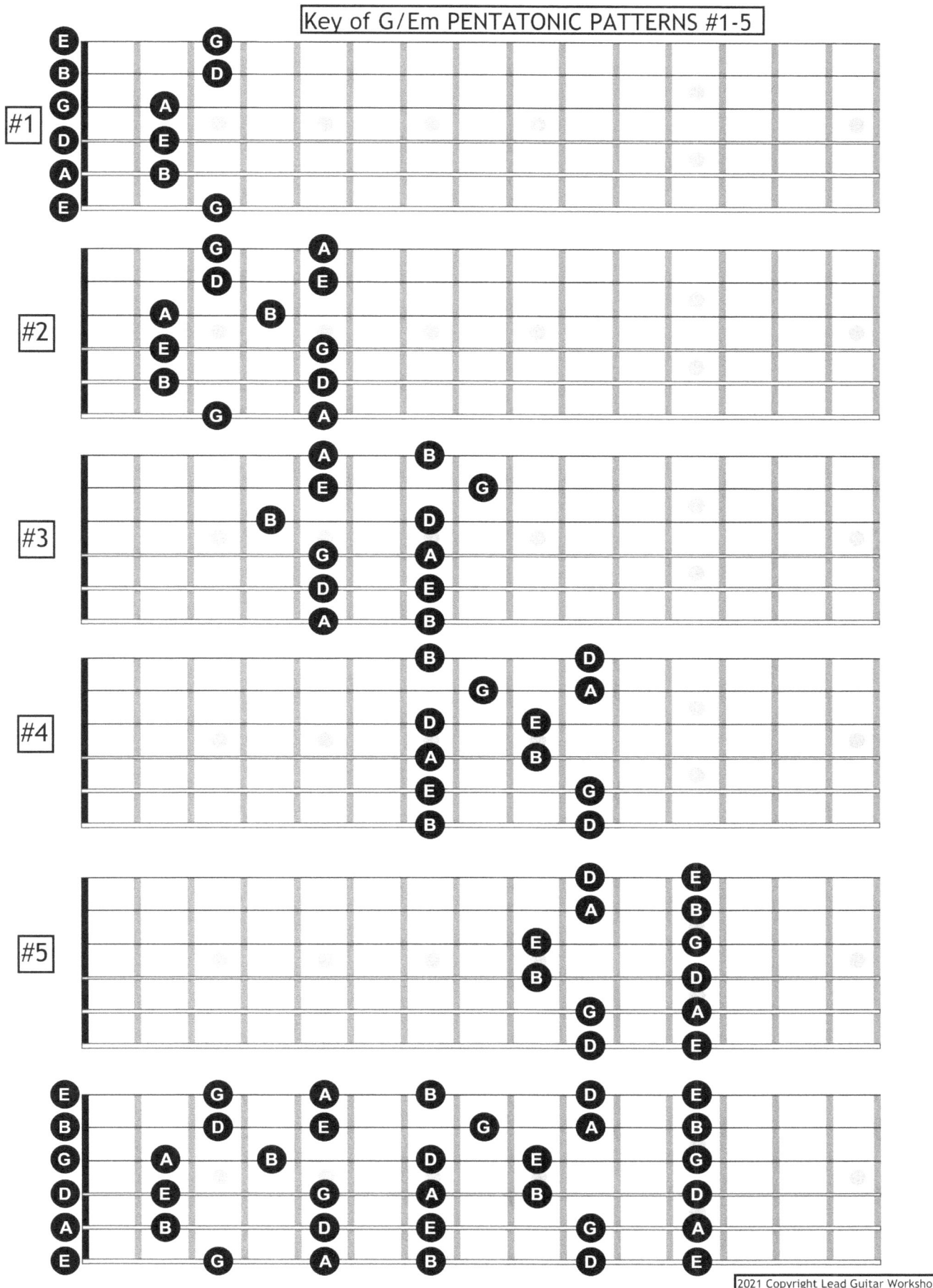

Key of G/Em PENTATONIC PATTERNS #1-5

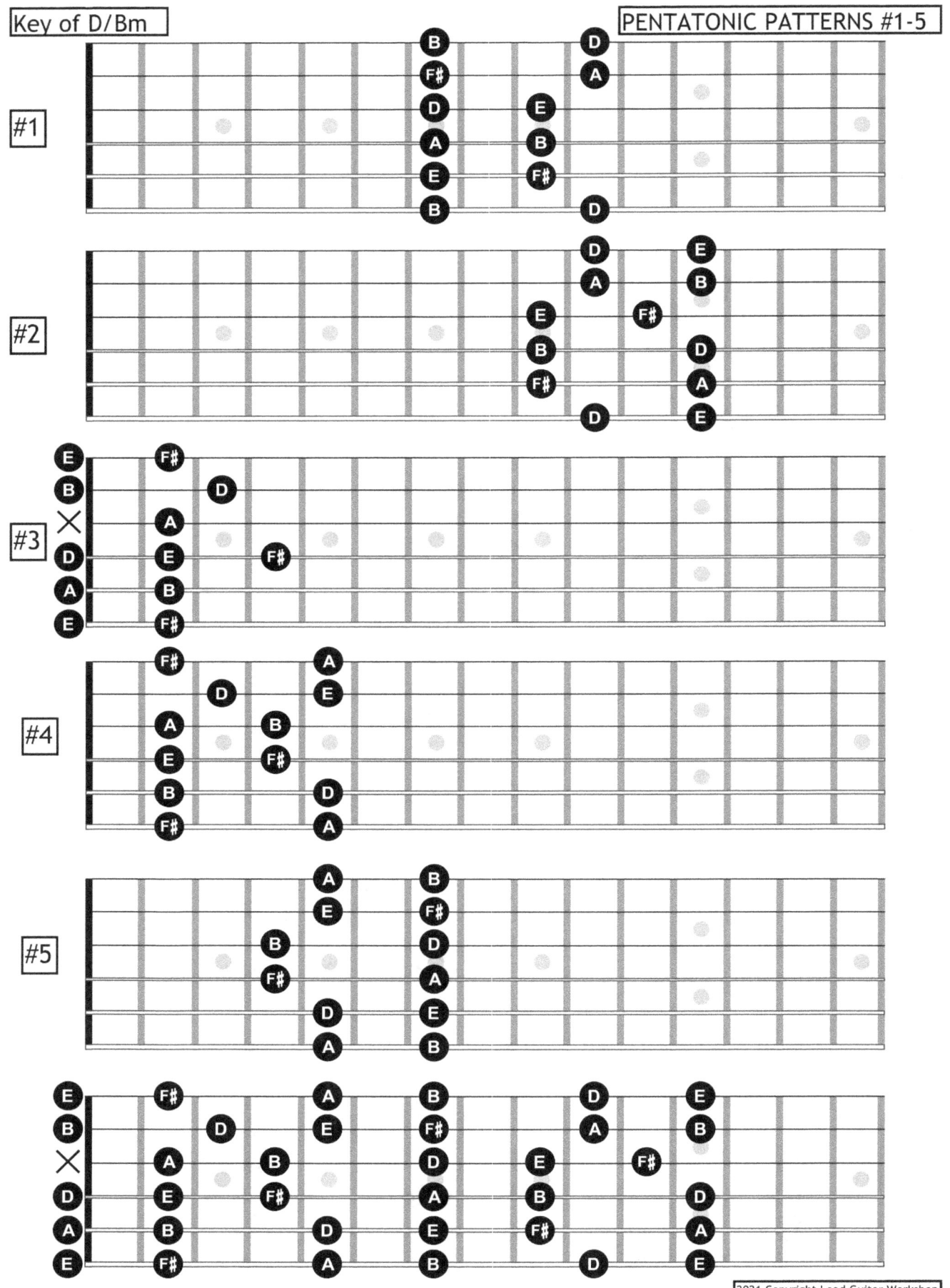

Key of D/Bm

PENTATONIC PATTERNS #1-5

#1

#2

#3

#4

#5

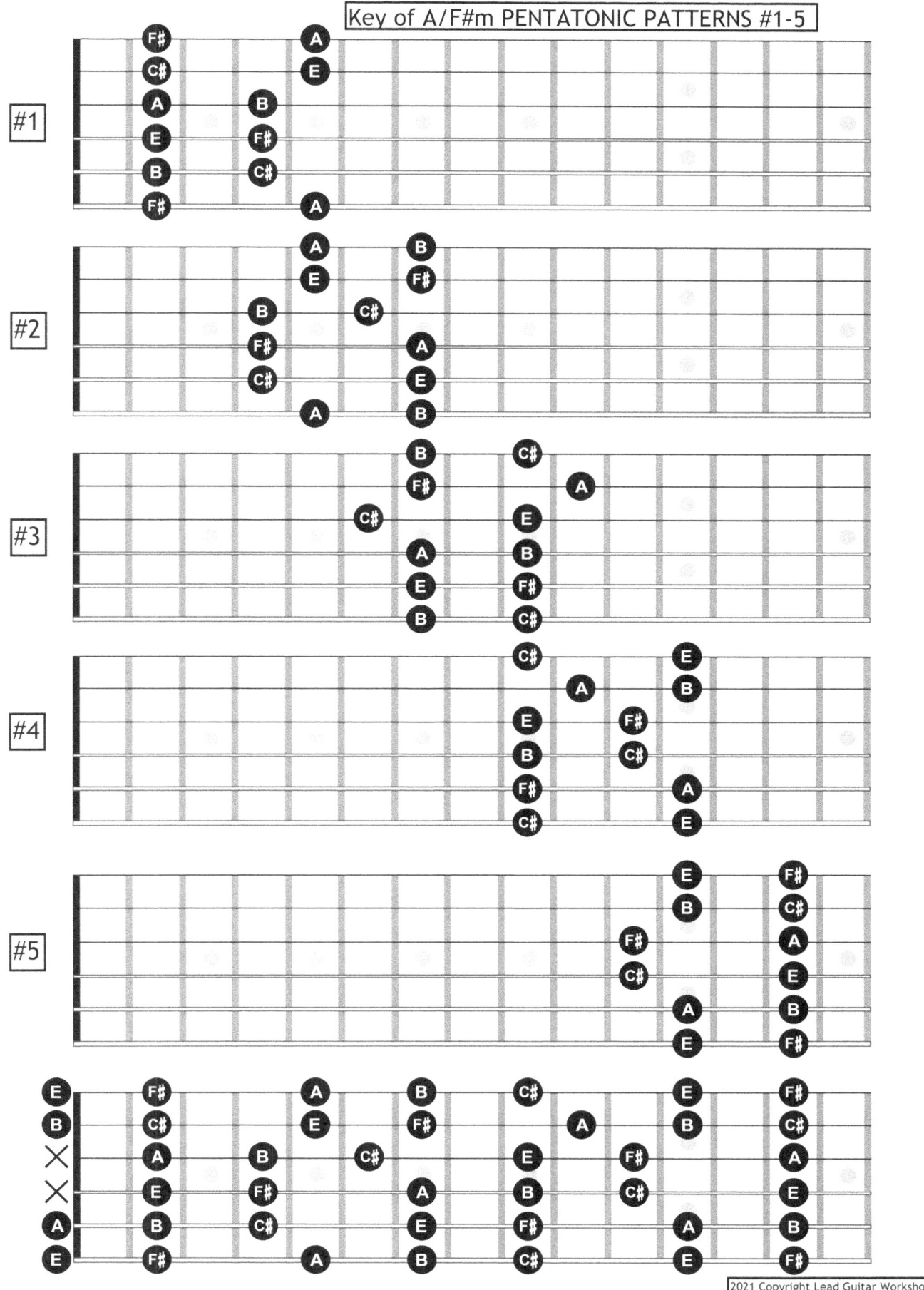

Key of A/F#m PENTATONIC PATTERNS #1-5

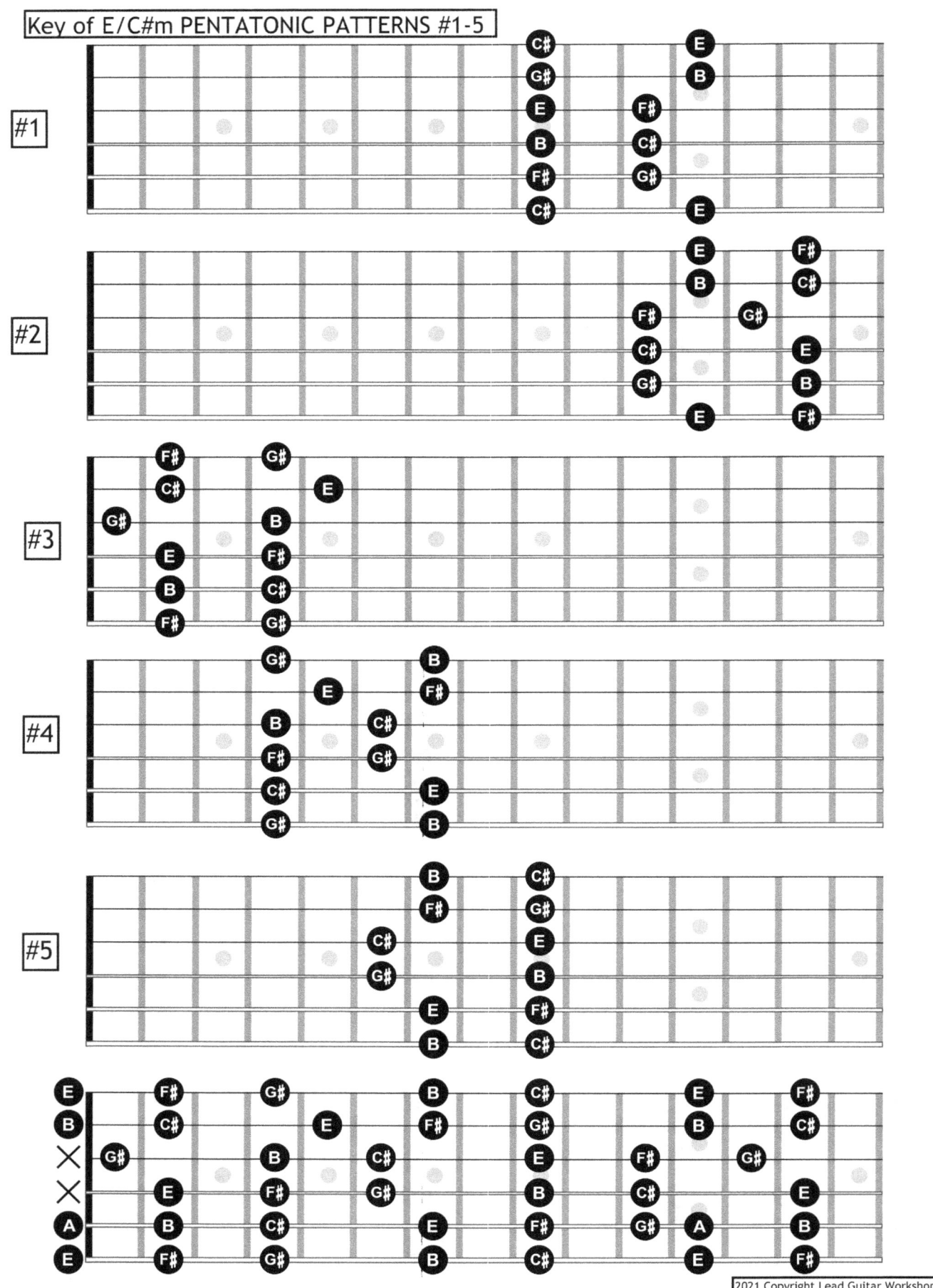

Key of E/C#m PENTATONIC PATTERNS #1-5

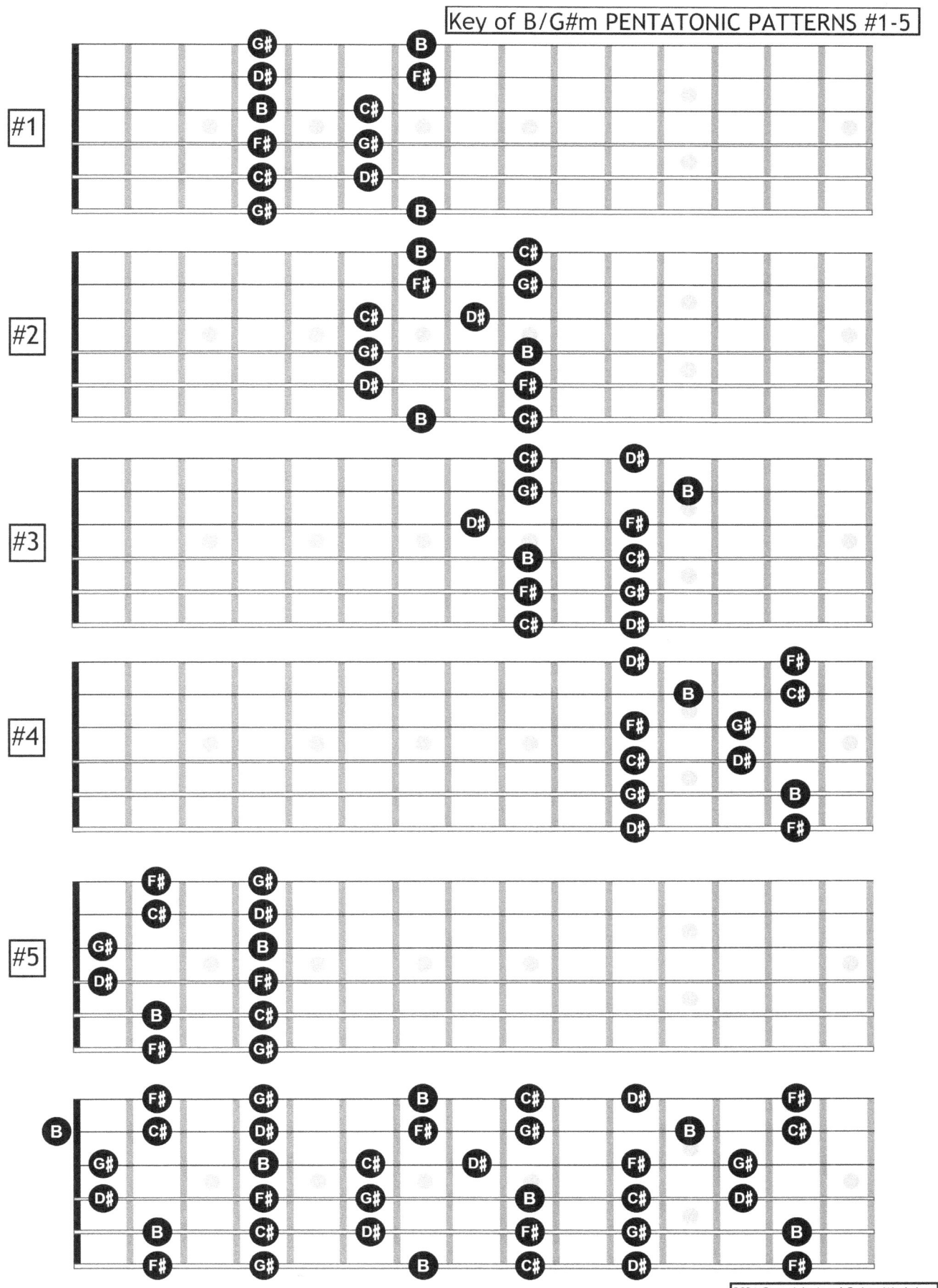

Key of B/G#m PENTATONIC PATTERNS #1-5

2021 Copyright Lead Guitar Workshop

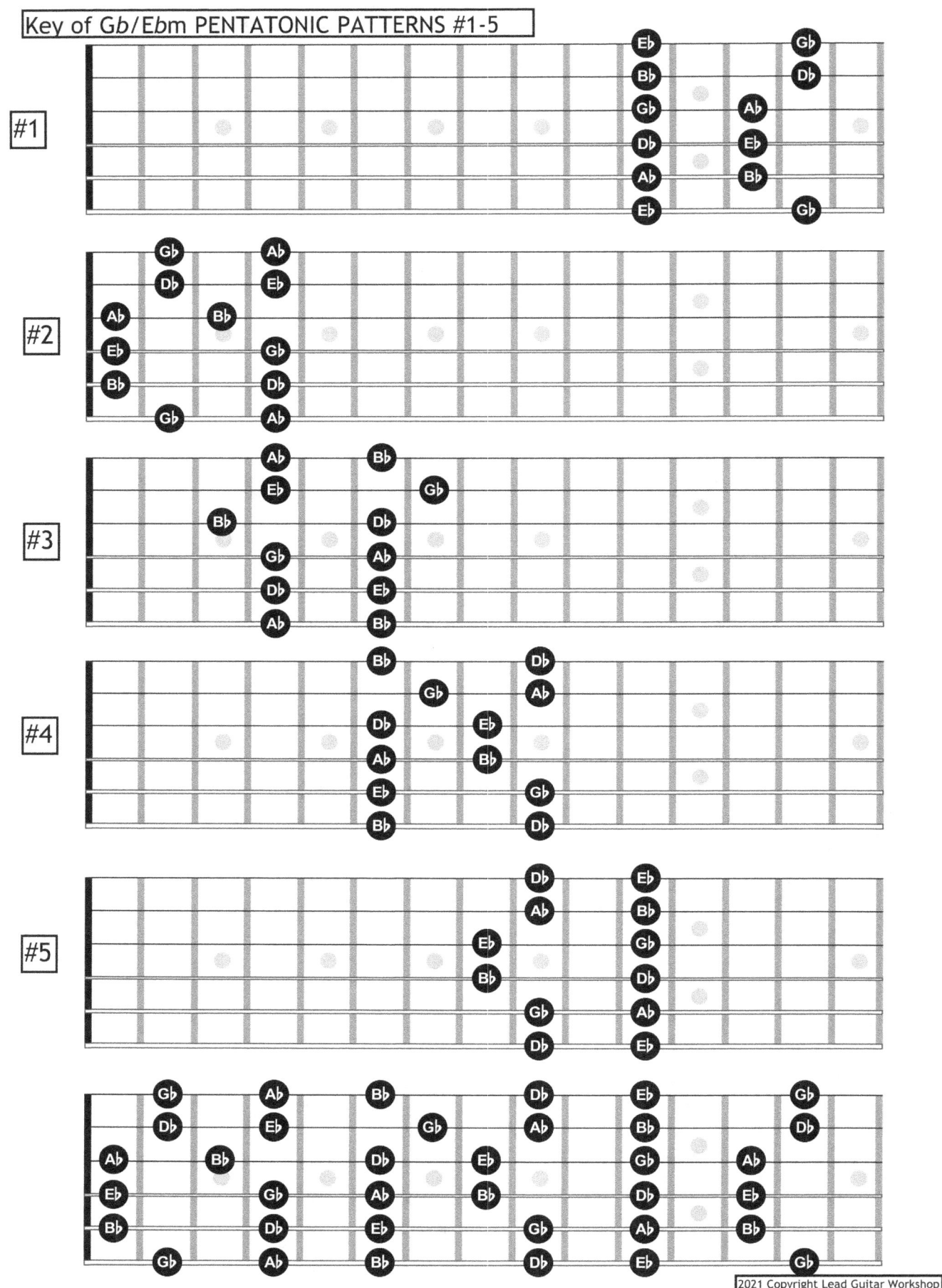

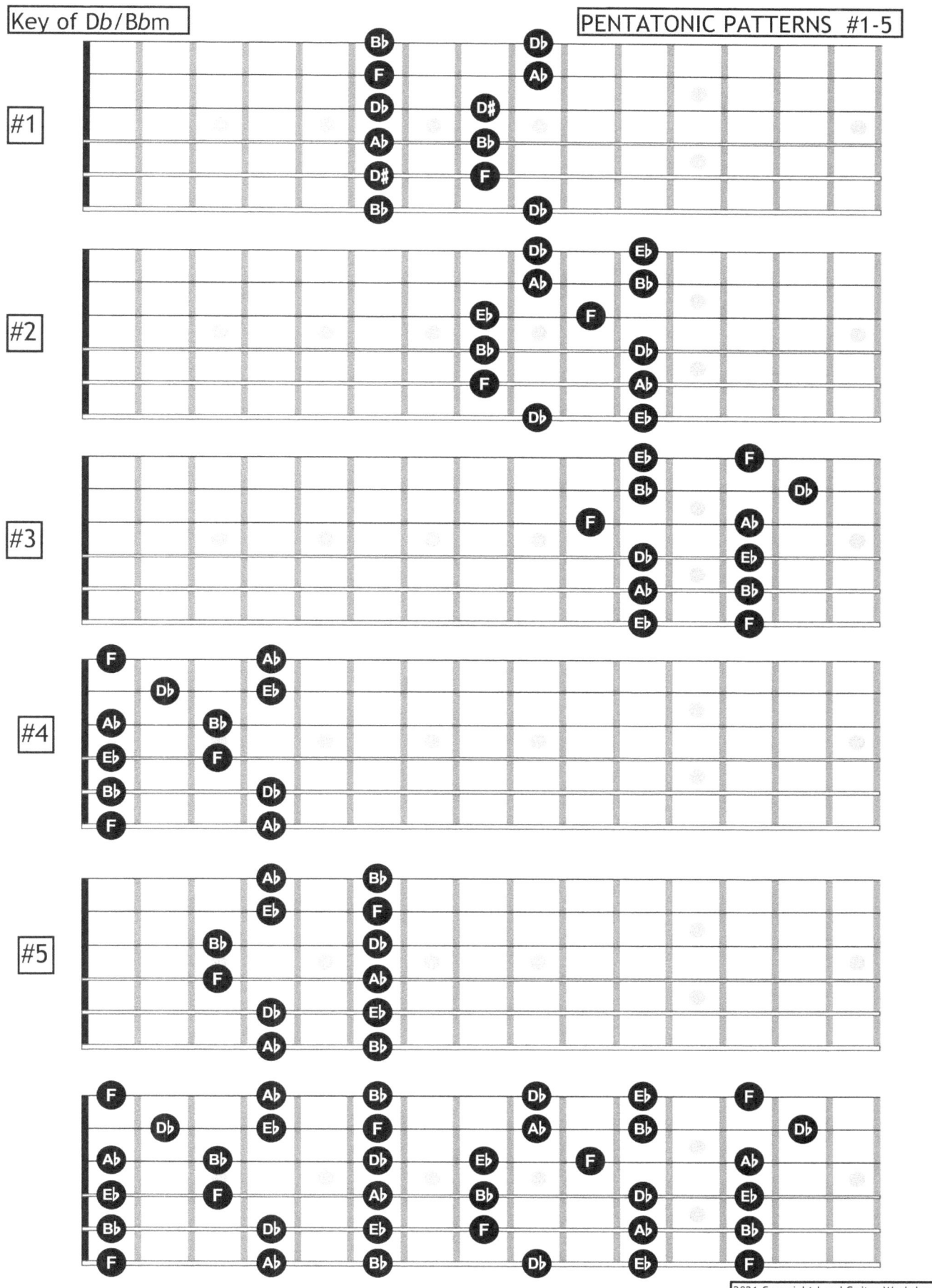

Key of Ab/Fm PENTATONIC PATTERNS #1-5

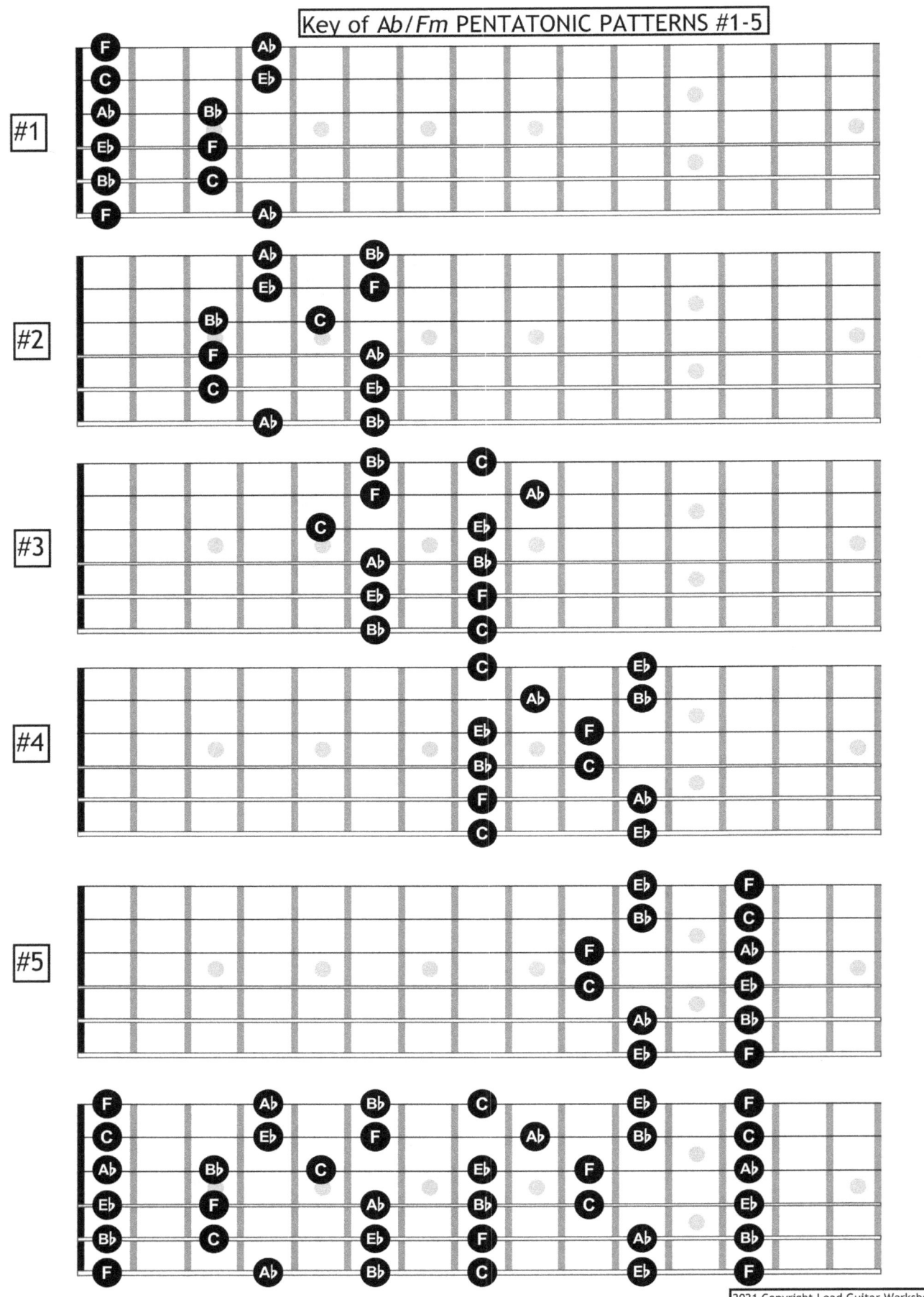

Key of E♭/Cm PENTATONIC PATTERNS #1-5

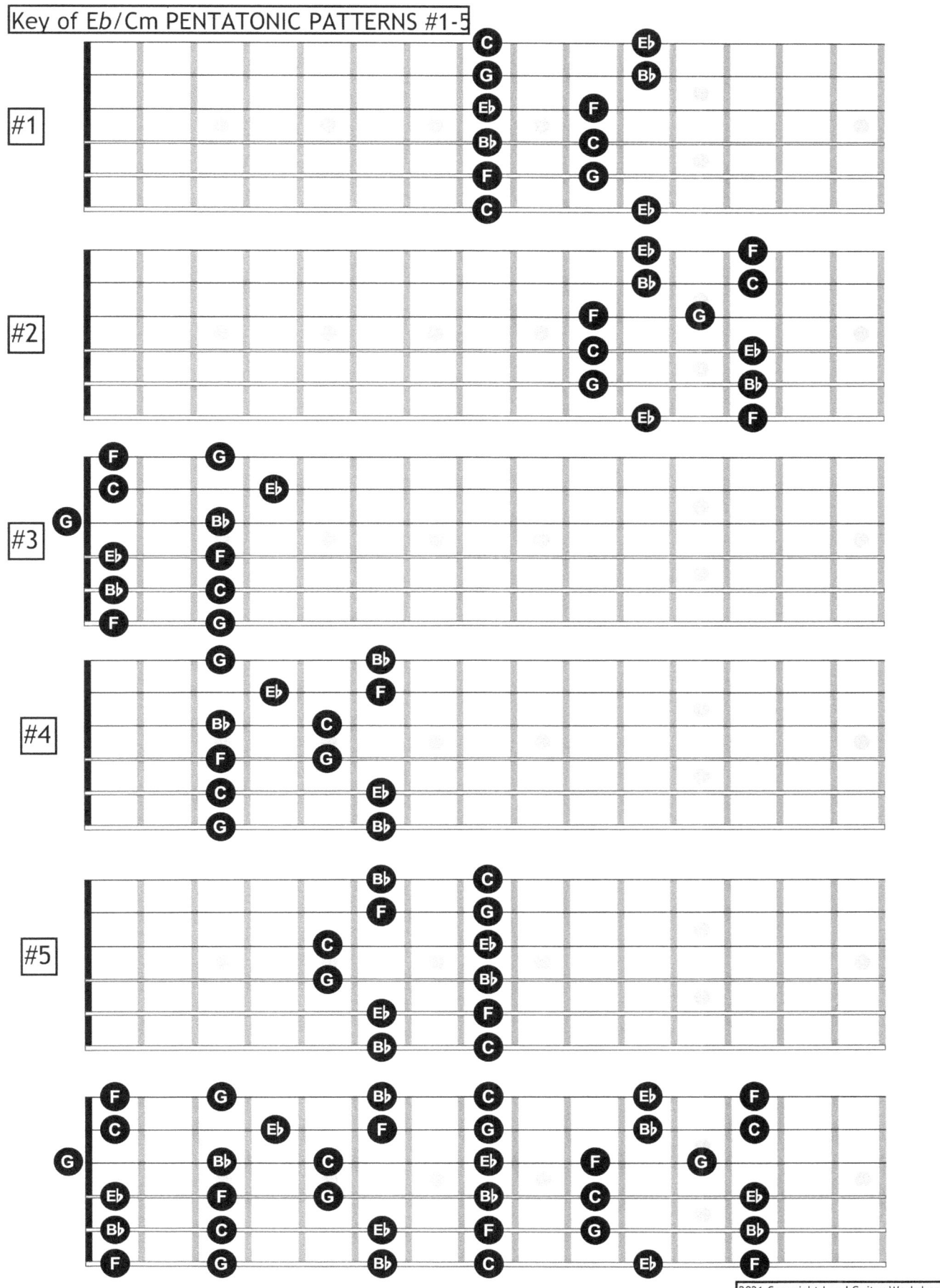

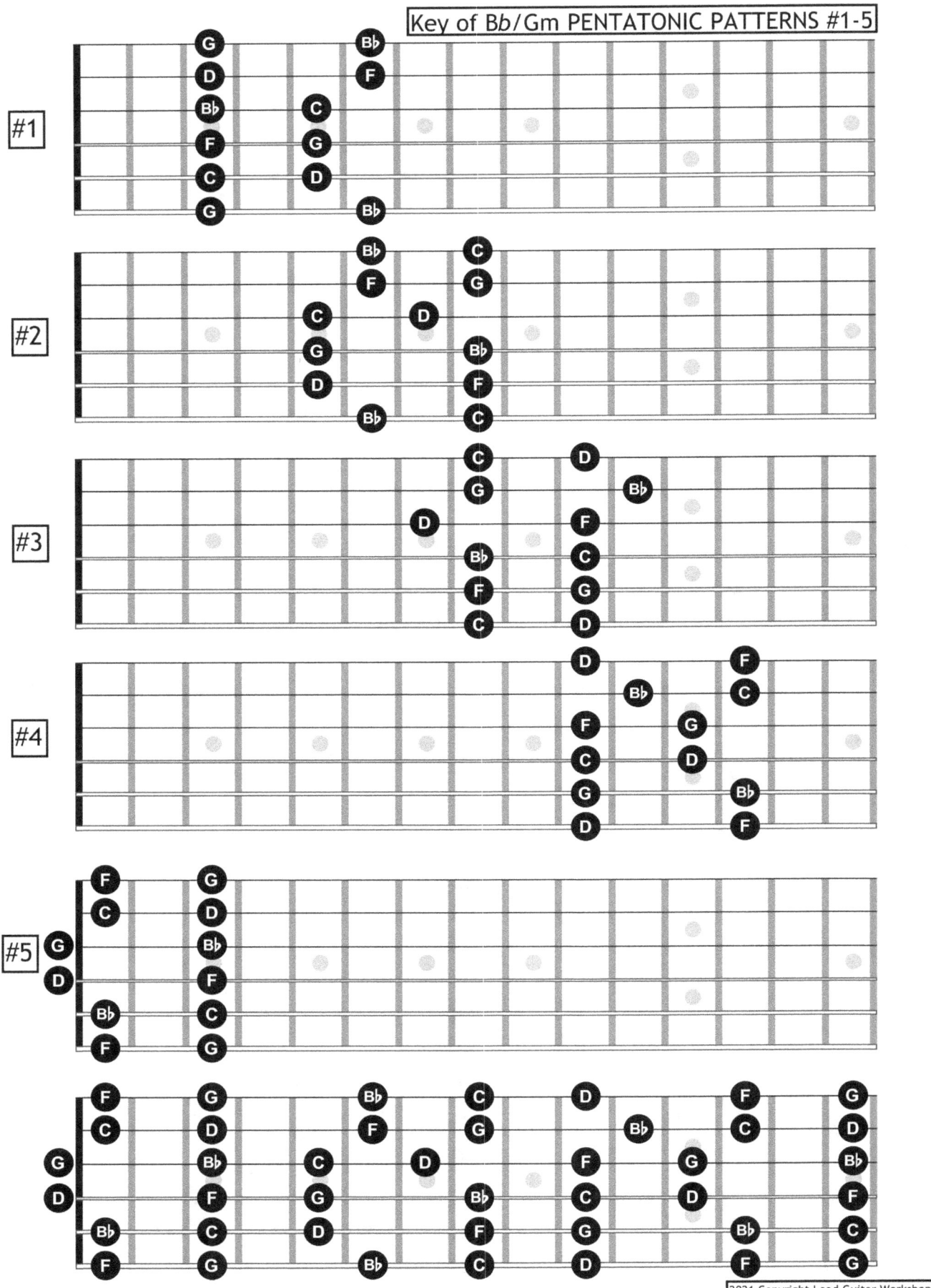

Key of B♭/Gm PENTATONIC PATTERNS #1-5

2021 Copyright Lead Guitar Workshop

Key of F/Dm PENTATONIC PATTERNS #1-5

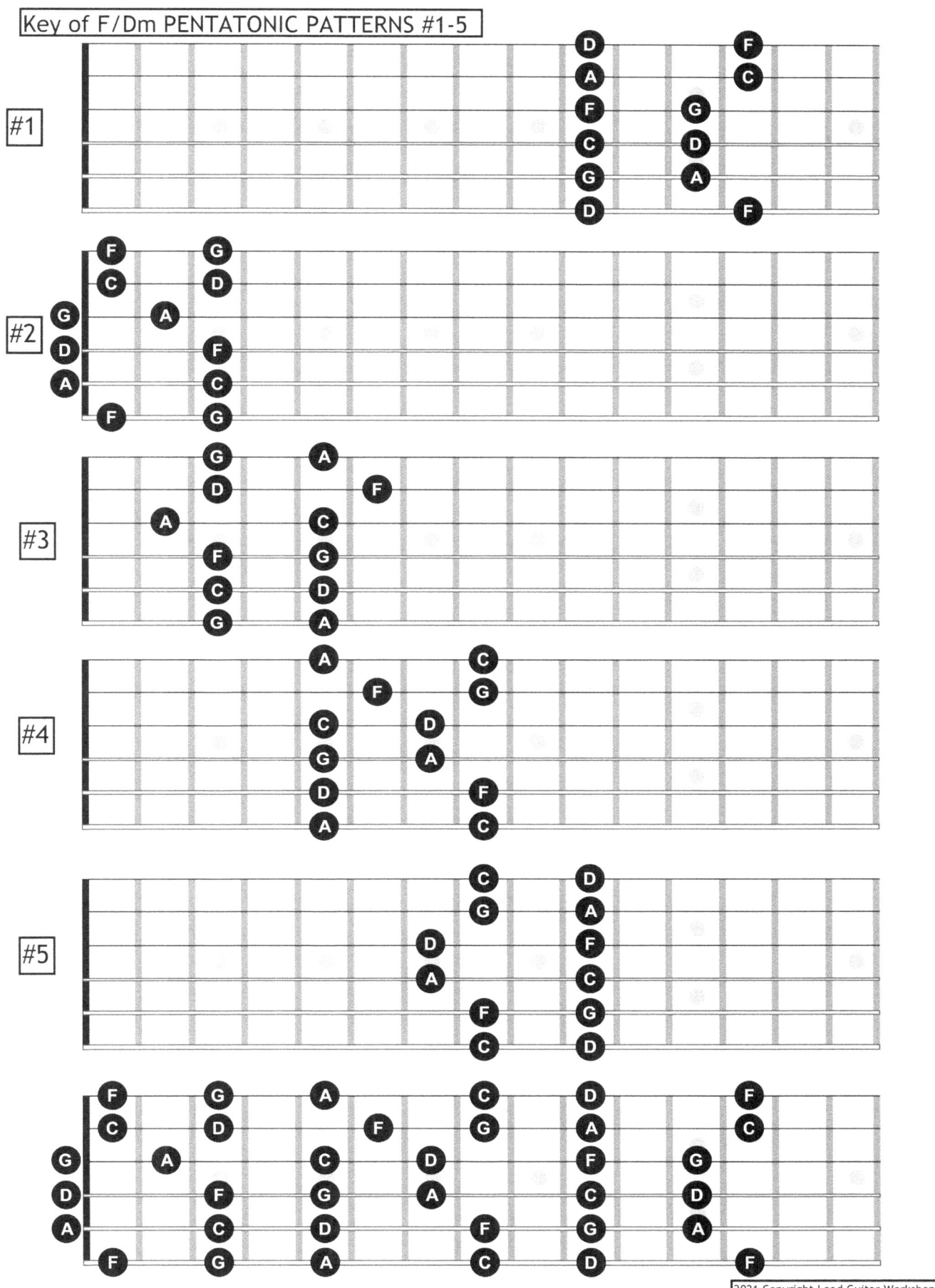

GLOSSARY

<u>Audiation</u> Inner Hearing but also the musical knowledge behind it, to hear the knowledge.

<u>Arpeggio</u> The notes of a chord played in succession rather than simultaneously.

<u>BPM</u> Beats-per-minute. How music tempo/beat/quarter-note is measured.

<u>Chord</u> Usually three or more notes played simultaneously.

<u>Chord Inversion</u> The notes of a chord rotating in order (example R35, 35R, 5R3).

<u>Chord Scale</u> The scale matched to a particular chord, using its chord tones and appropriate notes in between to best fit for playing the changes.

<u>Chord Tone</u> A single note, as part of a chord.

<u>Degree, Scale</u> The number in the scale at which a note lives. There are seven notes in the diatonic scale. They are numbered 1-7 for their degrees.

<u>Diatonic</u> meaning "of the key". Notes and chords only in that key.

<u>Diatonic Harmony</u> The seven chords that naturally occur in all keys and its resulting formula.   (I ii iii IV V vi viidim)

<u>Fingerpicking/Fingerstyle</u> Fingerpicking is using fingers only to pluck the strings on guitar. Fingerstyle might include thumb and/or fingerpicks.

<u>Gear</u> (LGW) Slang for describing the different rhythms. First gear is quarter-notes, second gear is eighth-notes; third gear is triplets; fourth gear is sixteenth-notes, and so on.

<u>Half-step</u> The smallest interval in music. It is one fret on a guitar, and a single piano key to the next (for example white to black)

Harmonic Rhythm The rhythmic pacing of chord changes; how often the chords change (for example every two beats versus every four beats).

Harmony Chords or notes being played simultaneously to produce a sonorous sound. Chord progressions and the underlying chord motion.

HO PO Short for Hammer-ons and Pull-offs

Hybrid Picking When you combine the use of a pick and the remaining three fingers to get a combination of flat pick and fingerstyle.

Inner Hearing Hearing music in your inner ear by memory even if you don't know it musically. (Happy Birthday, Hot Cross buns, and others)

Key One of 12 families built around the 7 note Major scale. Contains 7 chords, one for each of its own notes built by the Rule of Thirds.

Legato When a musician connects the notes of a phrase in a smooth and consistent sound without any silence in between the notes.

Lick A slang term used to describe a group of notes, usually used in a lead solo. These can be recognized by style, genre, person, and more.

LGW Lead Guitar Workshop

Melody One note-at-a-time succession of notes in a pleasing fashion. The signature of a song and the part that is copyright protected.

Mode A function of a scale/key. When a Key or scale is based on any one of its chords/notes. This changes the half-steps in relation to where they live in the scale, producing varying sounds of Major and minor chord progressions and scales.

Monophonic Producing one note-at-a-time only.

Muted String Ladder (MSL)(LGW) A picking hand exercise to improve rhythm and confidence in Down, Up, and Alternate picking across the strings

Musical Truth (LGW) A term to describe some of the fundamental rules in music that every musician follows regardless of instrument.

Neck Anatomy (LGW) Using octaves in a short to long connection to help navigate the fretboard and move around like other instruments do and not be tied to changing patterns. There are 2 pairs of "short to long" octaves (E and A string).

Pentatonic Meaning "five notes of the home." These are ancient five note scales believed to have originated in Asia. There are two main types, Major and minor, and they are in all types of music all around the planet.

Playing the changes A slang term a musician uses when they change their note choices/scales/arpeggios to match each individual chord instead of a "Global" sound of playing one scale for all the chords.

Polyphonic The ability to play multiple notes simultaneously. Pianos and guitars are polyphonic, the human voice is not.

Riff A slang term for rhythm guitar part made up of notes instead of chords. Think "Heartbreaker" by Led Zeppelin, "Crazy Train" by Ozzy.

Rhythm The pulse in music. The basis for everything music. The measured beat and its subdivisions.

Root The "main" note in a Key/chord/scale/arpeggio. The one everything else revolves around. The sound that comes home resolves to the Root.

Root Position When a scale pattern, arpeggio, or chord shape has its ROOT as the lowest note.

Rule of Thirds Stacking every other note in a scale to create a chord. Three notes for a triad and four notes for a seventh chord.

Self-Gen (LGW) Using your inner ear and inner clock to start and play music yourself, in time, especially with consideration of switching between chords and soloing.

Shell (LGW) A hand dexterity exercise to help overcome any guitar playing issue. It involves a fingering, a performance method, and rhythm.

Staccato Each note is sharply detached or separated from the others.

Tied In music notation when an arch connects two or more rhythms to create a sustained sound. Especially useful to achieve lengths of time not possible with traditional rhythms (for example a note that last 1 ½ quarter notes.)

Tonic The "main" note/chord. Often the key but not always. It is the note/chord that everything else resolves to.

Tresillo A Latin based rhythmic figure where 8 eighth-notes are grouped in 3 3 2 notes to total 8.

Triad A three note chord. Usually achieved by stacking every other note in a scale for a total of three notes.

Voice Leading A term used for connecting the chord tones of one chord to another with the notes moving the least amount necessary to make the chord change. This makes a really smooth sound.

Whole-step The second smallest interval in music. It is two half-steps in distance. Most scales consist of half-steps and whole-steps.

ABOUT AUTHOR

Michael Cerulo (aka Suke) is a guitarist and multi-instrumentalist whose life long love and devotion to music has given him a very distinct and identifiable sound. Whether it's his fluid guitar melodies, the warm organic tone of his flute, or his own recordings where he plays and produces all of the music, Suke's individuality, creativity and talent are evident in all of his creations.

Born in a suburb of Boston, Suke was raised in a musical family. His grandfather (George Lane) was a composer, multi-instrumentalist and bandleader during the late 40's and early 50's. All four of George's siblings were musicians as well, often being employed in his big band. The youngest brother helped start **Berklee College of Music**. Suke began playing guitar and taking music lessons when he was twelve. Being persistent, with an unbending intent to learn and grow, he then enrolled in Berklee College of Music in Boston. After graduating in '94, while also working for MOTU music software, Suke became a full time touring musician. Suke composed, played guitar and flute with his band **Schleigho**.

Schleigho (pronounced shlay-ho) was formed at Berklee in 1993 and was touring around the country a year later. The band's style is a mix of jazz and funk, with each of its four members contributing equally to bring about an unprecedented wall of sound. Being predominately instrumental, the band's incredible talent and versatility allows them to go from opening for the Allman Brothers to playing high scale jazz venues while satisfying the most discriminating of tastes. The band released their first CD (*self-titled*) in 1995, '*Farewell to the Sun*' in 1997 and '*In the Interest of Time*' in 1998. In 2000 the band signed with **Flying Frog Records (owned and managed by members of the Allman Brothers)**. Under Flying Frog Records they released '*Continent*' in 2000, and '*Live at HoDown 2000*' the following year. Schleigho has met with great success over the years; from amassing a substantial and dedicated national following to '*Continent*' breaking into the top 20 on CMJ and college Jazz radio charts. Averaging over 200 shows annually across the country, they have shared the stage with **The Allman Brothers band**, **Derek Trucks**, **Bela Fleck, John Scofield, Karl Denson, Maceo Parker, G. Love and Special Sauce, Galactic, moe. and Soulive**, to name a few. Schleigho has performed at the JVC Jazz festival (NYC), the Gathering of the Vibes, the High Sierra Music Festival, and the Berkshire Music Festival, among others, and are veterans of the club/college circuit and large festival scene for over 20 years.

Suke also performed for years with the band **Conehead Buddha**, which is a song structured improvisational fusion of hip-hop, rock, and jazz, flirting with many styles from drum and bass to latin and reggae. It's a high energy show featuring Terence and Shannon Lynch.

Another avenue he has been steadily involved with is the production of music for multimedia. For the last twenty years Suke has been developing his production and engineering abilities in his own project studio to further enhance his musical visions. He created *Tone Over Tone* in which he composes, performs, engineers, mix's and masters recordings to be licensed for multimedia applications. This area of music production allows for infinite amounts of creation and timbre. Using conventional instruments, modern technology and a thorough musical background, Suke now creates breathtaking music that utilizes almost any instrument in creation with lush sound design.

His sound is refreshing and his performance is intense. You can always hear diverse musical influences throughout his compositions and soloing. Music from the likes of Jimi Hendrix and Van Halen to John Coltrane, Roland Kirk, and George Benson. From Jeff Beck and Ozzy to Herbie Hancock, Mingus and Miles. From Igor Stravinsky to Square Pusher and Amon Tobin.

Suke currently resides in New York City with his family and has been the *Director of Lead Guitar Program at New York City's "Best" Guitar School* since 2004. He has taught over 15,000 lessons and classes amassing a staggering amount of teaching experience. Suke is also responsible for the musical evaluations of incoming teachers and has often taught the other teachers at the school. The hundreds of students and thousands of hours teaching have help sculpt and mold the success of his teaching methods.

Whether it's playing in a group context, performing, teaching or creating and producing music, Suke always incorporates a fine balance of taste and technique with a result that's not soon forgotten. He always keeps his eye and ear to the future while respectfully paying homage to his influences and tradition.

www.SukeCerulo.com

www.LeadGuitarWorkshop.com